Interdisciplinary perspectives on modern history

Editors
Robert Fogel and Stephan Thernstrom

**Those who stayed behind:
rural society in nineteenth-century New England**

Those who stayed behind

Rural society in nineteenth-century New England

HAL S. BARRON

Harvey Mudd College

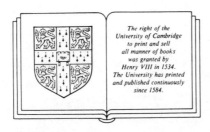

The right of the
University of Cambridge
to print and sell
all manner of books
was granted by
Henry VIII in 1534.
The University has printed
and published continuously
since 1584.

Cambridge University Press

Cambridge
New York   New Rochelle
Melbourne   Sydney

Published by the Press Syndicate of the University of Cambridge
The Pitt Building, Trumpington Street, Cambridge CB2 1RP
32 East 57th Street, New York, NY 10022, USA
10 Stamford Road, Oakleigh, Melbourne 3166, Australia

First published 1984
First paperback edition 1987

Printed in the United States of America

Library of Congress Cataloging in Publication Data
Barron, Hal S.
Those who stayed behind.

(Interdisciplinary perspectives on modern history)
Bibliography: p.
Includes index.
1. New England – Rural conditions – Case studies.
2. Chelsea (Vt.:Town) – History. 3. New England –
Population, Rural – Case studies. 4. Rural-urban
migration – New England – History – 19th century – Case
studies. I. Title. II. Series.
HN79.A11B37 1984 307.7'2'0974 83-26354

ISBN 0 521 25784 0 hard covers
ISBN 0 521 34777 7 paperback

For Kathy

Contents

Tables and illustrations

viii

Preface

The majority of people in nineteenth-century America lived in rural communities, but most of the social history of nineteenth-century America is not about them. This book is. Instead of following the long-standing emphasis on the frontier, however, I have written about those who stayed behind in settled rural areas. There, society was often shaped by population loss and little economic growth, quite unlike the rapid economic and demographic expansion so prevalent in the West and the cities. How such conditions came about and how they affected those who lived and labored under them are the subjects of this book.

In many respects, settled rural life offered a counterpoint to the more dominant themes being played out as the United States became an urban and industrial nation. Rural society was part of this great transformation, but the stability and homogeneity that developed in older agrarian communities contrasted sharply with the flux and diversity so common in the rest of American society. In the same vein, the persistence of family farming facilitated the retention and adaptation of older values to a greater degree than occurred in urban and industrial communities. City and country diverged during the course of the nineteenth century, but rural society and rural attitudes continued to influence American life, resulting in numerous political and cultural conflicts. Thus, it is important to understand the dynamics of older agrarian communities not simply because so many people lived there, but because they can also tell us much about the larger thrust of nineteenth-century American society.

In particular, this book is about those who stayed behind in the township of Chelsea, Vermont, between 1784 and 1900. Of all the states in New England, Vermont has been the least affected by urbanization, industrialization, and immigration, and it remained predominantly rural throughout the nineteenth century. I chose Chelsea as a case study because it has the most promising records of the many Vermont townships that experienced significant population loss during this period. From a historical point of view, this seems to be the community's sole distinction, and developments in Chelsea represent a pattern that was common in rural New England and

New York. Lessened growth was not simply another Yankee pe-
culiarity, however; it occurred throughout the agrarian North as farm
communities moved past the settlement period. Although the patterns
of change in Chelsea are not necessarily representative of these
broader changes in any statistical sense, they are certainly indicative
of the more general characteristics that distinguished settled rural
society from the rest of nineteenth-century America.

I think of this study as very much a part of the new social history
even though such a declaration is no longer as fashionable as it once
was. It tells a story of historical change, a narrative if you will, but
one that would be impossible to recount without the painstaking
analysis of quantitative data and the utilization of social-scientific
theories and methods. Whereas I hope I have gleaned as much as
possible from that often unyielding field, it was also necessary to
consult a wider variety of sources and to incorporate still other approaches in order to have a story worth telling. Ultimately, these
distinctions are trivial: This work will be judged not by the thickness
or thinness of its description but by the insights it offers into what
it meant to stay behind in rural America as the United States moved
on in new and different directions.

Scholarship, like farming, often gives the illusion of being a solitary
endeavor when, in fact, success in both owes much to the help of
friends, neighbors, and kin.

This book began as a dissertation in history at the University of
Pennsylvania where I was privileged to be part of an intellectual
community devoted to interdisciplinary scholarship in the best sense
of those words. The late John Shover first stimulated my interest in
rural history, Etienne van de Walle gave me many of the tools necessary
to undertake this study, and Michael Katz offered his perspective
as a leading practitioner of the new social history. My dissertation
director, Charles E. Rosenberg, has been my guide, and his sound
advice, keen insights, and the example of his own scholarship have
been both a source of inspiration and a pattern for emulation. Allan
Bogue read the manuscript and offered many valuable suggestions
for revision, which I hope I have incorporated. The manuscript and
its author have also benefited immeasurably from the critical comments
and friendly encouragement of Walter Licht, Tom Dublin, John Modell,
Dick Olson, Allan Winkler, and Martin Ridge.

In addition to intellectual stimulation and scholarly advice, there
has been much assistance of a more tangible nature. The initial
research for the dissertation was made possible by an Arthur L.

Penfield Scholarship from the University of Pennsylvania, and since that time I have received support from the Faculty Research Committee at Harvey Mudd College, the National Endowment for the Humanities, and the Arnold L. and Lois S. Graves Foundation. The staffs at a number of libraries and archives also made my work much easier: the Van Pelt Library at Penn, the Baker Library at the School of Business Administration at Harvard University, the Vermont Historical Society, the Vermont State Library, the Chelsea Historical Society, the National Agricultural Library, the Honnold Library of the Claremont Colleges, and the Henry E. Huntington Library. The people of Chelsea, Vermont, were open and helpful, belying any tight-lipped Yankee stereotype, and I especially want to thank W. Sid Gilman and the late Carroll Carpenter who let me use materials from their personal collections. The editors of *Agricultural History* have allowed me to use material in Chapter 4 that previously appeared in that journal. Frank Smith, my editor at Cambridge, somehow managed to turn the often traumatic process of publishing a book into an enjoyable experience.

And then there are kin. My parents, Bernard W. and Judith T. Barron, have been a constant source of support even though I became the other kind of doctor. I owe the most, however, to my wife, Katherine T. Kobayashi, for her thorough and incisive comments and for her love and understanding. It is a blessing to be married to such a talented and generous woman, a blessing of which I am mindful in this and everything else I do.

Hal S. Barron
Claremont, California
January 1984

1 After the frontier: theory, historiography, and the social history of settled rural America

Economic development and its social context are major themes in the new social history of nineteenth-century America, a century that witnessed the great transformation of American society and the emergence of the basic economic, geographic, and social contours of the modern United States. Employing methods borrowed from the other social sciences and utilizing new sources of data, historians in recent years have been able to delineate the dimensions of these changes with a scope and precision unattainable through more traditional approaches. Moreover, a greater awareness of social-scientific theory has facilitated the analysis of American trends in comparison with patterns of development in other societies and with respect to more general theories of human behavior and social change.[1]

The principal focus of this new social history, however, has been largely urban and industrial development. There are numerous studies of nineteenth-century urban social structure and social mobility, the creation of an industrial work force, the nature of the immigrant experience in the cities, and the changing roles of the family in industrial society. Yet relatively little attention has been paid to comparable issues in the development of northern rural society at a time when most of the population lived in the countryside and the United States was still predominantly rural. Obviously, urban and industrial growth was the most dramatic aspect of change in the nineteenth century and is more directly related to present-day conditions, but throughout the century, agriculture also went through significant transitions as farmers specialized in commercial crops and adopted more efficient forms of technology.[2]

The lack of a new social history for the rural North is due to a variety of intellectual constraints, both historiographical and theoretical. The particular historiographical traditions of frontier and agricultural history limit the comprehensive consideration of rural social development. As Robert Swierenga has noted, frontier, land, and agricultural history are the orphan children of American rural history and do not provide "a coherent, general framework for an overall history of rural development in America."[3] At a more general level, historians concerned primarily with broader theories of social change

1

have been little disposed to analyze conditions in the commercialized farm communities of the second half of the nineteenth century because of the nature of those theories. Consequently, notions about agrarian life in industrializing America are often confused and contradictory. This chapter attempts to elucidate the character of our present understanding of nineteenth-century northern rural society and suggests ways to broaden that understanding.

Any consideration of the state of nineteenth-century rural historiography must begin with the pervasive influence of Frederick Jackson Turner. Most social history of the rural North during the period has been written with an eye toward supporting or refuting his interpretations. Yet Turner's conceptual framework does not encompass the entire spectrum of rural development and is little concerned with theoretical questions about the impact of economic change on agrarian society. Instead, Turner emphasizes the relationship between one specific stage of rural development – the frontier – and the nature of American character and American institutions.[4]

Turner's theory of the frontier is an elaborate expression of the agrarian myth. In his argument, the frontier experience was the social equivalent of a medicine-show elixir – good for whatever ails. The process of settling the wilderness was capable of transforming landless eastern farmers and city dwellers into stouthearted and independent yeomen rooted to their new land. In place of older communities, which were stratified and characterized by social conflict, frontier communities were cooperative, egalitarian, and open to all, including foreign immigrants. The easy accessibility of free land and the upward mobility characteristic of the frontier also served to preserve the peace in older areas by acting as a safety valve for malcontents.[5]

Turner's critics, in turn, reject his version of the agrarian myth. They demythologize the frontier by emphasizing the continuity of commercial values and social conflict rather than the transforming powers of frontier life. New settlers were not self-sufficient yeomen but petty capitalists and speculators constantly on the move, buying, improving, and selling new parcels of land. In addition to farming, urban development and boosterism were critical components of the expansion of the frontier. Pioneers were not individualists but, in general, social conformists who sought to maintain rather than to abandon their cultural values. Instead of forcing cooperation and assimilation, the rigors of frontier life intensified conflict and divisiveness in the new communities and preserved older ethnic and class distinctions.[6]

The accessibility of the frontier and the availability of free land also seem to be more myth than reality. The impact of speculation on the price of land and the costs of starting a new farm meant that the frontier was really "open" only to a narrow spectrum of the nation's population. Certainly, few urban workers seem to have actually made the move, and recent historians have stressed factors other than a frontier safety valve to explain the relative lack of militant working-class consciousness in nineteenth-century cities.[7]

Although his detractors significantly revise Turner's vision of the frontier, his ideas remain central to their analyses. As a result, the historical literature is somewhat splintered, consisting of separate and extensive discussions of particular aspects of frontier society rather than a more holistic analysis. Each debate revolves around a single characteristic (conflict vs. cooperation or individualism vs. conformity), and the conclusions are skewed toward the extremes of an issue rather than toward a more complex middle ground. Ironically, even though some of the frontier historians are pioneers in the use of the quantitative methods so central to the new social history, they use only the theoretical framework developed by Turner.[8]

More important, the focus on the frontier precludes a comprehensive study of nineteenth-century rural development. There is little consideration, for example, of conditions in older rural areas. The frontier was a critical yet short-lived phase in America's rural history, but what happened after the frontier passed? As a result of Turner's influence, we have an east-to-west migration of rural historiography paralleling the movement of the original settlers.

Clearly, the study of United States rural history needs to move beyond Turner conceptually, temporally, and regionally. Agricultural and economic historians have given us extensive studies of nineteenth-century farming after the frontier within the context of the nation's economic growth and theories of economic development and economic behavior. At the macro level, the performance and expansion of the agricultural sector was a key aspect of America's economic advance during the nineteenth century. At the micro level, the character of farming changed dramatically as farmers specialized in commercial crops and improved the quality of the different factors of agricultural production.[9]

To a large degree, this revolution in American farming was intertwined with the industrial revolution. The rise of urban markets increased the demand for agricultural commodities and led to greater market orientation and more rationalization in farm operations. Clarence Danhoff surveys this transformation for all northern agriculture in his classic study *Change in Agriculture*; and Allan Bogue and Eric Lampard, for example, have studied corn-hog production and commercial dairying, respectively. In addition to the adoption of better farming practices and technological innovations, all these authors stress the importance of attitudinal and institutional change. The old-style farmer who marketed his surplus casually was replaced by the farm-operator–businessman who used his entrepreneurial skills to get maximum output from his resources. Support institutions such as marketing cooperatives, the agricultural press, agricultural societies, and government departments of agriculture at the state and national levels all emerged to facilitate their efforts.[10]

This literature, however, does not generally discuss the social context or consequences of economic development in the rural North, and important questions remain unanswered, indeed not even formulated. Were the revolution in farm production and the commercialization of agriculture accompanied by a revolution of social relationships in the countryside? Did change and continuity in rural communities parallel contemporary nineteenth-century urban patterns? How did change in rural areas affect the nation as a whole? What does the changing nature of agrarian life in nineteenth-century America imply for general theories relating economic development to social change?

The recent analyses of social change resulting from urban and industrial growth have been framed largely by either modernization theory or Marxist concepts. Both theoretical models describe the destruction of a traditional village society and its replacement by a new social order based on impersonal relationships and large-scale organization, but they place quite different values on this transformation. Modernizationists assume that this process was progressive, reflecting the awakening of a universal concert of liberal aspirations, which provided ever-expanding dimensions for individual freedom and accomplishment. In contrast, the Marxist historians emphasize disruption and alienation. The impulses behind social change were narrow class interests, which oppressed other groups and forced them into a continuous struggle to maintain cherished agrarian, artisan, and ethnic traditions.[11]

Recently, several American social historians influenced by the French *Annalistes* and British Marxists have begun to analyze rural social developments within these conceptual frameworks. In an important article, James Henretta seeks to reconstruct the *mentalité* of preindustrial American farmers. In contrast to the ideal type of the traditional European peasant, Henretta's husbandmen were not communally oriented as has been suggested by several colonial historians. Nor were they prototypical modern men or nascent capitalists whose acquisitive goals were frustrated only by the lack of sufficient markets to warrant completely commercialized agriculture. Rather, preindustrial American farmers were primarily concerned with the well-being and continuation of their family lines. They were not profit maximizers who strove to accumulate great wealth. Instead, they measured success by one's ability to pass on a freehold or competence to each of one's children – no more and no less.[12]

Two other authors, Michael Merrill and Christopher Clark, amplify Henretta's ideas more explicitly in terms of Marxist theory. Merrill attempts to define rural society in the North between 1750 and 1850 as the social product of a "household mode of production," which was distinct from either a simple commodity mode or a capitalistic mode of production. As Clark's work demonstrates, however, this mode of production was not incompatible with an increased involvement in the market. New England farm families, for example, welcomed the rise of putting-out industries during the first half of the nineteenth century but for traditional reasons. Proto-industrialization offered the rural family new means to preserve the older household system in the face of land scarcity and declining local agricultural opportunities.[13]

Henretta, Merrill, and Clark do great service by placing the social history of early nineteenth-century rural development within a broader theoretical context. Their interpretations facilitate the comparison of American trends with recent work on the emergence of a market economy in the European countryside. Similarly, American labor historians have also emphasized a household mode of production to explain artisan life in preindustrial cities. Finally, by elaborating new categories, this work has explicit implications for the more general theories of economic and social change. Pre- and proto-industrial American farmers were, to use a more modern agricultural term, hybrids. They were neither traditional peasants nor modern profit maximizers but rather transitional figures – in the market but not of it.[14]

But transitional toward what? All three authors assume that the rise of capitalism had the same disruptive social effects in the countryside that it had in the cities, but none actually studies conditions in commercialized rural communities. Clark asserts that the rise of centralized manufacturing and commercialized farming eventually undermined the viability of the older household system. He offers theory instead of evidence, however, to support his claim, and he fails to delineate the kind of social order that emerged as a result. Actually, within the scope of his study, Clark does not deal with greater market involvement in agriculture but focuses only on putting-out industries. Henretta also posits a decline in the orientation toward family goals, but he does not explain why ensuring the establishment and continuation of one's family line could not also be the primary goal within a thoroughly capitalistic order as well as in a preindustrial society.[15]

Like the frontier historian, ironically, Henretta, Merrill, and Clark focus on one specific phase of American rural development. Certainly the transformation from a developed noncommercial to a commercial rural economy was an important historical process, as was the settlement of the frontier, but an exclusive consideration of either tells us little about the nature of the settled rural conditions so prevalent during the second half of the nineteenth century. We cannot simply assume that social change in older rural areas paralleled urban and industrial trends.

Both this assumption of parallel development and the disinclination to study commercial agrarian society stem from precisely the same theoretical perspective that makes this new work so exciting. Modernization theory and Marxist analysis assume a rural-to-urban shift over time. Center stage, so to speak, moves from the country to the city. As a result, we have numerous concepts and empirical studies dealing with either the premodern rural society of peasants and villages (and their American variants) or the modern industrial order of workers and cities. In contrast to these emphases, however, there are almost no models to help us to understand social relationships in modern, commercialized rural communities or, for that matter, premodern urban settings. As two rural sociologists recently put it: "The classic nineteenth-century European writers in sociological theory devoted comparatively little attention to agrarian and rural life, concentrating their efforts instead upon explanations of the emerging urban–industrial sector."[16]

Rural sociology, a discipline devoted to the study of modern rural society, unfortunately offers historians little help in this regard. The field's particular institutional connection to agricultural experiment stations and extension services has resulted in work that is mainly applied and empirical with little overall synthesis. Instead, the discipline is characterized by a relative absence of theory and even, in the words of one critic, by an antitheoretical emphasis.[17]

To the extent that a theoretical perspective on modern rural society has been developed by rural sociologists, it is problematic. The concept of the rural–urban continuum, a variation of Ferdinand Tonnies's classic formulation of *Gemeinschaft* and *Gesellschaft*, or community and society, is the dominant theoretical framework in the discipline. Community is defined by localistic, personal, and informal inter-actions, whereas society is cosmopolitan, anonymous, and formal or bureaucratic. Although Tonnies intended these terms to represent two modes of human association that can exist simultaneously in the same geographic location, American rural sociologists have equated *Gemeinschaft* with the countryside and *Gesellschaft* with the city and made them mutually exclusive. The rural–urban continuum has been challenged significantly by recent studies, which find both kinds of attributes in rural as well as urban communities, but it continues to influence rural sociological research, which consists largely of mea-suring the differences between rural and urban society in terms of a wide range of characteristics.[18]

Although there are obviously many significant differences between modern urban and modern rural communities, the notion of a rural–urban continuum does not specify the causes of those differences. Instead, rural and urban are only descriptive and empirical terms without any explanatory power. Yet it is precisely those causal con-nections that are crucial to historians if they are to understand past rural society and explain the way it changed over time.

Even though there are few systematic studies of older farm com-munities, American historians have pervasive notions about the nature of that society because, in the absence of any appropriate interpretive construct, scholars have tended to superimpose urban and industrial patterns on the late nineteenth-century countryside. Whether they are primarily concerned with larger theories of social change or not, many historians implicitly, if not explicitly, tend to regard settled rural areas in much the same way as they interpret industrial de-velopment.

Writing about northern farming after the Civil War, agricultural historians detail the rise of large-scale operations that utilized increasing amounts of machinery and other capital investments. The surviving photographs from the 1890s of teams of twenty or thirty horses pulling great combines in the fields of California and the northern plains provide a graphic illustration of this trend. Similarly, the nature of farm labor changed as these new large-scale farmers reached beyond their families for workers and relied on wage labor or tenant farmers. As rural wealth became concentrated in fewer hands and new opportunities declined, the social structure of rural communities came to approximate the cities, and class divisions between farm owners, tenants, and laborers became more rigid.[19]

Yet commercial farm operations in the North during the second half of the nineteenth century were not, for the most part, factories in the field. They differed significantly from contemporary industries and do not begin to approximate the scale or organization of current American agriculture. There were huge farms, especially in the trans-Mississippi West, but these were not typical. Historians debunking Turner's vision of small frontier farmers and those interested in the technological evolution of farm machinery have overemphasized the small minority of large farms that used expensive machinery and hired great numbers of wage laborers.[20]

Instead, until the middle of the twentieth century the overwhelming majority of farms were family farms, which relied primarily on family members for labor and management. In his overview of the economic history of American agriculture, economist William Parker stresses the pervasiveness and constancy of the family scale of production from the colonial period to World War II. Although large-scale farms, tenancy, and hired labor were more prevalent in the West and the South, the older farm states in the North showed no inevitable trend toward those conditions. In his brief discussion of farming in *The Visible Hand*, Alfred D. Chandler explains the persistence of family management in contrast to the increasingly large scale of organization in industry:

> In the raising of corn, cotton, wheat, and other crops, biological constraints determined the time of preparing the soil, sowing, cultivating, and harvesting, and so set the overall processes of production . . . But the need almost never arose to devise organizational procedures to integrate and coordinate the processes. Therefore, the family was able to remain the basic agricultural working unit; and the farmer, his family, and a handful of hired helpers relied, until the twentieth century, on human and animal power to work farm implements and machines.[21]

The analogy to urban society also obscures significant differences in the social structure of rural communities. Farming communities were mainly collections of farm owners and their families. Although farmers hired outside labor, these workers were usually hired for only a short time period and rarely in numbers comparable to city factories. The frequency of wage labor and tenancy did increase during the late nineteenth century, but the social position of these laborers and tenant farmers was much more ambiguous than that of industrial workers. Often, for example, the tenant was the son or relative of the farm owner. There are not sufficient studies to delineate fully the rate of rural social mobility and its temporal, spatial, and ethnic variations, but those studies that do exist, especially the recent work of Donald L. Winters, indicate that the agricultural ladder toward farm ownership was a more well-traveled reality for northern rural workers than the occupational ladder was for laborers in nineteenth-century cities.[22]

But what about the attitudes or *mentalité* of the commercialized farmer and the nature of life in settled rural communities? Various authors note the increasing prevalence of urban cultural patterns and "modern" attitudes in the countryside. Lewis Atherton narrates the transformation of main street in the Middle West from a dynamic social force and cultural arbiter to a shrill mimic of the big city, and Wayne E. Fuller similarly chronicles the urban cultural inroads that resulted from rural free delivery. As has already been mentioned, Clarence Danhoff and Allan Bogue discuss the new attitudes of farmers themselves as they took a more calculating, rational, and business-like view of their farming operations.[23]

The case for the convergence of urban and rural culture during the late nineteenth and early twentieth centuries is by no means unambiguous, however. On the contrary, other studies indicate that the rise of the city and the ascendance of urban values were confronted by heightened resistance in the countryside. Robert Dykstra, for example, labels town–country conflict as the hidden dimension of American social history, and Stanley Parsons uses a similar social fault line to delineate the context of Populism in the Midwest. Rather than assume that commercial farmers acted as fully rational economic men, Anne Mayhew argues for a distinct set of rural values when she interprets farm protest between 1870 and 1900 as a reaction to the increasing market orientation of plains agriculture. Finally, Don Kirschner's study of state legislation in Illinois and Iowa indicates the persistence and increase of deep-seated rural animosity toward city ways well into the twentieth century.[24]

The characteristics of urban and industrial society, then, are not wholly satisfactory models for understanding developed agrarian society. Rather than capturing the essential features of commercialized rural life, the urban analogy obscures some of its critical and distinctive qualities. If the urban and industrial model is inadequate and mis-leading, however, so are the various notions of traditional, or pre-modern, village life. From the scattered evidence available, the nature of late-nineteenth-century rural society remains a puzzle, simultaneously exhibiting social and economic characteristics that have been associated with the pastoral village as well as with modern, capitalistic society.

Any attempt to resolve this seeming paradox must consider the fact that rural areas during the second half of the nineteenth century experienced fundamentally different patterns of development than did contemporary cities within the larger context of a commercialized, capitalistic economic and social order. In contrast to the rapid and continuous economic expansion typical of urban industry, economic growth in settled farm communities slowed down and leveled off. Whereas the population in the cities increased rapidly between 1860 and 1900, rural growth rates declined and many areas lost population. The key to an understanding of the social history of older farm communities, it would seem, lies in a detailed consideration of this lessened growth and its various social ramifications.

These different urban and rural patterns are strongly implied by theories of economic development. Throughout the second half of the nineteenth century, American cities expanded dramatically by creating new jobs and economic opportunities. Jane Jacobs defines this as the process of adding new work to old work, and Allan Pred, in his more formal model of American metropolitan growth, delineates a multiplier effect in which a city's manufacturing activity led to still other economic endeavors. Increased urban economic activity simultaneously enhanced the possibility of new inventions or innovations, which further accelerated the multiplier process to new levels, and this expansive spiral continued almost unabated until it ran into diseconomies such as high land costs resulting from overcrowding. Yet, in the case of high land costs, the adoption of still other forms of technology such as electric street railways permitted continued urban-industrial expansion in a more decentralized form.[25]

Like industry, the agricultural sector of the national economy grew significantly during the nineteenth century. Between 1869 and 1899, estimates of net farm output increased from $3.5 billion to $8.5 billion (American billion). This aggregate expansion, however, was due primarily to the development of new farming areas and their integration into the market and not to any continuous increase in the productivity of older farm regions.[26]

In contrast to the seemingly never-ending growth of cities and industries, agricultural development was limited by the supply of the least mobile and least flexible factor of production – land. Once a given location was settled and in farms, the number of family farm sites was near its maximum. To the extent that later adjustment to new market conditions and specialization in new farm products altered the local configuration of farm sites, they usually resulted in fewer local opportunities for farm families rather than more.[27]

Similarly, there was no local multiplier effect in rural areas. During the second half of the nineteenth century, mechanization decreased the number of rural "jobs" in older farm communities rather than increasing them. The adoption of new farm machinery and improved farming practices were mostly onetime changes, which shifted farm production to a new plateau but not into an upward spiral. Farmers plowed any increased returns back into their farms, bought new land from less successful neighbors, invested outside the community, or sent the money off with their children. In any event, the structure of the local economy did not expand appreciably as a result, and few new jobs were created.[28]

Interrelated with patterns of economic development, demographic growth rates in late-nineteenth-century urban and rural communities also diverged considerably. Between 1860 and 1910, the population in U.S. cities larger than 100,000 increased by 669 percent and went from less than one-tenth to almost a fourth of the total population. This phenomenal growth was due mainly to the ongoing in-migration of rural Americans as well as to the influx of youthful, urban-oriented foreigners in the "new wave" of immigration from southern and eastern Europe. As a result, the nation's urban population was young, mobile, and increasingly diverse.[29]

In contrast to the cities, rural population grew at a much slower rate, increasing only 98 percent between 1860 and 1910. Whereas in 1860, 80 percent of the country's population was rural, by 1910 that proportion had declined to just over one-half. This aggregate record of growth, however, is somewhat deceptive. In fact, an increasing number of older rural areas were losing population during the late nineteenth century. As Wilbur Zelinsky's study of rural counties demonstrates, depopulation began in New England and New York but spread throughout Ohio, Indiana, Illinois, Michigan, and Iowa by 1910. Even those areas that continued to grow often grew at a rate that was less than the rate of natural increase, indicating net out-migration.[30]

The causes of this population decline are varied. The pull of the cities and other newer rural areas has received the greatest amount of scholarly attention. Other causes of rural depopulation can be inferred, however, from sociological studies of twentieth-century farming areas. Calvin Beale points out that numerous agricultural workers were displaced by the widespread mechanization of farming.

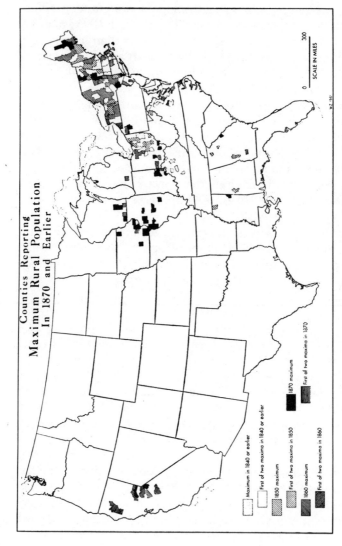

Counties reporting maximum rural population in 1870 and earlier. [From Wilbur Zelinsky, "Changes in the Geographic Patterns of Rural Population in the United States, 1790–1960," *Geographical Review* 52 (1962): 500. Reprinted with the permission of the American Geographical Society.]

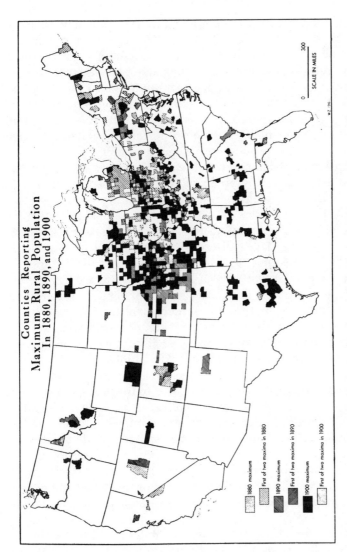

Counties reporting maximum rural population in 1880, 1890, and 1900. [From Wilbur Zelinsky, "Changes in the Geographic Patterns of Rural Population in the United States 1790–1960," *Geographical Review* 52 (1962): 500. Reprinted with the permission of the American Geographical Society.]

Historian John Saville also demonstrates that rural depopulation in England and Wales between 1851 and 1951 resulted in part from the displacement of rural artisans by the development of centralized urban industries. In addition to out-migration, the declining frequency of in-migration to older farming communities also caused them to dwindle. Because out-migration and in-migration were selective according to age, the age structure of depopulating rural communities became progressively older. As a result, the rate of natural increase declined as a larger proportion of the population was more likely to die and fewer inhabitants were in their family-forming years. Similarly, there is historical demographic evidence that absolute fertility (not just the number of women in their childbearing years) declined in northern rural areas after the settlement period had passed. Yet the exact configuration of these factors remains elusive. Sociologists as well as historians have preferred to concentrate on situations of growth and development rather than stagnation and decline.[31]

From the perspective of population growth as well as economic development, then, life in an older rural community was considerably different from life in a newly settled frontier, a commercializing agricultural region, or a major city – all of which were situations characterized by rapid rates of increase. In contrast to the continuous change inherent in these societies, older rural areas reached a kind of equilibrium. The dual phenomena of lessened economic and demographic growth are integrally related to the process of settlement and the structure of American agriculture in the nineteenth and early twentieth centuries, and they reflect an emerging balance between local land resources, the number of inhabitants, and outside market demand. It is also probable that unlike the social turmoil and divisiveness created by rapid change elsewhere, these older rural communities became more tranquil and homogeneous over time as local institutions and social norms also evolved into a state of equilibrium with demographic and economic conditions.

Certainly the notion of a social equilibrium is suggested strongly by literary depictions of older rural communities and small towns from the late nineteenth and early twentieth centuries. To regional novelist Sarah Orne Jewett, Dunnet Landing in Maine was permeated by tranquillity and was a welcome retreat from challenge and emotional intensity, and Zona Gale's fictional Friendship Village was capable of defusing any potential conflict and engulfing everyone in "universal togetherness." Other writers shifted away from this celebration of pastoral virtues to a revolt against the stifling life of the village, but the homogeneity and constancy of existence remained central themes.

Jewett's contemporary, novelist Mary Wilkins, saw rural New England as stale and lacking in vitality, and Harold Frederic and Hamlin Garland railed out against provinciality and conformity and emphasized the continuous dulling drudgery of farm life in New York and the Midwest. There is drama in rural fiction, but the tensions are internal and personal and not the result of the larger, more cataclysmic forces of change that dominate the urban novels of the same period.[32]

Thus, conditions in settled rural communities stand in marked contrast to our prevailing perception of rapid growth in nineteenth-century American society as well as to our theoretical presuppositions about the relationships between economic and social change. Obviously, older rural communities were not all the same. An Iowa corn-farming township in 1900, for example, did not replicate the experiences of a New England hill town of a half century earlier. At a more general level, though, the ramifications of lessened economic and demographic growth, especially the development of greater social stability, provide a more appropriate framework for analyzing developments in both areas than do comparisons to urban and industrial trends or the earlier stages of frontier settlement and the commercialization of agriculture. To comprehend the context and consequences of lessened growth in rural America, however, we need to move beyond theoretical speculation and literary stereotypes and look at the settlement and development of a community in rural New England, the first agricultural region to grow old.

2 The storm before the calm: growth and conflict in a developing rural community

Older rural society followed a different path of development in nineteenth-century America, and the first rural communities to diverge from the mainstream were the townships of northern New England that were settled during the second half of the eighteenth century. These communities began to experience lessened growth and population loss by the mid-1800s, a time when the West was developing rapidly and the colonial villages of southern New England were undergoing commercial and industrial revolutions.[1]

Until that happened, however, the rural communities of northern New England had much in common with the rest of American society. The process of settlement and the initial transition to a market economy in the early nineteenth century were both periods of growth and were accompanied by the same sorts of social tensions that affected the nation as a whole. That would change as local growth diminished and as the larger society developed in different directions, but to understand what those changes meant to those who stayed behind, it is first necessary to explore their experiences with growth and conflict in the early nineteenth century.

The township of Chelsea in Orange County, Vermont, is, in many ways, typical of the northern New England communities settled after the Revolution, and its beginnings reflect an oft-repeated pattern in the history of this frontier. In 1781, Bela Turner, a store owner, tavernkeeper, and state legislator from West Lebanon, New Hampshire, recruited seventy associates and applied for a charter from the government of Vermont to start a new township in the central part of that state. Rather than forming the nucleus of a new community, however, these grantees were primarily investors and land speculators, and only two of their numbers ever settled in the new township. Instead, the actual settlement of Chelsea began in 1784 when two distinct family groups, one from southern New Hampshire and the other from Connecticut by way of New Hampshire, established homes in different parts of the township. After this start, several hometown friends of the two families found their way to the new community, but a larger number arrived from different townships throughout

Connecticut, Massachusetts, New Hampshire, and southern Vermont
– the same areas that sent migrants to the other unsettled areas of
Vermont and the Hudson-Mohawk region in eastern New York.[2]

Chelsea grew rapidly during the early years of settlement. After
Vermont was admitted to statehood in 1791, a special federal census
counted 237 persons in 45 households, and by 1800, there were 146
households with 897 inhabitants. In typical frontier fashion, that
population was very young and very fecund. Only 7 percent of the
settlers were over forty-five years of age, and more than 40 percent
were children under ten. Moreover, the fertility ratio of those children
to women between sixteen and forty-five was 2,104 per thousand,
a figure comparable to other measurements of frontier fertility in the
region.[3]

These early settlers were almost universally farmers, and they
practiced the same kind of mixed agriculture prevalent throughout
northern New England. On 13 March 1798 the Chelsea town meeting
voted to raise taxes "in cash, wheat, Rye or Indian Corn," indicating
that grains were the principal crop. Viable crops in a wide range of
conditions, Indian corn and rye constituted the common bread of
the inhabitants, and wheat was grown successfully as long as the
native fertility of new lands held out. In addition to these field crops,
potatoes and a few head of livestock, especially milch cows and
sheep, helped to sustain the farmer and his growing family. Finally,
the forest provided fuel, lumber, and maple syrup, as well as potash,
which was a by-product of the arduous task of clearing the land and
was the main commercial commodity produced by these frontier
farms.[4]

Unlike earlier New England communities, late-eighteenth-century
settlements were usually not intended to be as a city upon a hill,
and Chelsea was neither a covenanted community nor the result of
colonization by a self-selected group of people. Rather, it was more
like later frontier communities, and the pattern of settlement was a
cumulative one – not entirely random but by no means purposive
in any collective sense. As a result, the early inhabitants of the
township embodied a variety of the divergent beliefs prevalent in
postrevolutionary New England and held different ideas about the
nature of their community. The most significant divisions among
them were religious, and throughout the first years of the nineteenth
century, local denominations often fought with each other for more
secular rewards in addition to spiritual salvation.[5]

As befitted a New England town, Chelsea's charter provided for
the public support of religion and education. Five equal shares or

tracts of land were set aside, one for each level of education, one
for the "Support of the Ministry," and a final parcel was reserved
for the "first settled Minister of the Gospel." According to the dictates
of the Vermont General Assembly, the land for the support of the
ministry went to the first organized religious society in the township,
in Chelsea's case, the Congregational Society. Founded in 1789, this
first church operated in the beginning on a very modest scale, and
for the first ten years of its existence never involved more than one-
third of the families listed in the first census. They had no regular
place for meetings until 1796 when the church began to use the same
room in which town meetings were held, and the first permanent
Congregational minister did not settle in town until 1799. In spite
of the modest scale of its operations, however, the Congregational
Society was the only organization in Chelsea before 1800, and its
lay leaders were consistently elected to local public offices. Of the
six founding officeholders in Chelsea, four were Congregationalists,
and of the first fifteen selectmen in the township, ten were associated
with the church.[6]

The Congregationalists were never a local majority, and as a denomination, New England Congregationalism between the First and
Second Great Awakenings was ill equipped to expand its membership.
The formality and lack of enthusiasm that characterized religious
services, as well as the undemocratic Calvinist doctrines of salvation,
held little appeal to frontier settlers who had recently experienced
a revolution against another, more secular standing order. Instead,
two diametrically opposed alternatives to hyper-Calvinism, Armin-
ianism and Deism, had much greater success in early national Vermont.[7]

By 1800 the township's population had grown to just under 900
people, and an increasing number of Chelsea inhabitants were affiliated
with the non-established denominations. Between 1792 and 1801,
twenty-three men submitted certificates from officials of other congregations in order to be excused from paying a tax to support the
Congregational Church. In 1802 the law was liberalized to allow
exemption from this tax solely on the basis of a personal affidavit
declaring disagreement "in religious opinion with a majority of the
inhabitants of the town." Seventy-four Chelsea taxpayers made this
declaration. In contrast, the total number of male and female members
in the Congregational Church remained under forty throughout this
period.[8]

Unlike the Congregationalists, Chelsea dissenters scattered to various churches in neighboring communities. The earliest tax exemption

was granted in 1792 to Jacob Norris, who traveled northeast to congregate with the Baptists in Corinth. Chelsea Baptists also went south to Tunbridge or west to Brookfield, and other dissenters belonged to the Universalist societies in Strafford or Tunbridge or to the Methodist Church in Vershire.[9]

As a result of this dispersion and the lack of any sizable local society, Arminian sectarians posed little challenge to the small but powerful Congregationalist faction. In 1798 a handful of Freewill Baptists from the western part of town ordained Samuel Hovey as their minister. Although their church was actually just across town lines in Brookfield and although Hovey was from that town, they performed the ceremony in Chelsea in order to qualify for the tract of land reserved for the first settled minister of the gospel. However, in spite of a town vote assigning the land to Hovey, the lot passed into the hands of the Congregational Church, which did not appoint a permanent minister until the following year.[10]

During the first decade of the nineteenth century, however, dissenters in Chelsea and throughout the state became more prominent and better organized. The Congregationalists lost their near monopoly on local offices, and several Baptists and other sectarians served as selectmen. Politically, the issue of public support of religion became the basis for partisan divisions in Vermont, and when the Jeffersonian Republicans wrested control of the state government from the Federalists in 1807, they abolished all connections between church and state. Similarly, in Chelsea, Republican candidates for state office and Congress began to capture a substantial minority of the local vote.[11]

The growing appeal of more free-spirited religion did not go unnoticed by local Congregationalists who sought to reunite the community under their control. Bothered by the divisions in Chelsea, the Congregational Church formed a committee in 1801 "to stir up the minds of members and visit members of other churches residing here to learn why they stand aloof from us." In 1809 the wave of Congregational revivals that began at the turn of the century in Connecticut and southern Vermont reached Chelsea, and under the direction of Calvin Noble, a new preacher and recent graduate of Middlebury College, this excitement brought forty-two new members into the fold, more than doubling the size of the congregation. A similar exercise in 1819 attracted forty-six converts. In both cases, however, many of these enthusiasts already had some family connections to the Congregational Church, and few if any came from dissenting families.[12]

In spite of the Congregationalists' new style, denominational divisions deepened and took on a new dimension in 1811 when Frederick Plummer, a traveling preacher, arrived in Chelsea and established a significant local following. Rejecting any name, these people simply called themselves "Christians" and demanded equal access to the county courthouse where the Congregationalists held their services. As a result, the established denomination commenced building its own church and met elsewhere until construction was completed. The "Christians" met in the courthouse, and eventually evolved into the local Methodist congregation, which built its own house of worship in the village in 1837.[13]

Although the Congregationalists and the anti-Calvinist denominations opposed each other in local affairs, there seem to have been few economic or occupational distinctions between the two groups. The usual impression conveyed by historians of religion is that the dissenting denominations attracted a poorer and lower class of followers than did the Congregational churches. Unfortunately, the earliest available indications of occupation and relative wealth in Chelsea are from the 1820 Census and 1837 Tax List, but according to this later evidence, the similarities between the two groups seem much more important than the differences. Both the Congregationalists and the rival societies consisted primarily of farmers and their families, and the dissenters were only marginally less well off. Other studies of the social basis of denominational affiliation in Vermont during this period also find few socioeconomic differences among the various branches of Protestantism in rural areas.[14]

The theological and ideological divisions, however, were profound. In rejecting Calvinist notions of predestination, Chelsea's "Christians," Methodists, Universalists, and Freewill Baptists adopted a perspective that was critical of social privilege and distinction more generally. Certainly this negative view of social privilege resonated with, and was reinforced by, the antiaristocratic tenets of Jeffersonian Republicanism, which infused every political issue of the day, raising the tone of partisan rhetoric to previously unheard levels of passion and derision. These beliefs and their political ramifications also entailed a different conception of the nature of community, which stressed individual freedom and responsibility over older views of corporate identity.[15]

Yet marked social distinctions were only beginning to emerge in Chelsea by the second decade of the nineteenth century. Rather, the township's early conflicts stemmed from the semirandom process of settlement, and the values and attitudes that led to conflicts were imported in the cultural baggage of the different settlers. In this vein, frontier Chelsea had more in common with nineteenth-century frontier communities than with the pioneer Puritan villages of the past. But, in addition to reflecting the settlers' backgrounds, these early conflicts also involved the future of the township and had important consequences for the nature of the community in which they and their children would make their homes.

By the 1820s Chelsea had moved beyond the settlement phase and had begun to take on the appearance of a developed rural community. In 1820 there were 1,462 people in 263 households, and the village center supported a number of nonagricultural occupations in addition to farming in the countryside. According to the census, forty-seven household heads worked at some kind of manufacturing and four derived their livelihood from commerce. Zadock Thompson's Vermont gazetteer of 1824 lists two gristmills, five sawmills, and two fulling mills for cleaning wool in addition to two clothier works, two carding machines, a small woolens factory, two trip-hammer shops, three stores, one tavern, and two tanneries. Two clergymen and three physicians also lived in the village, and because Chelsea was the shire town, or county seat, of Orange County, three attorneys' offices were located there. Another gazetteer from 1823 wrote that the village of Chelsea "is a place where considerable business is done."[16]

As is evident from the fulling mills and carding machines listed in 1824, Chelsea farmers, like so many others in Vermont in the 1820s, had begun to raise more sheep. Declining soil fertility, the Hessian fly, and the spread of wheat growing to more productive western soils virtually eliminated grains as a cash crop in the region. At the same time, however, increased demand from area woolen mills and the introduction of the long-staple Spanish Merino breed effected the widespread shift to sheep herding known as the "Merino mania." In 1836 Barry and Benton's *Statistical View of the Number of Sheep* . . . reported 5,752 sheep in Chelsea, an average of 31 per farm, and the Orange County sheep ranged "from Native to full blood Merino," and the wool was "usually well washed, but loosely put up." By 1840 the number of sheep in Chelsea had increased to 6,696, and the township's farmers produced 11,122 pounds of wool.[17]

Although it opened local farmers to outside market influences, the growth of commercial agriculture in Chelsea was not a complete agricultural revolution. Chelsea farmers continued to raise other livestock and a variety of field and garden crops and did not specialize exclusively in wool. Sheep raising was also not labor intensive and required less of the new and more disciplined work habits that were increasingly prevalent elsewhere. Although some small-scale manufacturing developed, Chelsea was by no means at the center of any great transformation. The township was connected by good roads to the larger towns on the Connecticut River and through them to the main regional centers, but it remained a secondary, rather than a primary, recipient of larger changes.[18]

This modest growth, however, stimulated further development, which was more prevalent in the village than in the countryside. Chelsea's largest population of just under 2,000 people was recorded in 1830 and remained at that level for the next two censuses. Of the 359 household heads enumerated in 1840, 63 engaged in manufacturing, 10 in commerce, 8 practiced the learned professions, and the remainder farmed throughout the township. The Bank of Orange County was founded in Chelsea in 1828 when it brought in Jason Steele, a young lawyer from Randolph, to be its cashier. Similarly, the Orange County Mutual Fire Insurance Company commenced operations in December 1839 and underwrote a half million dollars' worth of protection by the early 1840s. In addition to counting local sheep, Barry and Benton also listed Benjamin Grout's machinery for manufacturing fancy woolen fabrics, both "cassimeres" and "satinets," one of two such operations in the county. More shops and stores opened in the village, and Zadock Thompson's 1842 *History of Vermont* noted several new kinds of artisans plying their trades: tinworkers, cabinetmakers, a jeweler and watchmaker, and a printer, who began publishing the weekly *Tuesday News* in 1837 as well as a monthly periodical, *The Mother's Book and Young Ladies' Companion*.[19]

In contrast to the rough and ready equality of the frontier days, social distinctions were more apparent by 1840. According to the 1837 Grand List of Taxes, twenty-seven inhabitants were taxed for owning carriages or chaises, and six of them owned more than one vehicle. Amplius Blake, the merchant who topped the list with three and one-half carriages, also owned a store, a factory, and a potash plant and leased out three houses as well as three other farms including one of the most valuable in the township. Blake was the leading local stockholder in the Bank of Orange County, an investment of $6,575, and he had $3,000 on hand in cash or in promissory notes when the tax list was drawn up. Many of the others on the carriage list were engaged in a similar range of economic activities though on a reduced scale. Some of the leading farmers in Chelsea also owned carriages, as did the village doctors and lawyers and Sophia L. Noble, the Congregational minister's widow.[20]

The growing social distinctions between rich and poor and between the village and the countryside may have been symbolized by the smart gig or chaise in contrast to the sturdy wagon, but they were institutionalized by an organization that constituted still another faction in Chelsea's early history. Chartered in 1804, the George Washington Lodge No. 24 of the Free and Ancient Masons embodied the legacy of the Enlightenment in Chelsea. Although its complete list of members was kept secret, the sixteen men who served as masters of the local Lodge or represented it at state meetings between 1804 and 1830 give a good indication of the Masonic constituency. They included eight merchants and merchant-artisans, a physician, and a lawyer in addition to several farmers. Only two had claimed an exemption from the religious tax under the liberalized law after 1802, and none were members of the Congregational Church.[21]

As in other communities, the Freemasons in Chelsea were something of an elite group who wielded both economic and political power. Josiah Dana, for example, was a local merchant and Masonic master whose list of assets approximated that of Amplius Blake. He served his township as a selectman and a state representative, a county judge, a delegate to the state constitutional convention in 1814, and a presidential elector in 1828. In the same vein, one-half of the landlords, one-half of the largest creditors, and one-half of the principal stockholders in the Orange County bank from the 1837 Tax List can be identified as Masons, and all the Masons who can be found in that list owned carriages. The other Masonic masters were consistently elected to public office during the 1810s and 1820s, completely displacing the established Congregational leadership. In marked contrast to earlier years, none of the selectmen or representatives during this period belonged to the Congregational Church.[22]

Much of the Masons' ascent at the expense of the Congregationalists was tied to the decline of Federalism and the growing strength of Jeffersonian Republicans. In the aftermath of the War of 1812 and the Hartford Convention, Federalism with its close ties to New England Congregationalism became politically moribund. In Chelsea, political opposition to the Federalists and Congregationalists made for strange bedfellows, and a combination of Masons, non-church members, and religious dissenters began giving local majorities to Republican candidates as early as 1811. After 1816 the Jeffersonian party went unopposed. Rather than support the opposition candidate, however, local ex-Federalists simply did not vote and retreated from politics.[23]

One of these bedfellows began to kick in 1828 when the Antimasonic movement reached Chelsea and reactivated political divisions within the township. Antimasonry began in western New York in 1826 as a reaction to the kidnapping and probable murder of William Morgan, an ex-Mason who authored an "exposé" of the Masonic Order, and the first organized expression of Antimasonic sentiment in Vermont occurred just across Chelsea town lines in Randolph in the fall of 1827. The continuous discussion of the Morgan affair in the local papers gave the movement a wider momentum, and the March 1828 town meeting in Randolph witnessed an open dispute between local Masons and Antimasons. Chelseans were well aware of these events. Before Chelsea got its own Masonic Lodge in 1804, the Federal Lodge of Randolph was authorized in 1800 to meet in both towns. On the other side, two of the three leaders of the Antimasonic movement, the so-called Randolph Triumvirate, had ties to Chelsea; and one, Calvin Blodgett, later moved there to serve as county judge of probate.[24]

In Chelsea the issue came to a head during the protracted congressional election of 1828. The favored candidate was the incumbent and Chelsea's most distinguished resident, Daniel Azro A. Buck, whose father was also a U.S. congressman from 1795 to 1797 before he moved to Chelsea. According to one local history, the younger Buck was "probably the most popular man that ever lived in Chelsea, and one of the most popular in the state." Chelseans regularly elected him as their representative to the State Assembly when he was not serving in Washington, and his colleagues in Montpelier consistently voted him Speaker of the House. During the congressional election in 1826, Buck received all but one of the votes cast in the township.[25]

In addition to his public offices, however, Buck was also prominent in Masonic affairs. He had been the master of Chelsea's lodge between 1817 and 1818 and held the high position of grand secretary of the state's Grand Lodge between 1818 and 1828. During his 1828 congressional bid, Buck ran as an anti-Jackson, Adams Republican and received 213 votes in Chelsea, still an overwhelming local majority. His closest rival was the Jacksonian candidate with 54 votes, and William Cohoon, the Antimasonic candidate, garnered only 3 ballots. In the rest of the district, however, Buck's Masonic connections hurt him, and no candidate won the majority necessary for election. Actually, the Fifth District failed to elect a congressman in six subsequent elections held throughout the next twelve months. Although Chelsea voters regularly turned in a majority for Buck, the Antimasonic candidate steadily gained local support. Finally, at the eighth balloting on 2 November 1829, Cohoon won a plurality of Chelsea's votes (106 out of 235) and was elected to the Congress. This plurality disappeared in the 1830 elections, but Antimasons continued to get about a third of the total local vote until 1836.[26]

Although it is impossible to determine exactly who the first Antimasons were, certain characteristics are indicated by other studies. Politically, the Antimasonic vote represented a defection from the ranks of the Jeffersonian Republican faction and not a reinvolvement of the ex-Federalists. According to the leading historians of the movement, the Antimasons were probably religious dissenters drawn mostly from the Freewill Baptists. At a more basic level, Antimasonry in Chelsea and other communities was an attack on local privilege and a home-grown aristocracy centered in the village instead of the countryside. It was a movement against a new, secular standing order. Whereas during the 1810s it was possible for Masons and ordinary farmers to find common ground opposing an older social establishment, by 1830 the growing economic and political power of the Masons made such an alliance uneasy and unnecessary. Instead, the Antimasonic crusade in Chelsea pitted farmers against townspeople and reflected the social and economic differentiation that resulted from the emergence of a commercialized market economy.[27]

Growing Antimasonic sentiment forced many lodges, including the one in Chelsea, to disband after 1830. In spite of this new movement, however, a majority of Chelsea voters continued to send Buck as well as two other former Masonic masters to Montpelier throughout the 1830s, and as the 1837 Tax List indicates, Masons retained their economic position as well. In the wake of the political shuffling caused by the Antimasonic issue, the Republican-Democratic majority faced sizable opposition for the first time since 1815. During the 1830s, the old Federalist-Congregational faction became involved in local politics, and by 1836 had allied with the Antimasons under the Whig party banner. This local split between the Jeffersonian Republican-Democrat majority and the Whig minority remained constant until the formation of the new Republican party in the 1850s.[28]

For the first fifty years of its history, then, Chelsea grew rapidly and was dominated by social conflicts that manifested themselves in the arenas of religion and politics. Much of the early conflict was typical of any frontier community that brought together different people who believed in a variety of social ideas and doctrines, whereas the later fights stemmed from the growing social differences caused by the development of the local economy. These battles were part of larger wars waged in other places, and similar conflicts occurred wherever the diversity of the frontier or the expansion of the market economy stimulated social tensions. For Chelsea and for the larger society, the early nineteenth century was a period marked by economic and demographic growth in which growth and conflict went hand in hand.

By the 1840s that growth was increasingly a thing of the past. Chelsea's population was no longer as young as it had been during the settlement period, and the rate of natural increase had declined. Children under ten who had comprised 40 percent of the population in 1800 formed just over one-fourth of the local inhabitants in 1840, and adults over forty-five increased from 7 to approximately 17 percent. Similarly, fewer children were being born to those in their family-forming years, and the child–woman ratio in 1840 was roughly 1,200 per thousand, or 57 percent of the 1800 level.[29]

Economic development also slowed down. In 1840 the number of farmers in the community exceeded the number of farms that were available. Given the prevailing form of agriculture at the time, Chelsea's 24,000 acres were capable of supporting about 200 farms, and the 1837 Tax List recorded 186 entries of ten acres or more with at least one barn. Yet according to the 1840 Census, there were 278 household heads in town who were farmers and a total of more than 300 males over sixteen engaged in agriculture.[30]

Neither were local nonagricultural opportunities increasing. The first branch of the White River provided power for a number of smaller mills and shops, but it was simply not large enough to support substantial industrial expansion. That fate was sealed in 1846 when Governor Charles Paine, president of the newly chartered Vermont-Central Railroad, pursued his personal real estate and business interests and routed the line through his hometown, the small village of Northfield, Vermont. He ignored the easier eastern route, which would have gone through Chelsea or an adjacent township and north to Barre and the state capital at Montpelier. As a result, Chelsea's nearest rail connection was thirteen miles to the south in South Royalton. Before the issue was settled, a young Chelsea lawyer wrote about local reactions to a friend in January 1846: "The Rail Road is stirring up a dreadful commotion . . . They are perfectly confident that their road is the best, but now have given up nearly all hope that it will take the rails."[31]

Such a community was less able to hold on to its young men and women and found it difficult to attract large numbers of newcomers making their starts in life. Out-migration, lessened in-migration, and a lower rate of natural increase combined to hold the township's

Table 2.1. *Population change in Chelsea and other Orange County townships, 1790–1910*

Year	Chelsea		Interior Orange County townships[a]	
	Population	% Change	Population	% Change
1790	239		2,583	
1800	897	+ 275.31	6,589	+ 155.09
1810	1,327	+ 47.94	9,172	+ 39.20
1820	1,462	+ 10.17	—	
1830	1,958	+ 33.92	10,842	
1840	1,959	+ 0.05	10,829	− 0.12
1850	1,958	− 0.05	10,326	− 4.64
1860	1,757	− 10.26	9,573	− 7.29
1870	1,526	− 13.15	8,569	− 10.49
1880	1,462	− 4.19	8,953	+ 4.48[b]
1890	1,230	− 15.87	6,320	− 29.41
1900	1,070	− 13.01	6,039	− 4.45
1910	1,074	+ 0.37	—	

[a] Includes the townships of Corinth, Orange, Strafford, Topsham, Tunbridge, Vershire, and Washington.
[b] The rise between 1870 and 1880 and the sharp decline from 1880 to 1890 were due mainly to the boom and the bust of copper mining in Vershire Township (Vershire population: 1870, 1,140; 1880, 1,875; 1890, 754).
Source: John M. Comstock, *Chelsea, Vermont* (n.p., 1944), 40; and the published volumes of the U.S. Census of Population for 1790, 1800, 1810, 1830, 1840, 1850, 1860, 1870, 1880, 1890, and 1900. Figures for Orange County townships in 1820 are not available.

population constant between 1830 and 1850 and sent it into a steady decline during the second half of the century. Between 1840 and 1900 the population of Chelsea and other adjacent townships in the interior of Orange County decreased by more than 40 percent (Table 2.1). Of the state's 238 townships, over 100 lost more than a quarter of their population during this period; 70 townships, including ten urban areas with populations greater than 2,500, increased; and the remainder either did not change in size or experienced modest declines.[32]

This, of course, is the depopulation for which northern New England is so famous. Rather than viewing these changes as expected characteristics of older agrarian societies, however, the historians of the region have long spoken instead in terms of extraordinary decline and decay. In fact, the portrayal is so bleak that one gets the strong impression that rural New England was particularly cursed. Numerous adverse features of Vermont country life induced a Yankee exodus between 1808 and 1860 as waves of out-migrants escaped cold weather, barren soil, and high taxes and pursued the belief that greener pastures lay just beyond the western horizon. One 1927 study, "A Town That Has Gone Downhill," shows that Lyme, New Hampshire, farmers abandoned their hilltop acreage and either moved to valleys in other communities or to the western frontier. The implication is clear that the quality of life in Lyme went downhill along with its people. The most widely cited treatment of the twin phenomena of depopulation and abandonment of farms is Harold Fisher Wilson's classic study, *The Hill Country of Northern New England*. According to Wilson, the years between 1870 and 1900 were the "winter" of that region's social and economic history, and winters in Maine, New Hampshire, and Vermont are not insignificant matters. Actually, conditions were already beginning to chill during the "autumn" period between 1830 and 1870. Excessive competition from western agriculture and out-migration to the frontier and the cities made for difficult times in rural New England during the nineteenth century, and according to the traditional view, the result was a society that was atypically moribund and morose.[33]

But this interpretation is subject to question. The traditional view is often derived from the writings of biased contemporary observers who did not live in these older communities and tends to take their editorializing and anxious portrayals of "deteriorating" conditions at face value as evidence of social realities. Moreover, none of the authors make good use of available census information and often rely instead on misleading or inappropriate quantitative data.[34]

The traditional view also argues that population decline was related to economic adversity, that out-migrants left because of exceptionally poor economic conditions, and that their departure contributed in turn to further economic deterioration. Some of the region's population loss in the 1820s and 1830s did not result from economic adversity, however, but from an agricultural boom created by the increasing specialization in wool growing. At the height of the Merino mania, many northern New England farmers shifted out of wheat and mixed grain culture and took advantage of rising wool prices by raising sheep, a form of agriculture that was less labor intensive and used more land for grazing. As a result, Wilson himself noted that "sheep thus sometimes tended to crowd out human population."[35]

Later in the century, as developing railroads and industries altered the structure of the regional economy, rural communities in New

England followed divergent paths. One study of the Connecticut River Valley in Massachusetts utilizes a range of sources and differentiates between hill towns, valley towns, and industrial towns – categories that are also appropriate to Vermont and New Hampshire. In the two case studies of hill towns, Pelham and Shutesbury, population peaked in 1820 and began a steady decline throughout the rest of the century. Although the author makes the traditional argument relating economic hardship to population loss, economic indicators were almost constant in spite of this depopulation, real estate values remained virtually the same, and the number of farms in each community did not decline. Hadley and Hatfield, the two valley towns, were much more prosperous because of better land and easier access to urban markets. Yet the population in these communities also peaked and began to decline during the second half of the nineteenth century, and the number of farms and the value of farmland reached a plateau and stayed there. Finally, agriculture in the industrial towns of Ware and Westfield "adhered to the pattern characteristic of the hill and low-land areas." Although industrial expansion caused population and real estate values to increase markedly in both communities, the number of farms and the level of farm production were more constant.[36]

Other more recent scholarship also allows a more sanguine perception of rural New England during the second half of the nineteenth century. According to an anthropological study of Londonderry, Vermont, although the township's population declined by 30 percent between 1860 and 1900, the number of farms and the amount of land in use remained the same. An economist's study of New Hampshire's agricultural economy between 1870 and 1900 demonstrates a similar pattern of stability rather than decline. During the last three decades of the nineteenth century, the "winter" season, the number of farms in the state diminished by only 1 percent, from 29,642 to 29,324, and the total acreage in farms actually increased slightly. Average farm values and the value of farmland also remained more or less constant. Although New Hampshire farm incomes did not compare favorably with nonfarm incomes in the cities, farmers in New Hampshire were significantly better off than their midwestern counterparts because they were spared the burdens of debt and high interest rates and had easier access to nonagricultural goods.[37]

Thus it seems that reports of the region's demise during the nineteenth century are, to borrow from Mark Twain, greatly exaggerated. The slowed growth of New England's agriculture and the loss of rural population are certainly not mythical phenomena, but it is misleading to regard the region's rural development as either extreme or atypical. Rather, these patterns are better understood as "normal" characteristics of older agrarian communities. As in so many other aspects of American history, trends in New England anticipated analogous developments in other regions, and rural New England became the first agricultural area to grow old.

Although one can make the argument today that population loss and lessened growth were understandable features of settled rural life during the second half of the nineteenth century, many contemporary observers were ill equipped to think of these processes as being normal in any sense of the word. Instead, the contrast between decline in older farm areas and the dramatic expansion of the cities aroused significant anxiety and alarm. American culture then, as now, had little tolerance for a situation that did not give at least the illusion of rapid growth and progressive advance.

3   *The different meanings of rural decline in nineteenth-century America*

Population loss and economic stagnation in settled rural communities marked important departures from the prevailing tenor of nineteenth-century American society, and contemporaries reacted to these developments in quite different ways. During the second half of the nineteenth century, urban periodicals such as the *Atlantic Monthly* and the *Nation* often published articles that worried about "The Farmer's Changed Condition" and lamented "The Doom of the Small Town" and "The Passing of the Country Church," and Gilded Age spokesmen such as Josiah Strong considered rural decay a pressing problem, equal to the challenge of the cities. Gradually, these individual concerns manifested themselves in a wide range of organized, institutionalized, and professionalized activities such as the Country Life Movement, the Rural Church Movement, and the emergence of rural sociology as an academic discipline – all designed to improve and strengthen rural life by restructuring rural institutions and rural society.[1]

In contrast, those who were closest to settled rural society and most directly involved in agrarian life tended to be more sanguine. Agricultural periodicals in New England, for example, expressed relatively little anxiety about the nature of country life in the region as it lost population in the middle of the nineteenth century. Instead, reformers in Chelsea and other New England communities formed agricultural societies to promote better farming practices and other economic improvements. Even in the late nineteenth and early twentieth centuries, those who actually lived in older rural communities like Chelsea did not accept the diagnoses or the prescriptions offered by Country Life reformers.

These differing views of settled rural society reflected the divergence of urban and rural culture during the second half of the nineteenth century. As outside concern was shaped by the growing commitment to social science and professionalization, which epitomized the elusive search for order by the new urban middle class, Americans in rural areas continued to adapt older values to changing conditions. In the end, we have also accepted the outsiders' point of view even if late-nineteenth-century rural inhabitants did not. Both their lamentations

31

and their assessments have informed our own perceptions of the history of rural America during this period as well as our more general notions about the nature of rural life in a modern society. Yet this perspective is profoundly limited by the particular historical circumstances of its origins.

Although out-migration and depopulation had long been features of rural New England society, they did not become issues for public discussion until the middle of the nineteenth century. Many of the first Yankee migrants, no doubt, were bound for cities and factories, but this early rural-to-urban migration evinced only a small response. Instead, contemporary observers directed most of their attentions to the increasing numbers of their neighbors who succumbed to the "Western craze" and the "Genesee fever."[2]

According to the conventional wisdom of the time, New England farmers were attracted to the West by the cheapness, abundance, and fertility of western lands. In contrast to the played-out, thin, and stony topsoils of Vermont and New Hampshire, the *New England Farmer* and other agricultural periodicals frequently advertised frontier lands of "inexhaustible depth" and "unsurpassed fertility." Numerous testimonials of high yields by transplanted Yankees reinforced these descriptions, and the comparatively high property taxes in northeastern townships further enhanced the West's relative attractiveness. Most important, however, the value of much New England farmland had reached its peak by midcentury, and western lands not only were much cheaper but also held greater promise for speculative increase.[3]

This quest for greater and easier profits bothered New England agriculturalists, and beginning in the 1840s, editorials in regional farm periodicals began decrying the speculative urge. In an 1843 editorial on emigration, the *Maine Farmer* noted that "one of the hardest, and latest lessons of life, which the human race can be made to learn, is contentment – to be contented with the acquisition of a competent and comfortable subsistence by steady and honest industry." This belief intensified a decade later when a contributor to the *Country Gentleman* complained that few of the western migrants actually worked at "sober" farming and that, "instead of working, the community at large is speculating and 'prospecting.' " The editor echoed this thought in an addendum, noting that "true courage in this case seems to us to be, not in venturing with the multitude to the farthest lengths of speculation, but in daring to refrain from it when almost everybody else is more or less deeply involved."[4]

The virtues of competence and independence and the scorn for speculation expressed in the New England agricultural press embodied a kind of producer's ethic, which also held little truck with those who moved to the city. Henry F. French belittled this form of "social mobility" in an 1854 editorial entitled "Stick to the Farm":

> You are tempted to exchange the hard work of the farm, to become a clerk in a city shop, to put off your heavy boots and frock, and be a gentleman, behind the counter! You, by birth and education, intended for an upright, independent, manly citizen, to call no man master, and to be no man's servant, would become at first, the errand boy of the shop, to fetch and carry like a spaniel, then the salesman . . . to bow and smile and cringe and flatter – to attend upon the wish of every painted and padded form of humanity . . . and finally, to become a trader, a worshipper of mammon . . . compelled to look anxiously at the prices current of cotton and railroad stocks, in order to learn each morning, whether you are bankrupt or not, and in the end, to fail, and compromise with your creditors and your conscience, and sigh for your native hills.[5]

In addition to pointing out the moral, if not always the financial, failings of those who left, New England agriculturalists tried to stem the tide of this exodus by improving the economic position of local agriculture through agricultural reforms. Local farmers' clubs, county and state agricultural societies, and, later, state boards of agriculture provided the institutional framework for most of their efforts in conjunction with the continuing editorials and reportage of the agricultural press.[6]

The Orange County Agricultural Society, for example, was founded in Chelsea, Vermont, in 1846 and was one of a wave of county agricultural societies begun throughout New England during the 1840s and 1850s. In contrast to the learned character of earlier organizations of gentlemen farmers, these new groups were grassroots organizations. In Chelsea the 108 local members of the Orange County Agricultural Society included a sizable percentage of the township's husbandmen drawn from those with small operations as well as those with larger farms, and a dozen artisans and a handful of merchants and professionals also joined.[7]

The primary purposes of these agricultural societies were to hold annual exhibitions and to disseminate the latest state of the agricultural art. The annual fair of the Orange County society in Chelsea in September 1849 awarded 300-odd prizes in more than 100 categories of agricultural produce, mechanical arts, and household manufactures.

In all, the whole range of rural activities was recognized: from a twenty-five-cent discretionary award to nine-year-old Lucy Lovejoy for her two pairs of woolen hose to five dollars to the township of Tunbridge for fielding the best five pairs of working oxen from any one town.[8]

New England agricultural reformers held high hopes for these agricultural societies. In his 1845 article, "New England Emigration," S. C. Charles wrote: "I trust that a brighter day will dawn upon us, when State and county agricultural societies are formed throughout our land. They are beginning to wake up the farmer to the importance of scientific agricultural knowledge in the cultivation of land." State legislatures, recognizing the need to strengthen local farming to combat out-migration, willingly (but not generously) provided a modicum of financial support to the county societies. By 1871 the legislatures in Massachusetts, Maine, New Hampshire, and Vermont had all created state boards of agriculture to further aid the development of that industry. Charles H. Heath no doubt expressed the beliefs and attitudes of those involved when he addressed the founding meeting of the Vermont State Board of Agriculture in 1871:

> The first object of the Board must be to do those things that will tend to increase the population and wealth, as well as the mental and moral improvement of the state . . . For want of that encouragement and those opportunities which it is hoped will result from well applied and united efforts of this sort, many of Vermont's best sons have left her borders and have gone to organize and build up new communities in the West.[9]

These agricultural reformers were convinced that farming in New England could be just as attractive as in the West. The key to economic viability lay in more intensive techniques rather than in the exploitative soil mining that characterized much of American farming. The complaint of old, worn-out soils was false according to the *New England Farmer* in 1845. Certainly the fields of old England were much older, but by careful husbandry they continued to yield abundant harvests.[10]

In his prizewinning essay, which he delivered at the Orange County Agricultural Society Fair in 1849, Waldo M. Spear of Braintree, Vermont, sang the praises of manure and provided a detailed recipe adapted to local soil conditions:

> Thus to take three-fourths of muck, one-fourth animal manure, add one bushel of salt and one of lime to the cord, and let it remain in the compost heap until well rotted and mixed thoroughly . . . Thus every farmer should make from one to two hundred cords of compost yearly. And instead of having hay crops of barely one ton to the acre, we can have three.

Later in the century, state agricultural board officials and other speakers at annual institutes for local farmers repetitiously expounded on the virtues of specialization, careful cultivation, and the adoption of manuring and other scientific techniques. Their maxim to New England husbandmen was to make two blades of grass grow where one had grown before.[11]

Throughout the nineteenth century, agricultural improvers also cautioned against an overly rosy picture of western opportunity. In his address to the Vermont State Board of Agriculture in 1871, Charles Heath voiced another commonly held belief, which was expressed often in the agricultural press, when he noted: "Our own advantages have been overlooked while an exaggerated idea of the West, inconsistent with the true facts of the case, have drawn from us those very men, who, if retained, would have elevated Vermont to a much higher position than she now holds on the roll of states." Other writers in Vermont and New Hampshire were quick to point out that New England states rather than the West received the highest yields per acre of wheat and corn, and that one could make as much profit from a 100-acre dairy farm in Vermont as one could make raising corn on 100 acres in Iowa. A few stressed the noneconomic amenities of older settled areas, which were not available on the frontier, and an 1843 editorial entitled "Emigration from New England" made the following point:

> But every such removal must be attended, among our rural population, with immense sacrifices and privations. In the education and training of their children, and their domestic comforts and social privileges, they will forego advantages which it will be all but impossible to repair; in respect to health, they are almost sure to suffer; and in the power of acquiring by industry and frugality an honest competence, nay, more than that, a reasonable independence, they can seldom better their condition by removal.

Speaking to the Agricultural Society of Rutland County, Vermont, in 1848, George Perkins Marsh called the Yankee emigrant "the deserter who abandoned the blessings of a well-ordered home in New England amidst rural beauty . . . to live among the miry sloughs, the puny groves, the slimy streams which alone diversify the dead uniformity of Wisconsin or Illinois." Other agricultural reformers, like L. D. Mason, continued to express many of the same sentiments more than thirty years later.[12]

The attitudes expressed by New England agriculturalists continued to hold sway in the region throughout the second half of the nineteenth century, but they represented a curious combination of values that was increasingly at odds with the larger urban society. On the one hand, agricultural spokesmen advocated responding to market pressures and adopting rational scientific techniques to increase productivity and maximize profits. On the other hand, they advised contentment with a competence or a modest independence and berated those who went after greater or quicker returns. Such a blend of attitudes resists easy categorization as traditional or modern, yet it continued to inform the lives of settled rural New Englanders as American society underwent its great transformation.

The county societies and the reformers connected with farm periodicals and state boards of agriculture did much to improve husbandry in northern New England, but they did little to reverse or even abate the trend of rural depopulation, which intensified during the second half of the nineteenth century. From their statements and proposed remedies, though, it is clear that these agricultural improvers did not regard continued out-migration as an indictment of rural New England society or of rural life more generally. They felt none of the panic over rural decline and none of the compulsion to reshape the entire fabric of rural life that others would feel toward the end of the century. Instead, they chastised those who left the region and criticized their wrongheaded values and their betrayal of the producer's ethic. More important, agriculturalists regarded population loss mainly as the result of an imbalance of economic opportunities between rural New England and the West, which they sought to redress through specific agricultural reforms.

Ultimately, the spokesmen for rural New England remained secure in the fact that theirs was still an agrarian nation. For whatever reasons, most of the emigrants moved to other rural areas, and the agrarianism that Waldo Spear expressed at the end of his address in Chelsea in 1849 continued to ring true:

> Would you be strong? go follow the plow.
> Would you be thoughtful? study the fields and flowers.
> Would you be wise? take on yourself a vow
> To go to school in Nature's sunny bowers.
> Fly from the city; nothing there can charm:
> Seek wisdom, strength and virtue on a farm.[13]

By the end of the nineteenth century, however, that confidence in rural life met new and significant challenges as the degree and scope of rural depopulation increased markedly. Declining agricultural communities were no longer confined to New England and New York, and contemporary observers were well aware of the change. In an essay in the *Forum* in 1895, Henry U. Fletcher noted that more than half the rural townships in Ohio, Indiana, and Illinois lost population between 1880 and 1890, and the rate in Iowa was not far behind. Even more alarming, however, was the new perception that migrants from the Northeast and the Midwest were not moving primarily to other rural areas but to the cities. This "drift to the city" combined with increasing foreign immigration to urban areas and signaled a fundamental shift in the nature of American society that earlier migrations did not imply.[14]

Anxiety over urban growth at the expense of the countryside, though long a fixture of Jeffersonian agrarianism, increased markedly during the closing decades of the nineteenth century. Rural depopulation was no longer discussed principally by agricultural reformers, however, but by conservative social critics who were distressed by the new directions of social change. Whereas earlier writers stressed the ill effects of city life on individual health and morality, now commentators worried that the future of the nation as a whole was at stake. In his widely discussed book *The New Era*, Josiah Strong devoted a whole chapter to "The Problem of the Country" and expressed grave concern about rural migration to the cities:

> Vast movements of population are of profound significance both in their causes and effects. While we hear much of the millions of aliens who are flooding our shores and foreignizing our cities, but little is said of a movement hardly less momentous, whose consequences, though not so obvious, are perhaps equally far-reaching. I refer to the tide of population which is setting so strongly from country to city, and which is depleting the one and congesting the other, to the detriment of both.[15]

Sharing Strong's concern, other writers regarded this state of affairs as a threat to the nation's future well-being. An 1892 essayist stressed the dependence of the city on the countryside. "Sociologists tell us," he wrote, quoting some published conventional wisdom of the day, "that 'only the agricultural class possesses permanent vitality; from its overflow the city population is formed, displaced, renewed.' 'Any city population, if left to itself, would die out in four generations.' 'The city is an inland lake, fed by constant streams, but without an outlet.' " Continuing this aquatic metaphor, he prophesied, "as are the fountains [i.e., country], so will be stream and lake."[16]

Others, more apocalyptic in their outlook, cited ominous historical precedents. In his discussion of "The Farmer's Changed Condition" in the *Forum* in 1891, Rodney Welch noted that, before the decline of the Roman Empire, farmers of wealth and culture left their estates in the care of others and moved to the cities, which afforded them greater opportunities for pleasure. Anticipating the maxim that those who forget the past are condemned to repeat it, Welch went on to mention a rural–urban shift in France just before the French Revolution. "With little doubt," he stated, "it was the cause of that event."[17]

In addition to worries about the national welfare, the declining quality of life in depopulated rural communities was also cause for concern. As the size of a farm township declined, roads deteriorated, property values depreciated, and local institutions fell into disuse and disrepair. There "comes a tendency toward degeneration and demoralization," as Josiah Strong explained, wherever rural population decreases.[18]

The problems of the rural church were one focal point of this concern. More than the schools or local government, the church was regarded as the key institution in the country community. Consequently, the declining numbers of active congregations and the diminished numbers of members and worshipers indicated a severe threat to the welfare of rural society. To quote an 1891 author, a New Hampshire-born professor at the University of Iowa:

> Many churches have dwindled into insignificance, or have been blotted out altogether, owing to deaths and removals, with no corresponding additions. In scores of towns houses of worship are closed, to all appearance finally, or are used for non-religious purposes, while others are in the hands of Catholics, or are too far gone for occupancy of any sort . . . The home mission societies regard some of these towns in as much need of missionary work as the rudest frontier settlements.[19]

The president of Bowdoin College sounded an even more alarming note the following year with an article entitled "Impending Paganism in New England." Such problems extended to the Midwest as well. According to the *Andover Review* in November 1890 there were "more villages in Illinois without the gospel than in any other state in the Union."[20]

Even more haunting than the specters of rutted roads or dilapidated churches was the sorry state of those who stayed behind. In his discussion of midwestern population decline, Henry U. Fletcher delineated the negative results of selective out-migration:

> One by one, family by family, their inhabitants slip away in search of other homes; a steady but hardly perceptible emigration takes away the young, the hopeful, the ambitious. There remain behind the superannuated, the feeble, the dull, the stagnant rich who will risk nothing, the ne'er do-wells who have nothing to risk. Enough workers remain to till the soil, to manage the distribution

of food and clothing, and to transact the common business of life; but the world's real work is done elsewhere.[21]

The long-term consequences were positively lurid. Josiah Strong and former clergyman and popular writer Rollin Lynde Hartt likened isolated New England to the depravity of poor whites in Alabama and Tennessee. According to Strong, the isolation and depopulation of one New England town resulted in "the same illiteracy, the same ignorance of the Christian religion, the same vices, the same 'marriage' and 'divorce' without reference to the laws of God or man, which characterize the mountain whites of the South." Later, eugenicists such as Charles B. Davenport formalized this impression and viewed feeblemindedness and sexual immorality as the hereditarian hallmarks of declining and degenerating rural communities. The twentieth-century sociologist Edward A. Ross rejected the concept of folk degeneration as being a narrowly biological one and emphasized instead the broader notions of folk depletion and deteriorating conditions caused by the departure of the natural leadership from rural communities. In the end, however, the results were the same:

> Let no one imagine that the symptoms of folk depletion are confined to the stagnating counties of New England. This phenomenon has a wider range than most people suspect . . . In parts of southern Michigan, Illinois, Wisconsin, and even as far west as Missouri there are communities which remind one of fished-out ponds populated chiefly by bull heads and suckers.[22]

Rural society, in those areas losing population at least, had lost its place as the fount of independent, republican virtue. Before urbanization, according to Rodney Welch, life in the country was as "refined and cultured as that of the towns . . . In short, farmers constituted a class from which men could be selected who were, by virtue of their intellect and learning, competent to fill public position." By the end of the century, many observers were convinced that people of that caliber had left the countryside for the city. In those areas where out-migrants were replaced by newcomers, the incursion of foreign stock and the rising incidence of tenancy exacerbated contemporary anxieties about rural decline. Troubled by the increasing numbers of foreign tenants, an 1891 commentator noted: "In entire counties in Illinois and Wisconsin the English language is scarcely heard outside of the large towns." The vision of a society like that in Europe was bothersome. In place of sturdy Yankee yeomen, America would soon have an illiterate rural peasantry, "possessing the rights of citizenship" but unable to speak English and "utterly incapable of performing or comprehending its duties."[23]

These anxious portrayals of rural decline were not entirely accurate descriptions of contemporary conditions. Many of these social critics were projecting their doubts about urban society on rural communities that were far removed from their experience. Others mostly lamented the decline of their own importance rather than that of their community as a whole. Ministers who decried the abandonment of religion, for example, often seemed to be more concerned with the institutional trappings of faith than with faith or Christian morality itself. Amos N. Currier's depiction of closed and rotting church buildings prompted one New England farmer to respond: "If religion has declined among our people, there has been no accompanying decline of morality. The ministers have lost much of their influence chiefly because they have been educated away from the people." Similarly, concern about religious decline was confined to the established Protestant denominations. Though Catholicism and evangelical revivalism were thriving in many rural communities, social commentators did not consider them legitimate religious expressions. Catholicism was a corrupting foreign influence, and the various holiness sects were rejected because they were unorganized, illiterate, and lower class. In his article "The Future of Rural New England," Alvan F. Sanborn felt that the two new churches in his town were a step backward because the congregations were fundamentalist and narrow. James E. Boyle took a dim view of similar trends in the Midwest when he noted: "But never have I found a case where these self-proclaimed 'sanctified' people have convinced their neighbors of their sanctity."[24]

The middle-class biases of most of these observers colored their perceptions. In contrast, several farmers who responded to the more hyperbolic depictions were less concerned about the extent or effect of social decline. T. H. Hoskins rejected any nostalgia for a golden past and noted in 1891 that "the comfort and prosperity of the earlier generations of our farmers are exaggerated. There was as much debt, as little general advance, and very much more vice among New England farmers fifty years ago than now." Rather than expressing any regret about the loss of a leadership class, one resident of a remote hill town celebrated in his community's egalitarianism. He shared little of the others' uneasiness over the declining vitality and the increasing poverty of rural life. Instead, he was happy to be isolated from the mainstream:

> This isolation helps keep out the feverish spirit which troubles most American communities. There is little ambition of any sort among us; and the modern principle that every man ought to labor everyday, and through the whole of every day, finds no

acceptance whatever in our corner of New England . . . In short
we prefer to take such amusements as we can get, day by day,
rather than to expend all our efforts in merely striving to better
our material condition . . . It would be easy to quarrel with this
kind of philosophy; and yet the result is that, although poor, we
enjoy what is accounted the best gift of wealth, namely, leisure.[25]

Although farmers and other settled rural inhabitants did not share
this anxiety over rural depopulation and decline, it was no less
heartfelt. Conservative social critics mourned the passing of small
New England and midwestern towns as the cultural arbiters of
American life and expressed increasing alarm over the transformation
of American society into predominantly urban forms. If, as has been
asserted, "the great casualty of America's turmoil late in the century
was the island community," then this was its swan song.[26]

As a result of these expressions of alarm, a new generation of in-
tellectuals and reformers turned its attention to the problems of rural
life and offered a new perspective and new solutions based on the
precepts of social efficiency and social-scientific analysis. Certainly,
the earlier efforts to increase the economic efficiency of farming
continued and expanded. Local farmers' institutes grew and evolved
into the agricultural extension system created by the Smith–Lever
Act in 1914. The Hatch Act in 1887 and the Adams Act in 1906 also
provided federal support for agricultural research designed to increase
farm productivity. What is significant about the attempts to remedy
rural depopulation in the late nineteenth and early twentieth centuries
is that, for the first time, they included a substantial number of
measures addressed specifically at the social problems of country
life.[27]

The men and women who advocated these reforms, known loosely
as the Country Life Movement, were a new breed. Very few were
farmers, and though many were born in rural communities, hardly
any lived in the countryside as adults. Instead, they were educators,
professors, and clergymen who resided in urban areas and academic
centers. Much in line with more general portrayals of Progressive
reformers, the Country Life activists were relatively young and very
well educated, often with degrees from leading colleges and universities, and most were members of scientific or social-scientific
professional organizations. In short, they were members of the new
middle class.[28]

The Country Life reformers also had a different perception of rural
problems. Though they were inspired by the concerns of the previous

decade, they did not share in its anxieties. Rather than accept the subjective and anecdotal approach of earlier observers, rural reformers attempted a more detatched and scientific assessment of the situation. Much like their contemporaries concerned with urban social problems, they believed that systematic surveys were the only basis from which to implement effective social reforms. As a result of such surveys, a more careful analysis of census statistics, and a perspective rooted in sociological and economic theory, the Country Life reformers came to regard rural depopulation as something much less ominous than the doom of American civilization. Rather, it was a temporary adjustment in the transition to a new industrial order whose negative aspects could be ameliorated through specific reforms. Unlike their predecessors, these new reformers were bothered not at all by the vision of an urban-industrial social order.[29]

No single work better illustrates this new perspective or had a greater influence on contemporary reformers than Wilbert L. Anderson's *The Country Town: A Study of Rural Evolution*, published in 1906. Though a minister by profession, Anderson was clearly an advocate of the social-scientific approach and well attuned to the contemporary works of sociology and economics, as his numerous references to Adna Weber and Franklin H. Giddings attest. From the first sentence of his preface, it is clear that he differed significantly from earlier rural commentators:

> Science has the difficult task of correcting the illusions of the senses. The heavens and the atoms alike deceive the observer, and in history, also, things are not what they seem. The social fact thrusting itself upon impression has another character when placed under the laws of progress. One group of observations has peculiar need of interpretation – radical changes in the rural population meet the eye everywhere, of which crass misjudgment passes from lip to lip and from page to page of print . . . It is time to attempt a careful survey of this whole region, into which adventurers have pressed rashly, and from which explorers have brought disheartening reports.[30]

In Anderson's view, the growth of the city and the development of an industrial economy did not cause the deterioration of the countryside. Rather, the mechanization of agriculture created a surplus rural population, which moved to the cities, and this growth of urban areas in turn created new markets for rural farmers. Thus, city and country were not antagonists but interrelated components, each contributing to the welfare of the other. As Anderson put it: "The growth of the city, therefore, assures a corresponding rural development and prosperity. Nothing is more devoid of economic intelligence than the representation of the city as growing continuously through the gregarious instinct of man, until the country ceases to be significant in comparison." The migration of rural people was a healthy consequence of the shift from the "age of homespun" to the "age of machinery," and as such it was only an intermediate phase in the achievement of a new economic equilibrium. Based on his analysis of census statistics, Anderson felt that the period of rural population loss would soon draw to a close.[31]

In spite of some depopulation, Anderson contended that most rural areas were not really suffering, and his analysis of local conditions provided a more evenhanded assessment than previous appraisals. He noted, for example, that out-migration from depopulating communities was selective of those at the bottom of the social scale as well as those at the top. As Anderson put it: "The net result of these changes is a gain in homogeneousness; in the country town the dream of equality is nearer realization today than ever before."[32]

The decay of local institutions, though often a consequence of extensive depopulation, was not an inevitable result. Citing studies of church membership, Anderson noted that churches can and did grow in many declining townships. As he stated: "More depends on the vitality and activity of the church than upon the fortune of the town in keeping or losing its people." To remedy the decay where it had already occurred, Anderson proposed a program of social reconstruction of local institutions, primarily the church, and placed his faith in the good middle-class farmers who remained while others left.[33]

Thus, the utilization of a more systematic analysis enabled Anderson to qualify earlier views of rural–urban migration and its impact on rural society. At the heart of his perspective was his ability to view rural trends as interdependent with a broad range of societal changes. One intellectual historian has recently suggested that this sensitivity to interdependence was the conceptual paradigm that defined late-nineteenth-century social-scientific thought and distinguished it from previous social analyses. For Anderson and other Country Life reformers, their awareness of societal interdependence provided the means to transcend the apocalyptic quality of earlier interpretations of rural change and to focus instead on specific areas in need of reform. Even Josiah Strong changed his mind. In his introduction to *The Country Town*, Strong expressed his admiration for Anderson's book and, in contrast to his earlier views on the subject, agreed with Anderson's conclusion "that there is no scientific reason for the popular notion that the rural population is under a fatality of evil."[34]

Though the survival of rural life was assured, its social vitality was not. Even Anderson had not been so sanguine as this. Among the Country Life reformers, there was the pervasive feeling that urban life was more attractive than rural life because more country people appeared to be moving to the cities than was warranted by economic considerations alone. As one rural sociologist wrote:

> The fact that the country people are leaving the country for the life of the city is very strong evidence of their judgement that, taking everything into consideration, life in the city is preferable to country life at the present time. The problem before us now is to develop a life in the country which will be as satisfying economically, socially, and spiritually as the best life to be found in urban communities.

Rural institutions and patterns of social interaction were backward and "socially inefficient," and life in the country did not give the people what they wanted (or, more to the point, what the reformers felt they needed). In the hopes of making country life more attractive and better able to compete for inhabitants, rural reformers sought to reconstruct local institutions and to create a new social fabric in rural communities. In place of the older and declining sources of social order, they sought to institute new patterns of authority based on criteria of professionalism and social efficiency.[35]

The Rural Church Movement was a major aspect of Country Life reform. Taking their cues from the social gospel and the urban trend toward institutional churches, rural church reformers worked to revitalize established Protestantism. The basis of the country church's problems, they felt, was the people's loss of faith – not a loss of theological faith but a loss of faith in the church as a social institution. The excess of denominationalism, which characterized many rural communities, was at the root of this social ineffectiveness. In place of several weak denominational churches, reformers advocated one large union church or cooperative congregation. Such an institutional base would facilitate the broader social role that they envisioned for the church within the community. The rural church should become the social center of the community in addition to its spiritual core and thus enhance the sociability of rural compared to city life. In addition to organized social activities, the rural church must also elaborate a program of local reforms and base all its activities on a scientific study of local conditions.[36]

Such surveys of rural religious and social conditions formed the major activity of the Rural Church Movement, and national denominational and interdenominational organizations sponsored numerous sophisticated social-scientific studies. The earliest and most influential of these surveys was *The Country Church: The Decline of Its Influence and the Remedy*, which was a study of Protestant churches in Windsor County, Vermont, and the rural parts of Tompkins County, New York, and was published in 1913 under the auspices of the Federal Council of Churches of Christ in America. One of its two authors, Charles O. Gill, was a country minister who, fifteen years earlier, had established his own church in a Windsor County township that had been without a minister for more than twenty years. His co-author was his more illustrious cousin, Gifford Pinchot, a noted apostle of Progressive reform. Stimulated by Theodore Roosevelt's establishment of the Commission on Country Life in 1908, the two cousins began their study in 1909 and meticulously gathered and analyzed data on changes in church membership and attendance, changes in contributions measured in current and constant dollars, ministers' salaries, and equipment. They related this information to variations in local soil quality and social and economic conditions, as well as to differences in the specific programs of the individual churches. As a result of their efforts, the Federal Council of Churches of Christ in America created a Commission on Church and Country Life, which Gill left his pulpit to administer. He and Pinchot later co-authored a similar but much expanded study of organized religion in Ohio entitled *Six Thousand Country Churches*.[37]

Many of the rural church activists were professional sociologists. Warren H. Wilson, a minister and an early Ph.D. student of Franklin H. Giddings at Columbia, headed the Department of Church and Country Life of the Presbyterian Board of Home Missions and, in that capacity, directed numerous rural county surveys. Similarly, Edmund deS. Brunner began his career as a rural sociologist as the director of the Town and Country Division of the evangelical Interchurch World Movement and later headed the Institute of Social and Religious Research. In these positions, he oversaw a comprehensive study of 25 typical rural counties and the partial study of more than 1,000 others and encouraged the publication of a multitude of volumes on rural social and religious issues. Thus, a large number of the leaders in the first generation of rural sociologists, including Paul L. Vogt, Newell Sims, Edwin L. Earp, and C. Luther Fry, had very close ties to the Rural Church Movement.[38]

The other thrust of the Rural Church Movement was the professionalization of the rural ministry. Church reformers felt that much of the resistance to their ideas came from the country pastorate. George F. Wells noted in his investigation for the Carnegie Institute: "Perhaps the most pathetic and deplorable phase of the entire social problem of the rural church lies in the fact that the country clergymen themselves as a class do not understand the problem of their churches as social and capable of solution." In Wells's opinion, there was an increasing deficiency of "efficient" clergymen, and as a remedy, rural church reformers stressed better training for country ministers. Toward this end, Edwin L. Earp, professor of sociology at Drew Theological Seminary, and Dean G. Walter Fiske of Oberlin Theological Seminary offered courses specifically on rural problems to help correct the predominantly urban orientation of seminary education.[39]

The rural school was the second institutional focus of the Country Life Movement. Paralleling the measures advocated for the rural church, reformers proposed consolidation and professionalization as the solutions to the rural-school problem. In light of the social decline of numerous rural communities, educational reformers such as Ellwood P. Cubberly and Harold Fought felt that farmers were no longer capable of managing their own schools. Instead, schools should be taken out of local politics, consolidated, and put under the control of expert county superintendents and well-trained teachers. The consolidation of one-room rural schools would facilitate such educational innovations as grading and curriculum expansion, as well as the construction of new school buildings as well lit, ventilated, and equipped as the most modern and efficient urban schools.[40]

Rural-school reformers also proposed basic changes in the curriculum. Farmers, it seems, were not even capable of teaching their children how to farm properly. The poor attitudes and unscientific practices that father instilled in son were, in the eyes of many Country Life reformers, causes of the migration away from farming. To remedy this problem, they urged the adoption of a strong vocational curriculum that would teach scientific agricultural methods and thereby elevate the status of farming to that of a profession in the minds of rural students. Gill and Pinchot called for the establishment of agricultural high schools in *The Country Church*, and vocational programs in agriculture and home economics were important elements of the attempts to combat social and economic inefficiency in the countryside. A leading historian of education recently summed up the school reformers' ultimate vision: "In the form of a one best system designed by professionals the rural school would teach country children sound values and vocational skills; the result was to be a standardized, modernized 'community' in which leadership came from the professionals."[41]

In addition to changes in specific rural institutions, Country Life reformers were concerned at a more general level with the entire process of socialization in rural communities. Dean G. Walter Fiske defined this as the "civilizing process in which individuals, by merging their rights, interests, and functions, develop community efficiency through group action." Again, the Country Lifers looked to the city for their example, because the urban environment, they believed, had the advantage of developing this process more rapidly and thoroughly. The "Challenge of the Country," to quote the title of Fiske's book, was to "teach the country the secrets of socialization, so that the social efficiency of urban life may be reproduced in the country."[42]

The efforts to improve rural recreation provide one of many examples of this goal and pattern of emulation. Noting that there was a playground in every factory town, Warren H. Wilson stressed the need for comparable rural facilities. Likewise, adult recreation should also be organized. The casual meetings in the country community were, Wilson felt, "a wholly insufficient socializing experience . . . there is little of politics or religion and nothing of art, literature, social reform." Instead, Wilson and others advocated dramatic clubs, athletic leagues, and pageants analogous to the group activities in a European village or a planned urban community.[43]

It is ironic in light of the previous generation's fears of evolving into a peasant society that these rural reformers should look to European village festivals as one source of their programs. The greater irony, however, is related to the Country Life Movement's notion of urban society. Various scholars have shown that their fellow reformers in the cities held a pristine vision of rural community, an Arcadian myth, in their minds' eyes as they advocated garden cemeteries, urban parks, planned housing, zoning, and similar reforms. In contrast, Country Life activists subscribed to an equally fallacious view of city life and created a myth of urban social efficiency.[44]

In spite of the lack of a central umbrella organization, the Country Life Movement institutionalized a community of interest concerned with the problems of rural society through numerous conferences and publications. The first rural conferences were held mainly at the state level, but President Theodore Roosevelt's appointment of the Commission on Country Life in 1908 gave the movement a national scope. By 1917 both the American Academy of Political and Social Science and the American Sociological Society had sponsored symposia on rural conditions and published the proceedings. Through their papers and proposals, Country Life reformers sought to bring American rural society into congruence with the dominant urban way of life by developing centralized, efficient social institutions. That they had little direct connection with the rural communities they wanted to reshape was not a hindrance in their eyes but a further indication of their own objectivity and a further testimony to the efficacy of social science as the basis of a planned society.[45]

Eventually, however, they wound up talking only to themselves. Few of the movement's social reforms were successful, and after World War I, the zeal for rural reform waned along with the rest of the Progressive impulses. Instead, energy was increasingly channeled into legitimizing the new academic discipline of rural sociology. As a result, the organization of conferences, the taking of rural surveys, and the development of a college curriculum concerning rural issues gradually became ends in and of themselves. When the Purnell Act of 1925 provided federal funds for the study of rural social conditions to be administered by the Agricultural Experiment Stations, the discipline took still another step away from its religious and reformist origins.[46]

Few at the local level shared the Country Life reformers' assessments of their problems or their desires to restructure community institutions. The only reforms that struck responsive chords were those that offered some immediate economic benefits to the farmer, and even here the positive response was far from unanimous. Agricultural extension work, the movement for good roads, the development of rural cooperatives, and rural free delivery, which did much to alleviate the oft-cited economic and social isolation of rural life, were all advanced but not usually initiated by the Country Life Movement.[47]

In contrast, the Rural Church Movement found little grass-roots support. The country pastorate resisted social-gospel interpretations of their churches' problems, and rural parishioners continued to subscribe to theological fundamentalism rather than moving toward a broader social role for their churches. Thus, the reformers' drive for federated congregations made little headway. The federal census of religious bodies did not consider their number significant enough to be recorded separately until 1926. In 1926, federated churches in Vermont, the state with the largest number, accounted for only 6 percent of the Protestant congregations. In all of New England, the region with the greatest concentration of these churches, federated church members comprised just 1 percent of all affiliated Protestants.[48]

Though the drive toward consolidated schools was ultimately more successful than the movement for cooperative churches, it too met with local resistance. In Vermont, the issue first came up in 1885 when the state legislature asked all townships to consider abolishing their district school systems in favor of a more centralized township school system. Only fifteen townships in the state agreed to do this, and Chelseans voted down the proposed reform in 1886 by more than 3 to 1. Those in nearby Thetford were even more adamantly opposed to the new system, prompting one local school official to declare: "There is a mistaken notion, too widely prevalent, that our educational system is almost, if not quite a failure. Such is not the case, our schools have been unjustly condemned by those who know not of what they speak." Quoting from one scholar's extensive research on the subject: "The impetus to consolidate rural schools almost always came from outside the rural community. It was rare to find a local group that 'had sponsored or spearheaded the drive for re-organization.' "[49]

Rural Americans resisted educational reform for a variety of reasons: Changes would be expensive; they would lose control of their schools; they resented the reformers' condescending attitudes, and they simply did not share their urban assumptions. Even the work of local groups to bring about school consolidation did not imply an awareness of, or an accord with, the broader ideological perspective of the reformers. In Chelsea and other depopulating rural communities, the eventual consolidation of schools was a response to the diminishing number of schoolchildren rather than an attempt to reform local education. According to a case study of an Ohio township, residents of Kingsville in Ashtabula County did not advocate consolidation to improve the quality of local schools. Rather, they felt that transporting students to an existing school in a central location would pose less of a burden to local taxpayers than constructing new decentralized school buildings.[50]

Local farmers also voiced fundamental disagreement with the perspective of rural reformers in letters to the editor and other discussions of the Country Life Movement in the agricultural press. Often they expressed resentment toward the incursion of self-proclaimed experts who had little knowledge of the day-to-day realities of farming or rural life. To the extent that there were any problems with life in the country, farmers believed that they were economic, not social. The real social problems were in the cities. In 1908, the year Theodore Roosevelt appointed his Commission on Country Life, the Worthy

Overseer of the Patrons of Husbandry proposed tongue-in-cheek that the Grange appoint a "Commission on City Life" to investigate social conditions in urban areas. The consensus from the countryside was clear: "Farmers could take care of themselves; the real need was for more money in the farmers' pockets."[51]

By rejecting the Country Life Movement, rural inhabitants did more than empty their shotguns at some unwanted urban interlopers. They rejected an entire world view – a perception of the nature of the industrial revolution and a vision of a progressive society planned by social scientists and run by professionals. Though many in the cities also rejected this perspective, it gained increasing support, both active and tacit, among the urban middle classes. Along with laborers and immigrants, then, farmers had different perceptions of the impact of industrial capitalism and different notions of how to lead their lives.

Just what those perceptions and notions were and how they came to be is difficult to tell. In depopulating farm areas, the problem is compounded because regional historians have treated the anxious descriptions of the 1890s and the self-serving analyses of the Country Life reformers as evidence of social reality. A better approach would be to study the behavior of the rural men and women who experienced these changes directly. What impact did the dramatic economic and social upheavals of the second half of the nineteenth century have on their lives and the nature of their society? It is to these questions that we now turn as we focus on a case study of an older rural community that suffered extensive population loss.

4   Quitting the farm and closing the shop: the economy of a settled rural community

On Friday evening, 11 February 1876, in Chelsea, Vermont, Colonel John B. Mead, an agricultural reformer from the neighboring town of Randolph, delivered the closing address at the State Board of Agriculture's institute for area farmers. His talk, "Opportunities for Young Farmers," concerned the widespread exodus of young men from their fathers' farms and voiced a familiar theme. Young men, Mead warned, "quit the paternal acres, upon arriving at their majority, their heads filled with visionary schemes for rapidly getting wealth, which, to a vast number, through erroneous education, is the 'chief end of man.' " To Mead, like many other agricultural writers of the time, this picture was depressing indeed. "I venture the assertion," he said, "that in ninety-nine cases of every one hundred where young men leave the farm to seek the good they would possess and enjoy, sooner or later they will candidly admit that the same goal might have been reached, both in honors and in wealth, through the patient continuance in well doing at the home of their boyhood."[1]

Whether they agreed with Colonel Mead's assertions or not, the good people of Chelsea must have provided an attentive audience, for the problem of young men quitting the paternal farm was one they knew only too well. Of the 153 young males between five and fourteen years of age listed in the U.S. census returns for Chelsea in 1860, only 36, less than 25 percent, were still present in 1880. Because the numbers of those leaving had long exceeded those coming in, Chelsea, along with many other rural Vermont townships, was in the midst of an extended period of population decline.[2]

From the perspective of national development, this out-migration was part of a larger redistribution of population that accompanied the expansion of the United States economy in the nineteenth century. According to economic theory, modern economic growth depends on such internal migration to reallocate the supply of labor to areas of greater economic opportunity. Whereas the stream of migration from northern New England definitely facilitated national economic growth, its effect on the small rural communities that supplied the migrants is less clear-cut.[3]

At a more local level, the traditional view of northern New England

51

during the nineteenth century paints a picture of economic decline that coincided with the loss of population. Yankees left northern New England because they were attracted by new opportunities: the rise of the West and the lure of the city. At the same time, price competition from western agriculture caused the local farm economy to suffer. Thus, throughout the century, farms in New Hampshire and Vermont were deserted, mills and shops were closed, and the depopulated township quickly went downhill.[4]

For all its emphasis on the importance of these outside economic forces, however, the traditional view fails to give an accurate depiction of local economic conditions and does not explicitly consider their relationship to out-migration. In *The Hill Country of Northern New England*, Harold Fisher Wilson uses only state level statistics from the agricultural census to impute changes in the local economy. Similarly, none of the monographs on specific communities that lost population use manuscript schedules or even published county-level data to delineate local trends. Instead, Wilson and the others base their interpretation primarily on contemporary observation, much of it hyperbole about "abandoned" farms or editorializing about the decay of old New England.[5]

In contrast, a closer study of Chelsea between 1840 and 1900 shows that both the agricultural and nonagricultural sectors of the local economy did not experience wholesale decline in the face of constant population loss. At the same time, however, the gradually diminishing number of local inhabitants did not allow continued development. Rather, the local economy slowed down and stabilized as both farmers and villagers adjusted to outside economic changes as well as to local demographic realities. The lessened growth and stability that gradually emerged from this equilibrium between local and translocal factors were typical characteristics of settled rural economies, and many of the developments in Chelsea occurred throughout the region and were repeated later in other older rural areas.

Chelsea at midcentury was a typical middle-sized rural Vermont township. The village contained the usual array of institutions: a bank, a post office, several general stores, a string of workshops, a hotel and a livery stable, an academy, two churches, a jail, and a courthouse. There was no large-scale industry, and only a few small factories produced for outside markets. Instead, village artisans, merchants, and professionals provided goods and rendered services to area husbandmen. From their shops, blacksmiths shod horses and fabricated agricultural machinery, and local shoemakers and tailors outfitted the farmers and their families. Merchants bought and sold, teamsters hauled to and fro, and along the streams, millers sawed wood and ground grain. The village doctors and dentists ministered to the farmers' bodies, and the Congregational and Methodist clergymen cared for their souls.[6]

Agriculture was the principal economic activity in the township, and the land in Chelsea was hilly, much like the terrain in many of the New England townships that lost population during the nineteenth century. In spite of the hills, however, farming was viable. As Zadock Thompson wrote about Chelsea in 1824, "the surface is considerable uneven, but the soil is, in general, warm and productive," and he noted in 1842 that "all kinds of grain common in Vermont, are raised with tolerable success." According to present-day studies, Chelsea's land-class index rating ranks in the middle group of Vermont townships. The majority of its 24,000 acres are termed "fair to good farm areas"; 30 percent is rated poor to fair, and 10 percent is deemed unsatisfactory for modern dairy farming. As an 1892 survey of agricultural conditions in Orange County reported: "There is but little land in this County unfit for agricultural purposes. Where by reason of being rough or stony it is unfit for tillage, it affords excellent pasturage."[7]

At midcentury, Chelsea farmers took advantage of that pastureland and, like most Vermont husbandmen, relied primarily on livestock rather than cereal crops. The 1840 Census counted 340 horses, 971 swine, and 1,710 cattle in addition to 6,696 sheep, and the principal field crops were oats and hay to feed the farm animals. These animals and their products were the focus of the Orange County Agricultural Society fairs during the 1850s, and the biggest cash prizes were given for numerous categories of horses, cattle, oxen, milch cows, and sheep, and butter, cheese, and wool were also well rewarded. Area farmers also displayed maple sugar and orchard fruits and won smaller prizes for potatoes, onions, beets, pulse, and similar vegetables.[8]

On the eve of the Civil War, Martin S. Carpenter's farm exemplified the mix of wool, butter, and maple sugar production that characterized Chelsea's agriculture. At the age of thirty-one, Carpenter owned a 140-acre farm worth $2,100, three horses, a yoke of oxen, four head of cattle, one hog, four milk cows, and twenty-five sheep. He must have been particularly proud of his oxen because he had entered them in the competition at the 1858 Orange County Fair. From these animals, valued at $600, he produced 120 pounds of wool, 500 pounds of butter, and 100 pounds of cheese, and meat and hides worth in all about $200 in that year's market. He harvested 125 bushels of potatoes worth $40, and his 40 acres of woodland yielded 400 pounds of maple sugar for an additional income of $50. Carpenter planted only small amounts of grain and other food crops; instead, most of his labor went toward the 30 tons of hay he grew to feed his livestock.[9]

Because his own family was so young, Martin Carpenter had to turn to others for additional labor. Martin's twenty-four-year-old brother, Alvah Carpenter, recorded in a diary for 1861–3 that he had spent much of his time working on Martin's farm in addition to his own. Alvah's terse entries give muted testimony to the arduous toil and the seasonality of work on these nineteenth-century Vermont farms. The yearly cycle began toward the end of April when Alvah used his brother's prized oxen to draw manure out to the fields. The Carpenter brothers spent the next few months manuring, harrowing, plowing, sowing, and hoeing their field crops. "Harrowed and manured in the hill," "Martin helped plow with horse," "sowed wheat," "planted corn in the forenoon," and "planted potatoes," Alvah wrote often during May. In June and the first part of July, he sowed barley, planted beans, and hoed all the different crops.[10]

Haying commenced around the third week in July, and it represented the busiest time of the year. Depending on the weather, Alvah was able to mow all or part of the day and got in from one to five wagonloads. This was an involved operation that demanded more than one man, so several neighbors and relatives swapped labor during the haying season. In addition to working with his brother Martin, Alvah noted help from his other brother, Nelson, and from fellow townsmen Lewis and Israel, and he, in turn, worked for them in their fields.[11]

During September and October, the Carpenters harvested the other crops with less frequent outside help. They got in oats, wheat, and barley, which they thrashed, and they also cut up and husked corn, dug potatoes, and picked apples. This was the time to begin readying for winter, so Alvah stacked firewood in the sheds, repaired his sleigh, banked the house, and worked on the barnyard. He made provisions for wintering some of his sheep with neighbors and butchered a few hogs to sell and to provide meat for the coming months.

The winter months were not as filled with work as the fall had been, and Alvah made more frequent trips to the village as well as a number of day journeys to Montpelier and other nearby towns. Interspersed with these excursions, he chopped and drew firewood for next year's fuel and worked on the roads around his farm. In

A Chelsea farm late in the nineteenth century. [Reprinted from W. S. Gilman, *Chelsea Album* (Chelsea, Vt., 1980).]

April the maple sap began to run, and the various sugaring-off festivities signified the beginning of spring and another cycle of crops.

In spite of the continuous depopulation of Chelsea between 1840 and 1900, the structure of local agriculture changed very little. Chelsea remained predominantly an agricultural community. According to the censuses of 1840, 1860, 1880, and 1900, at least two-thirds of the male household heads were farmers or farm laborers. In the local tax lists, agricultural land regularly accounted for more than two-thirds of the assessed value of all real estate between 1855 and 1890. The farms, like most farms in the northern United States at that time, were family units owned and operated by the head of the family. Throughout the period, more than 90 percent of the farm operators were heads of households, and fewer than 10 percent of the farms were ever rented for cash or shares.[12]

The number of farms, their size, and their location also changed very little. Between 1840 and 1900, Chelsea always contained about 200 farms, and from 1850 on, local tax lists regularly assessed around 23,000 of Chelsea's 24,000 acres as land in farms. Though it does not record the number of farms per se, the 1837 Tax List has 186 entries of 10 acres or more that had at least one barn. The agricultural census counted 187 farms in 1850, 209 in 1860, 219 in 1870, 220 in 1880, and 195 in 1900. Of the 209 farms listed in 1860, 179 were core farms operated by male farmers who were the heads of their households rather than by widows or persons with major occupations other than farming. In 1880 there were virtually the same number of core farms, 175. The distribution of farm sizes was also fairly constant. The average size of the core farms was 121 acres in 1860 and the largest farm was 325 acres, compared with an average size of 128 acres and a maximum of 320 acres in 1880. A comparison of the H. F. Wallings map of Chelsea published in 1858 with the map from the Beers atlas of 1877 shows the same number of farms and the identical spatial distribution of those farms over a twenty-year span. Finally, property values also remained static. The mean value of the core farms rose only a little between 1860 and 1880, from $2,083 to $2,178, and the assessed value for all farmlands decreased slightly from $12.61 per acre in 1855 to $11.13 in 1885.[13]

The output of local agriculture also did not change significantly until the late 1890s. From the 1850s until the close of the century, wool, butter, and maple sugar remained the primary farm products in more or less fixed proportions. The core farmers clipped 23,000 pounds of wool in 1860 and 21,200 pounds in 1880. Dairying yielded 52,500 pounds of butter and 9,500 pounds of cheese in 1859 and 60,500 pounds of butter and 1,700 pounds of cheese in 1879, and boiling maple sap resulted in 61,750 pounds of sugar in 1859 and 63,200 in 1879.

Martin Carpenter's farm was a little larger in 1880 and he sheared more sheep, but he, too, continued to produce the same mix of products. Alvah was still on his farm nearby and recorded exactly the same tasks and the same seasonal cycle of work in his 1880 diary that he had written twenty years earlier. Although the brothers saw each other frequently, they did not work together as often because both had able-bodied sons to help them out on their farms. During haying season, however, Alvah and his son again swapped labor with his neighbor who had a good workhorse, and Martin's sons came by to get in three loads of hay from the old pasture.[14]

After the already depressed price of wool fell even more in 1894, Chelsea farmers quit raising sheep altogether. In 1897 there were

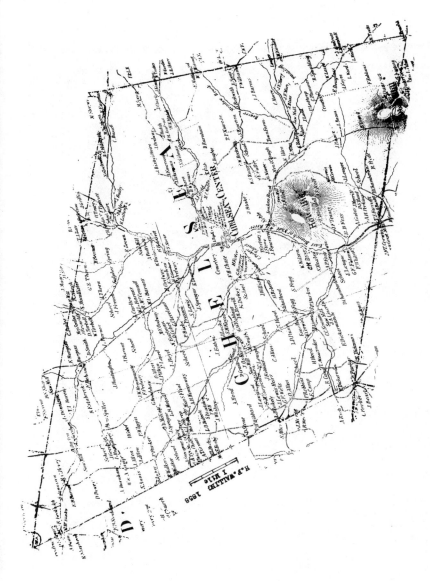

Chelsea, 1858. [Reprinted from H. F. Wallings, *Map of Orange County Vermont* (New York, 1858).]

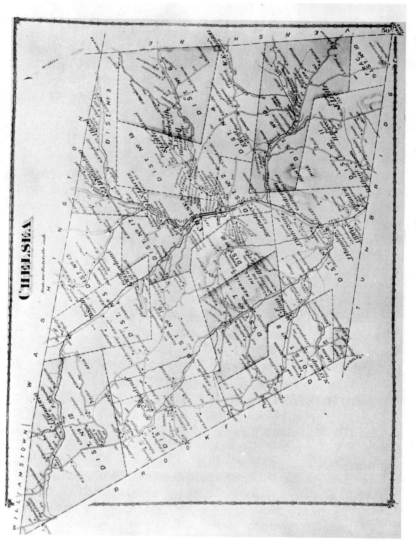

Chelsea, 1877. [Reprinted from F. W. Beers, *Atlas of Orange County Vermont* (New York, 1877).]

only 752 sheep in the township, an 84 percent drop from the 4,686 sheep recorded in 1880. Though the recent construction of a creamery in town with a separator and a licensed Babcock butterfat test operator reflected the new primacy of local dairying, there were only 17 percent more milk cows in 1897 than in 1880. The collapse of the wool market and the general depression of the period caused local land values to decline markedly, and, consequently, there were slightly fewer farms in 1900 than in 1880. Few farms appear to have been abandoned, however, for in all of the lists of abandoned farms published by the State Board of Agriculture between 1891 and 1900, only two were in Chelsea. Moreover, local tax assessors continued to assess and tax the same amount of farmland throughout the period, indicating little deserted property.[15]

The stability of Chelsea's agriculture over most of the second half of the nineteenth century, and the lack of abandonment in the wake of falling wool prices, belie the images of long-term economic decline and deserted farms that characterize the traditional view of rural Vermont during these years. Instead, the constant number of farms and level of farm production suggest that agricultural development in Chelsea had reached the limits of its growth and had leveled off.

This appearance of constancy and stability, however, masks a series of dynamic but subtle adjustments by Chelsea farmers to local population decline and outside market conditions. After the Civil War there were strong signals from the marketplace to change the prevailing form of agriculture from sheep raising to dairying. According to T. M. Adams, the author of the classic price series for Vermont agriculture, "by 1868 wool prices were nearly down to their pre–Civil War level, while the general index of all farm products was still 88 percent above it." Wool, which sold for 40 cents a pound during the 1850s and shot up to 85 cents during the Civil War, was selling for less than 30 cents a pound by the end of the 1870s. In contrast, butter increased from 15 cents a pound in the early 1850s to a peak of 37 cents after the Civil War, and it averaged more than 25 cents during the 1870s (Table 4.1).[16]

As the price of butter improved and that of wool deteriorated, the profitability of switching to dairying became increasingly apparent. Agricultural writers of the period uniformly agreed that the cost of feeding one cow for a year was equivalent to keeping eight sheep. During the 1850s, when wool was 40 cents and butter was 15 cents, forty average sheep in Chelsea produced 160 pounds of wool worth $64.00 and 30 lambs worth $75.00 for a total of $139.00. In contrast, five average cows yielded 450 pounds of butter worth $67.50 and

Table 4.1. *Real prices received by Vermont farmers, 1850–1899 (1860–4 = 100)*

Years	Wool	Dairy	Maple sugar	Livestock	Cost of farm labor
1850–4	103	111			
1855–9	93	117			
1860–4	100	100	100	100	100
1865–9	66	130	95	121	105
1870–4	72	130	99	112	111
1875–9	68	125	93	109	111
1880–4	76	137	105	116	126
1885–9	71	132	103	122	141
1890–4	68	139	90	114	138
1895–9	54	134	101	123	143

Note: To compute real prices, the prices of the different farm products and the cost of farm labor were divided by Adams's index of prices paid by Vermont farmers for goods and services. For purposes of conciseness, only the average levels for each five-year period are presented in this table.
Source: Thurston M. Adams, "Prices Paid by Vermont Farmers for Goods and Services and Received by Them for Farm Products, 1790–1940; Wages of Vermont Farm Labor, 1780–1940," University of Vermont Agricultural Experiment Station, *Bulletin* 507 (1944).

five calves worth $40.00 for a total of $107.50. By the 1870s, however, wool was 30 cents and butter was 25 cents, and the same forty sheep brought in $123.00 and the cows earned $145.00.[17]

Yet, in Chelsea, as in other area townships that were losing population, farmers did not specialize exclusively in dairying and capitalize on changing prices. As we have seen, farm production remained almost constant between 1860 and 1880. Even after wool prices fell to 16 cents and local wool raising collapsed in the 1890s, Chelsea farmers did not make any large-scale move into butter production. To paraphrase a famous Vermonter of a different time and place, dairying in nineteenth-century Chelsea was "the road not taken."[18]

In light of the tremendous price advantage, it is surprising that Chelsea farmers did not produce more butter and less wool. Few factors appeared to hinder that transition. Chelsea's land was not particularly unsuited for dairy farming. On the contrary, surveys of present-day agriculture place Chelsea among the most intensive dairying townships in the state. In 1880 the majority of the most valuable farms raised cows and sheep on the same land, and the Beers atlas from 1877 shows that these leading dairy, wool, and mixed farms were adjacent to each other and scattered throughout the township. Similarly, plotting these farm sites on the U.S. Geological Survey map reveals little difference between the different types of farms with respect to their elevation, slope, or accessibility to water supply.[19]

The local supply of capital was also not crucial because a shift to dairying did not require significant additional expenditures. Neither wool nor dairying required a large outlay of capital for farm equipment. Because the hilly terrain precluded the widespread use of expensive horse-driven machinery, the value of farm implements per farm was only $110 in 1880, only a fourth of the mean value of livestock. Whereas the most heavily capitalized farm had $500 worth of machinery, it had well over $5,000 worth of livestock. Chelsea husbandmen also were not locked into wool production because their sheep were a fixed capital investment. On the contrary, both sheep and dairy cows were easily and frequently sold as farmers replaced their stock every few years. In 1879 local farmers sold 850 sheep and 140 head of cattle, or about 20 percent of the recorded animal population.[20]

The structure of the local market and the transportation network in Chelsea did not prevent specialization in dairying. As local farmers' records and newspaper accounts show, the village merchants bought both wool and butter from Chelsea farmers to resell in Boston and smaller urban markets in New Hampshire. Neither wool nor butter decayed rapidly and therefore did not require rapid transportation, so the lack of direct railroad connections did not favor one product over the other.[21]

Though they continued to produce the same products, Chelsea farmers were not especially conservative and resistant to change. On the contrary, more than 100 Chelsea men were members of the Orange County Agricultural Society in the 1850s, and later reports from the State Board of Agriculture demonstrate that local husbandmen were progressive and alert. At the 1883 institute for local farmers in a session on "The Practical Value of Nitrogen in the Farm Economy," a Chelsea farmer, Willis Scales, described his own experiment with fertilizers and showed his homemade blend to be cheaper and more effective than commercial brands. Other Chelsea meetings witnessed debates on what grains to use as feed and whether Jerseys or Holsteins made the superior butter cow. On one evening, the ladies took over the discussion to compare notes on the finer points of making butter, and "a very interesting time occupied in its consideration, lasting until a late hour."[22]

Chelsea farmers probably did not have any great preference for

FARMERS' MEETINGS!

→A T←

CHELSEA, VT.,

JANUARY 3D AND 4TH, 1888,

→UNDER THE DIRECTION OF THE←

BOARD OF AGRICULTURE.

PROGRAMME.

TUESDAY, January 3d.
FORENOON.

10.00	Address of Welcome.	
10.30	Our Principal Farm Crop.	By W. W. Cooke of Burlington
11.30	Discussion.	

AFTERNOON.

2.00	Economy in Stock Feeding,	By M. W. Davis of Westminster
3.00	Discussion.	

EVENING.

7.00	Music.	
7.15	Strawberry Culture,	By Wm. Chapin of Middlesex
7.45	Are Jersey Cattle Profitable,	By H. W. Vail of North Pomfret

WEDNESDAY, January 4th.
FORENOON.

10.00	Can Potatoes be grown with Profit,	By Wm. Chapin of Middlesex
10.45	Care and Raising of Horses,	By H. H. Hill of Isle LaMotte
11.30	Discussion.	

AFTERNOON.

2.00	The Dairy and Dairy Stock,	By Rollin C. Smith of Pittsford
3.00	Discussion.	

EVENING.

7.00	Music.	
7.15	The Farmers on Education,	By Pres. M. H. Buckham of the University of Vermont

ALL MEETINGS FREE.

The ladies are especially requested to attend all the sessions. All present are invited to join in the discussions.

Burlington, Vermont.

W. W. COOKE, SEC'Y OF BOARD.

Broadside announcing meetings for farmers sponsored by the Vermont State Board of Agriculture in 1888. (Chelsea Historical Society.)

raising sheep instead of switching completely to dairying. Older farmers, mindful of high wool prices in the past, or just too set in their ways to change, might have continued tending to their flocks even though wool prices declined. But the correlation coefficient between age and the number of sheep in 1880 is only $r = -.02$, indicating that there was no tendency for older farmers to have more sheep than younger farmers. Chelsea farmers may have been reluctant to abandon pastoral work rhythms for the more confining and demanding tasks related to dairying, specifically the need to bring in the cows and milk them twice a day, every day. Although there is no evidence that speaks directly to this point, Chelsea farmers had always done some dairying. The increased amount of labor required for an expansion of local dairying was indeed a problem but not because Chelsea farmers were averse to more work. Rather, they just did not have enough hands to do it.[23]

Chelsea farmers continued to rely on sheep during the second half of the nineteenth century in spite of lower prices for wool because that was their best strategy for coping with the declining local supply of labor and the high cost of retaining local workers or of bringing in other laborers from outside the community. John Lynde of nearby Williamstown made this point in an 1874 report when he commented on the stagnant condition of agriculture in Orange County. "Several causes have combined to produce this state of things," Lynde said, "the most prominent of which is the scarcity and high price of labor," which he attributed to the "growing desire of our young men to leave the farms for the store, the work-shop, or the far West."[24]

In Chelsea, according to the 1860 Census, 163 males between fifteen and seventy other than the household head lived and worked on local farms; by 1880 that number had declined by almost 20 percent to 133. In the township as a whole, there was a supply of 161 young men between fifteen and twenty-four in 1860, but by 1880 that pool had shrunk to 119, less than three-fourths of its previous size. Hiring labor from outside the family or the community had also become more expensive, and Adams's price series shows a definite upward trend in the real wages of Vermont farm laborers during the second half of the nineteenth century. During the 1850s, farmhands got between 75 and 80 cents a day with board, but when John Lynde made his report in 1874, they were earning $1.25 plus their keep.[25]

The shorter supply and higher cost of farm labor favored continuing wool production rather than switching to dairying because raising sheep used less labor than raising milch cows and was becoming

Table 4.2. *Number of sheep per farm, 1860 and 1880*

Size of flock	Farms, 1860		Farms, 1880	
	N	%	N	%
0	36	20.1	59	33.7
1–24	67	37.4	41	23.4
25–49	41	22.9	43	24.6
50+	35	19.6	32	18.3
Total	179	100.0	175	100.0

Source: Manuscript Schedules, U.S. Census of Agriculture, 1860 and 1880.

even less labor intensive during this period. On the other hand, changes in dairying practices during the second half of the nineteenth century required increasing amounts of farm labor. Ultimately, Chelsea farmers were unwilling to pay the wages necessary to shift into dairying because the increasing productivity of their sheep allowed them to compensate somewhat for lower wool prices while using less labor.

Chelsea farmers produced equivalent amounts of wool in 1860 and 1880, but they used 20 percent fewer sheep in 1880. In 1860 there were 5,305 sheep on the township's 179 core farms for an average of 30 sheep per farm, and the largest flock was 225 sheep. In 1880 the largest flock was only 135, and the 4,294 sheep averaged 25 per farm. Although some of the smaller farmers got out of wool altogether, the more substantial growers continued in the same numbers. The key was the increasing productivity of local sheep. In 1860 the average clip per sheep on the core farms was 4.1 pounds of wool, and by 1880 that yield had risen almost 25 percent to 5.1 pounds. Consequently, Chelsea farmers could maintain the same level of wool production in 1880 using fewer sheep and, more important, less labor to care and grow feed for those sheep (Table 4.2).

The increasing productivity of local sheep was not the result of the introduction of new breeds to Chelsea farmers; rather, it stemmed from the more widespread diffusion of superior stock already present in the community before 1860. At the 1849 Orange County Fair held in town, three Chelsea farmers won seven of the sixteen first- and second-place prizes awarded for sheep. At the fair in 1858, five local husbandmen entered full-blooded Merinos and won all of that year's prizes. According to the 1860 Census, two farmers averaged yields of 10 pounds of wool per sheep and one got 13, both figures among the best recorded anywhere at that time. In 1880 the highest return

Table 4.3. *Average output of sheep per farm, 1860 and 1880*

Wool per sheep (lb.)	Farms, 1860		Farms, 1880	
	N	%	N	%
2–2.99	25	20.2	1	0.9
3–3.99	39	31.5	12	10.6
4–4.99	31	25.0	38	33.6
5–5.99	21	16.9	44	38.9
6–6.99	8	6.5	18	15.9
Total	124	100.0	113	100.0

Source: Manuscript Schedules, U.S. Census of Agriculture, 1860 and 1880.

was 12 pounds of wool per sheep, indicating that the breed itself had not made marked improvements during the twenty-year interval. Instead, the combined pressures of declining prices for wool and the lessening supply and increasing cost of labor stimulated the adoption of better breeds (Table 4.3). An important twentieth-century study emphasizes similar market pressures to explain the diffusion of the innovation of hybrid corn in Iowa. Certainly Ezra A. Carman was aware of a comparable dynamic in 1892 when he referred to the depression of wool prices earlier in the century and wrote:

> Wool-growing was not generally profitable, and there was a general reduction in flocks. It cost $1.25 to $1.50 to keep a sheep a year and the general average did not exceed 3 pounds in ordinary wool-growing flocks, which at 40 cents would amount to $1.20, or less than the cost of growing. But in flocks which sheared 5 to 6 pounds of well-washed wool there was a living profit which measurably sustained the industry.[26]

In contrast to the labor savings inherent in the utilization of better breeds of sheep, dairying was becoming more labor intensive, and nineteenth-century Vermont agriculturalists emphasized varied labor-intensive practices as the key to successful dairying. Certainly the initial selection of good milkers was important, but more important was the care and feeding of the cow. In 1878 E. R. Skinner of Tunbridge centered his talk about dairying on two texts of great import: first, "No man can afford to keep a poor cow," and second, "No man can afford to keep a cow poor." At other institute sessions on dairy farming, several speakers pointed out the necessity for year-round milking and "winter butter" in order to compete with western farmers; and all stressed the closer and more time-consuming processing of

Table 4.4. *Number of milk cows per farm, 1860 and 1880*

	Farms, 1860		Farms, 1880	
Size of herd	N	%	N	%
0	5	2.8	11	6.3
1–4	139	77.7	125	71.4
5–9	33	18.4	28	16.0
10–14	0	0.0	8	4.6
15–19	1	0.5	1	0.6
20+	1	0.5	2	1.1
Total	179	100.0	175	100.0

Source: Manuscript Schedules, U.S. Census of Agriculture, 1860 and 1880.

the butterfat needed to make the top quality "gilt-edge" product that could command higher prices.[27]

An economic historian has shown recently that labor requirements per cow on eastern farms increased by 68 percent between 1850 and 1910, and "there were no devices or economies of herd size to offset these time-increasing forces." Instead, the greater output that accompanied the commercialization of dairying during this period was due not so much to the use of better breeds of milk cows but to the longer milking periods and the reliance on better care and feeding practices such as those advocated by Vermont agricultural improvers. In Chelsea, the average cow produced 91 pounds of butter in 1859, and increased to 105 pounds in 1879. But, unlike the increasing productivity of sheep, higher dairy yields came mainly from greater inputs of labor.[28]

Longer milking periods and better feeding also increased the derived demand for hay and grain and the labor required to produce it; and this increased demand was more characteristic of dairying than wool growing. Partial correlation analysis illustrates these trends, using the number of cows or the number of sheep as the dependent variable and controlling for the variance caused by the number of other animals and the size of the farm. The second-order partial correlation coefficient between the number of milk cows and the amount of hay grown increased in strength from $r = .43$ in 1860 to $r = .61$ in 1880. For sheep, the partial correlation with hay was weaker and increased less, from $r = .28$ in 1860 to $r = .34$ in 1880. Similarly, the second-order partial correlation coefficient between the number of cows and the amount of hired labor in 1880 was $r = .62$, whereas the comparable statistic for sheep was only $r = .22$.[29]

Table 4.5. *Average output of milk cows per farm, 1860 and 1880*

Butter per cow (lb.)	Farms, 1860		Farms, 1880	
	N	%	N	%
1–74	51	29.7	32	20.4
75–99	38	22.0	34	21.7
100–24	51	29.7	52	33.1
125–49	17	9.9	8	5.1
150–74	10	5.8	17	10.8
175+	5	2.9	14	8.9
Total	172	100.0	157	100.0

Source: Manuscript Schedules, U.S. Census of Agriculture, 1860 and 1880.

With adequate labor further out of reach in 1880 than in 1860, Chelsea farmers decided not to negotiate any transition to dairying. According to the 1880 Census, there were actually 25 fewer milk cows in the township than in 1860. Though a handful of farmers kept larger dairy herds, most Chelsea farms held the same number of cows in both years (Table 4.4). Because increased yields depended more on increased labor inputs than on improved breeds, the productive capacity of most local milkers changed much less than that of the sheep (Table 4.5). Clearly, Chelsea farmers stayed with wool instead of expanding their dairy operations because that was their best strategy for coping with the declining supply and increasing costs of labor.[30]

For the farmers in Chelsea and the other depopulating townships in northern New England, this strategy was, at best, a holding action, and it trapped the local agricultural economy in a vicious circle. Unlike the Midwest where farmers could adopt labor-saving machinery, these hill farmers had no such technological alternative to counteract the high price and short supply of labor. Instead, they adopted the less promising tactic of staying with wool, and as wool prices declined, farm values stagnated and local farming became less attractive, increasing the likelihood of continued out-migration and lessened in-migration.

Those who owned farms or expected to own farms stayed, but the opportunities available for other young men and women were not attractive enough to stem the tide of departure or to induce sufficient in-migration. Although wages for agricultural laborers in Vermont rose significantly during the late nineteenth century, Chelsea farmers were less willing and less able to pay them. Besides, industrial wages were higher and rose at a faster rate, and outside commercial employment multiplied. More important, only a fixed number of farms existed in Chelsea for either dairy or wool production, so unless one stood to inherit his family's farm or could afford to buy another farm that came on the market, the possibility of eventual farm ownership was better elsewhere.

To the many farmers who stayed in the isolated townships of Vermont and New Hampshire, then, John B. Mead's admonitions to their children to stay on the farm embodied a sentiment they agreed with even though they knew that his analysis was overly optimistic. On the other hand, the knowledge that their departed sons and daughters were fueling the growth of the national economy would have probably come as little consolation. Instead, they were forced to struggle constantly just to hold even ground, for they were caught in a web of less benign interactions, which, if not beyond their comprehension, was certainly beyond their control.

Like the agricultural side, the nonagricultural sector of Chelsea's economy also underwent a series of adjustments to both outside economic conditions and local population loss. In contrast to the seeming stability and constancy of local farming, however, the internal structure of the village economy changed significantly during the second half of the nineteenth century. Unlike the traditional view of northern New England's history during this period, though, these changes did not indicate a situation of widespread economic decline and decimation. Rather, the net result of the various adjustments within the local nonagricultural economy was one of lessened growth but continued overall economic stability.

The decline of local industry in Chelsea was one of the most immediate consequences of outside economic developments. Geographic conditions never did favor the development of large-scale enterprise because the township's source of power, the first branch of the White River, was not large enough or steady enough to sustain factories that could compete with bigger plants elsewhere. The most waterpower generated by any local mill in the nineteenth century was only thirty-four horsepower; and only one of the four establishments in the 1870 Census of Manufactures that used waterpower was in operation more than six months of the year. In winter, the stream froze, preventing production, if not ice skating by the local youths. The spring thaw also caused problems. When Elliot Densmore's sawmill flume was carried off by high water, a nearby newspaper reported that his major loss was not the $100 cost of repairing

Chelsea village in the 1860s. [Reprinted from W. S. Gilman, *Chelsea Album* (Chelsea, Vt., 1980).]

the damage but the week's sawing time he lost while replacing the flume. "The stream is so small on which his mill stands," noted the paper, "that the loss of one week's time in the spring is quite a damage to him."[31]

In spite of this imperfect power supply, the ready availability of raw materials from local farms did give rise to several smaller manufacturing firms, which produced for outside markets. As competition from outside manufacturers accelerated, however, the position of these small local factories became increasingly precarious, and none lasted long enough to become permanent fixtures on Chelsea's landscape. As noted earlier, Barry and Benton's 1837 *Statistical View of the Number of Sheep* . . . listed B. Grout of Chelsea as a manufacturer of "cassimeres and satinets." The local tax list of that year appraised his mill building at $1,000, the fourth highest appraisal of any mill, farm, shop, or store in the community. Though Benjamin Grout was in the prime of his life, by 1850, he and his family had left town, and no comparable factory was listed in the Census of Manufactures.[32]

The largest manufacturing firms recorded in 1850 shared similar fates. G. W. Townsend and E. Townsend owned a chair shop and employed three workers who manufactured 5,000 chairs worth $2,250. The business probably netted close to $1,000 that year, yet by 1855, the Townsends were out of it and owned farmland rather than commercial property. In 1860 they were gone from Chelsea altogether, and no chair-making factory was recorded that year or in any subsequent census. Daniel Atwood's boot and shoe shop, which also employed three men, closed its doors between 1850 and 1860. Though his industry did not rely on waterpower, Atwood was at a serious disadvantage with respect to the larger shoe manufacturers in New Hampshire and Massachusetts because of Chelsea's lack of direct connections to distant markets.[33]

The most explicit account of industrial failure in Chelsea is, perhaps, the saddest. An Irish immigrant family, residents of the township since the early 1850s, bought farmland with stream frontage and built a woolens factory in 1868. By 1870 the Watersons were doing a brisk business and running the largest factory in Chelsea. They employed seven workers, produced $2,000 worth of wool cloth, and contracted for $1,440 worth of custom carding and weaving. Net profits for the year exceeded $1,000. In 1874, even though the father and one brother had died, R. G. Dun & Company gave James Waterson a sterling credit rating. In 1879, however, the business was struggling, the factory was mortgaged, production was only occasional, and Waterson was "in no position for credit." He mortgaged the farmland on which the factory stood in September 1880 and died a few months later, a broken man at the age of forty-eight.[34]

By 1880 manufacturing for outside markets had become a thing of the past in Chelsea. Though all four of Chelsea's largest manufacturing concerns produced goods from raw materials that were in abundant local supply, they were hampered by an inadequate source of power and poor transportation connections. The small size of these local firms made them victims of not only the seasonal change in climate but also the periodic depressions in the business cycle that followed the Panics of 1837, 1857, and 1873. Local industry was simply unable to hold its own against the economies of scale accruing to the bigger mills and factories on the larger streams and in the more central locations.

Local boosters did not give up without a fight, and during the second half of the nineteenth century they mounted several efforts

Table 4.6. *Trades and tradesmen in Chelsea, 1850–1900*

Year	No. of trades	No. of tradesmen
1850	24	88
1860	20	69
1870	16	60
1880	18	67
1887	12	52
1900	10	30

Source: Manuscript Schedules, U.S. Census of Population, 1850, 1860, 1870, 1880, 1900; 1887 data from Hamilton Child, *Child's Orange County Gazette, 1762–1888* (Syracuse, N.Y., 1888), 33–43.

to stimulate economic development. In 1851 the town raised a large tax to help pay for a bridge that extended the road from Chelsea across the White River at Royalton to the new railroad depot on the other side. Chelsea contracted for a telegraph line to that depot in 1868, prompting a nearby newspaper to remark: "It is hoped that the onward march of progress will not end with this, but that the businessmen will press on until they have a railroad running there." Money was appropriated in 1871 to survey a railroad route from Montpelier to South Royalton by way of Chelsea, and the township voted to buy stock valued at $15,000 to aid the Chelsea, Tunbridge, and South Royalton Railroad Company in 1892, but the spur line never materialized. In a similar vein, the township exempted new industries from taxes for a period of ten years during the 1890s, but this too came to naught. Although one shoe factory took advantage of the tax break and commenced operations in April 1892, its proprietor went bankrupt six months later.[35]

The village artisans who produced primarily for the local market also did not fare well during these years. Between 1850 and 1900, both the number of trades practiced in Chelsea and the number of men who plied them declined markedly (Table 4.6). Obviously, the failure of local industry accounts for some of this decline – three shoemakers and three chairmakers lost their place of employment between 1850 and 1860. Similarly, three tanners supplied the local demand for shoe leather in 1850, whereas only one was required a decade later. Depopulation also reduced the size of the local market for the artisan's goods. More important than the negative impact of faltering local industry and local population loss, however, was the

Table 4.7. *Occupational groups in Chelsea, 1850–1900*

	1850	1860	1870	1880	1887	1900
Merchant	15	18	22	23	22	25
Professional	17	13	13	17	15	12
Displaced crafts						
Shoemaker/cordwainer	14	8	7	7	3	2
Tailor	5	5	1	3	2	0
Chair maker	5	2	0	0	0	0
Tanner	3	1	1	1	0	0
Cabinetmaker	2	0	0	1	0	0
Gunsmith	1	0	0	0	0	0
Machinist	1	0	0	0	0	0
Stable crafts						
Wheelwright/carriage maker	4	5	6	2	2	3
Saddler/harness maker	3	2	2	7	5	2
Tinsmith	2	2	4	3	2	1
Service trades						
Blacksmith	9	9	8	9	9	4
Teamster	5	2	3	2	3	4
Miller (saw & grist)	5	3	2	2	3	4
Construction trades						
Carpenter	17	22	18	18	18	5
Painter/plasterer	3	2	4	6	4	5
Mason (stone & brick)	0	2	1	1	1	0

Source: Manuscript Schedules, U.S. Census of Population, 1850, 1860, 1870, 1880, 1900; 1887 data from Hamilton Child, *Child's Orange County Gazette, 1762–1888* (Syracuse, N.Y., 1888), 33–43.

displacement of local craftsmen resulting from the growth and reorganization of outside manufacturing. The trades that suffered the most significant decline in Chelsea were those in which the product was increasingly mass-produced elsewhere (Table 4.7).

The development of the shoe industry is the best example of this trend. The growing national demand for shoes prior to the Civil War stimulated the widespread adoption of a sewing machine capable of sewing leather and other labor-saving devices. This technological shift moved shoe production out of the local artisan's workshop and away from the older putting-out system and moved it instead into centralized, highly capitalized factories. Similar developments characterized the growth of ready-made clothing and the centralization of the woodworking industry after the Civil War. Indeed, of all the trades and businesses in Chelsea recorded in the R. G. Dun & Company credit ledgers, the lot of the shoemakers and tailors was clearly the least enviable. Four of the seven men engaged in these trades between 1850 and 1890 went bankrupt, and the other three were credited for only small amounts. Of these three, all shoemakers, one migrated after two years to the larger shoe manufacturing town of Haverhill, Massachusetts, and the other two were young men and given credit only because their fathers were prosperous farmers. The declining fortunes of local artisans were also evident at the Orange County Fair. In 1849 prizes were awarded for the best boots, shoes, and examples of tailoring under the larger category of "Mechanics Arts." At the 1858 fair, however, these awards were no longer made, and only a handful of craftsmen were recognized.[36]

Though the rise of centralized mass-production industry displaced numerous local artisans, it also expanded the economic role of local merchants who sold the new factory-made goods. By the 1880s, general-store owners such as John B. Atwood had added "ready-made clothing, hats, caps, boots and shoes, ladies' ready-made garments" to his traditional stock of groceries and dry goods. In 1850 a lone gunsmith handcrafted firearms for Chelsea townfolk. In 1887, however, Charles A. Densmore sold centrally manufactured rifles and pistols as part of a larger watch and jewelry business. In contrast to the diminishing number of artisans, the number of retail merchants in Chelsea remained constant and even increased slightly in spite of the overall loss of population (Table 4.7). The R. G. Dun & Company credit ledgers also indicate that local retailers were not doing poorly. Of the sixteen firms listed between 1850 and 1890, most merchants showed some increase in their assets over time. Unlike the sorry record of the shoemakers and tailors, only one retailer failed and only two were given poor credit ratings. Thus, the distributive sector of Chelsea's economy was stable and experiencing some growth at the expense of local craftsmen and manufacturers.[37]

Other occupational groups were also stable, belying any notion of wholesale collapse. Doctors, lawyers, and other professionals continued in more or less the same numbers between 1850 and 1900. Many of the trades listed in Table 4.7 did not decline. As long as the agricultural economy did not decline, there was a fixed demand for millers, teamsters, and blacksmiths. Consequently, the numbers of these tradesmen who provided services for area farmers did not fall off until the 1890s. The almost constant numbers of carpenters, painters, and, to a lesser extent, masons indicate that there was also a continuous level of construction in Chelsea until the turn of the century. Finally, all three handicrafts that did not decline produced goods that were not manufactured extensively elsewhere. Sleighs, the mainstay of the wheelwright or carriage maker's trade, were too bulky to have been imported from faraway factories. Similarly, the tinsmith's stovepipes and the saddler's harnesses had to be custom-made to meet the particular needs of the individual customer and were not widely mass-produced.

Thus, Chelsea's nonfarm economy did not experience the decimation posited in the traditional accounts of the period. Small local industry and village artisanship fell on hard times, but this decline was due primarily to outside economic changes, not to the local loss of population. As such, this transition from a productive to a distributive economy characterized the nonfarm sector of many rural communities in the late nineteenth century, whether they were declining in size or not.

Nevertheless, the size of the local market did shrink during this period, and the dwindling number of local customers effected more subtle changes in the businesses of local craftsmen and merchants who continued to work in Chelsea. As a rural sociologist has shown in a study of a present-day Iowa farm community, alterations in the internal organization of local businesses are common economic adjustments to local population loss. In Chelsea, local tradesmen adopted several strategies to compensate for the declining demand for their wares. Several artisans relied increasingly on custom work and repair jobs instead of the manufacture of their main stock-in-trade. In 1850 Chester A. Bass, a carriage maker, made most of his money from the thirty-six double or single sleighs that he crafted, and custom work accounted for less than 10 percent of the value of his annual product. In contrast, the two carriage makers listed in the 1870 Census of Manufactures produced a total of only fifteen sleighs (they also made a few buggies and two lumber wagons) but earned a third of their income through custom jobbing and repair work.[38]

Rather than relying solely on the production of a single line of goods, other local craftsmen diversified their businesses as a ploy against declining local demand. Usually the direction of diversification followed their primary occupation. Ira Thompson, one of the few shoemakers left in town in 1887, was a dealer of leather and "findings" in addition to making and repairing shoes. Hamilton W. Dearborn served the community in that decade not only as a carpenter and builder but also as an undertaker who manufactured and sold his own coffins. Similarly, Byron Berry was both a harness maker and a carriage trimmer. Others, like the local wheelwright, who manufactured shingles and ran a planing mill and a general repair shop along with his main trade, pursued more disparate endeavors.[39]

The growing availability of ready-made merchandise also made it easy for some artisans to diversify by becoming involved in retailing in addition to manufacturing. H. W. Dearborn, the carpenter and undertaker, was listed as a carpenter in the 1880 Census. He expanded his operations during the 1890s to in lude selling furniture and referred to himself in 1900 as a dealer or merchant. Joseph and Oscar Tracy, two brothers, bought out the local tinsmith's shop in 1858 from its previous owners, who had taught Oscar the trade. In 1860 the Tracy brothers worked with tin and sheet iron and produced pans, sap pails, and stovepipes. In 1880, though they had expanded the scope of their operation to include copper work, they produced less. Yet, three years later, R. G. Dun & Company rated them as the "heaviest firm in town" and estimated their worth at $20,000 – a far cry from the modest shop and the $1,500 assessment recorded in 1858. Retailing, not manufacturing, had become the mainstay of their business. In 1887 the *Orange County Gazette* listed Oscar Tracy first as a dealer of hardware and iron stoves (an item that is in perpetual demand in Vermont) and only second as a manufacturer of tin, sheet iron, and copper wares. He also sold mowers and other agricultural machinery and farmed sixty acres. Though Oscar Tracy was listed as a tinsmith in the 1860, 1870, and 1880 censuses, in 1900, he, like H. W. Dearborn, also became a merchant.[40]

In addition to changes in the internal structure of their businesses, part-time farming provided another hedge against the diminishing size of the local market. According to the 1860 Census of Agriculture, only eleven farms were operated by nonfarmers. By 1880 that number had more than doubled to twenty-four; and in 1900, in spite of a slight overall decrease in the number of farms in Chelsea, twenty-six farm operators had a primary occupation other than farming. These farms were considerably smaller and less valuable than the farms that were operated by farmers. In 1879 none yielded farm produce worth more than $300 (the average for farms operated by farmers was over $550), and the majority were less than ten acres. To the artisans and small merchants who owned them, however, the farms provided an added and needed measure of security.[41]

Though it was far removed from the epicenter of the economic upheavals occurring elsewhere in the nation, Chelsea's local economy definitely felt tremors and shock waves throughout the second half of the nineteenth century. Through a series of adjustments to both local and external conditions and changes, the total amount of economic opportunity available in the township became more or less fixed. The number of farms in Chelsea remained constant and the exodus of young men and women and the high price of farm labor prevented local farmers from specializing exclusively in dairying and led them instead to continue a reliance on the older mixture of farm products. The technological developments that created many of the attractive outside opportunities also lessened possibilities for further growth in Chelsea's nonagricultural economy. As local industry and artisans were superseded and displaced, village merchants augmented their role in the township's economy, but there was no economic expansion. Just as depopulation prevented specialization by Chelsea farmers, it also pushed local tradesmen and shopkeepers into a range of economic activities in order to continue making a living. In the end, Chelsea's economy became stagnant but stable, a far cry from both the excessively bleak portrayals of northern New England during this period and the rapid economic expansion characteristic of cities and newer rural areas during the second half of the nineteenth century.

The agricultural economy also remained stable in many other areas throughout New England and New York in spite of significant population loss. As has already been mentioned, a recent economic study demonstrates the viability of New Hampshire farming at the close of the nineteenth century, and the number of farms and the amount of land in use also did not change in Londonderry, Vermont, even though the township lost 30 percent of its population. County-level census data show more or less constant numbers of farms in Orange, Addison, and Windsor counties, which experienced the biggest population declines of the fourteen counties in Vermont. Finally, the farming population in Marathon Township in eastern New York also lost almost 40 percent of its population during the second half of the nineteenth century, yet the number of local farms stayed the same.[42]

Changes in the nonagricultural economies of rural communities in the region also paralleled trends in Chelsea. James M. Williams's 1906 sociological study of a rural community in Oneida County, New York, chronicles the declining number of manufacturing establishments during the nineteenth century, which was coupled with an increase in the number of retail stores. Although manufacturing waned in Marathon, New York, the number of retail establishments in the village trebled after the Civil War, and Dryden Township in nearby

Tompkins County followed a similar pattern. Commenting on analogous developments in Londonderry, Vermont, one scholar has written:

> The post-1850 manufacturing decline was caused by the displacement of such community-based industries as tanning and wool carding and cloth dressing by urban manufacturing centers, part of a national trend. The rise in both service and retail operations after 1860 was also a spinoff of national industrialization . . . Although manufacturing declined because of these influences, service and retail businesses became more diversified. Decline in opportunities in one economic segment was compensated by an increase in another.[43]

As local economic opportunities became fixed and the potential for future growth lessened in these older rural communities, the distinction between those who had a foothold in the local economy and those who did not loomed even larger. Gradually, the local population came to consist predominantly of only those individuals who had or could expect just such a foothold, and a certain population stability developed during the second half of the nineteenth century that paralleled the emerging constancy of the local economy.

5   *The ties that bind: migration and persistence in a settled rural community*

The high degree of geographic mobility and the extensive population turnover that characterized Americans and their communities during the nineteenth century are among the most significant findings of the new social history, and the relationship of this mobility to questions concerning social structure, political power, the nature of community, and class consciousness is a pervasive theme in much of the recent literature. The empirical bases for such findings and the settings for their larger implications, however, almost exclusively have been situations of rapid economic and demographic growth. Whereas most historians regard industrialization, urbanization, and western expansion as the hallmarks of nineteenth-century development, such growth was by no means a universal phenomenon, and throughout the century an increasing number of older rural communities experienced population decline and slowed economic development as resources shifted to new areas of growth. Yet we know little about migration and persistence trends in these older farming communities or the social consequences of those trends. We cannot simply assume that the high level of nineteenth-century mobility was continuous throughout American society or that such flux was a constant element of American culture.[1]

In Chelsea, given the overall loss of population and the lack of economic growth, one would expect to find more out-migration and less persistence than in the growing communities. Certainly the traditional historical view of a widespread exodus from New Hampshire and Vermont supports such an expectation. However, persistence rates in Chelsea do not reflect excessive out-migration. They were higher than persistence rates measured in other nineteenth-century American communities – urban or rural – and they indicate that these Vermonters were becoming even more likely to stay put over the "wintry" second half of the century in spite of local economic stagnation and the increase of outside opportunities.

This seeming paradox is the focus of this chapter. In Chelsea, decades of selective out-migration and decreasing in-migration left a larger percentage of the township's population who were less likely to move on because of extensive economic and social ties to the

78

Table 5.1. *Persistence in Chelsea, 1840–1900, in percentage*

	1840–60	1860–80	1880–1900
All males	—	28.5	30.0
All adult males[a]	—	30.9 (37.6)	32.2 (45.0)
Male household heads	32.1 (42.1)	34.3 (42.5)	32.2 (51.3)
Farm operators	—	39.0 (48.3)	39.0 (56.0)

Note: Dash indicates not available. Figures in parentheses are for males aged 20 to 49.
[a] Twenty or more years of age.
Source: Manuscript Schedules, U.S. Census of Population, 1840, 1860, 1880, 1900, and U.S. Census of Agriculture, 1860 and 1880.

community. Moreover, unlike their contemporaries in the cities or on the frontier, those who stayed in the township experienced few dramatic changes over the course of their lives. Both the relative lack of turnover of Chelsea's population and the comparative stability experienced by individual inhabitants are in marked contrast to the general view of American society during the nineteenth century and are extremely important, if little understood, characteristics of older rural communities.

To pursue these issues, general persistence rates were computed for all males, all males over twenty, all male household heads, and all male farm operators in Chelsea for two time periods: 1860–80 and 1880–1900 (Table 5.1).[2] In addition, general rates were calculated for men between the ages of twenty and fifty in each of the categories to lessen the effect of mortality. These calculations were also made for male household heads for the period between 1840 and 1860.

In spite of the fact that these figures measure persistence over a twenty-year interval, they approximate the decadal rates found in many contemporary nineteenth-century cities (twenty-year urban persistence rates can be assumed to be much lower). The comparisons with other rural areas are even more striking. Between 1860 and 1880, 31 percent of Chelsea's adult males remained in the township. In Trempeleau County, Wisconsin, however, only 27 percent persisted between 1860 and 1870, and the rate for the entire twenty-year period was a little more than half of Chelsea's, or 16.8 percent. Farm operators consistently had the highest persistence rates in rural areas. Yet farmers in Chelsea were much more likely to remain than were their counterparts on the expanding midwestern frontier (Table 5.2).[3]

Table 5.2. *Persistence of Farm Operators, in percentage*

	1860–70	1860–80
Trempeleau County, Wisconsin	31.9	18.4%
E. Central Kansas	31.0	20.7
Eastern Kansas	26.0	22.1
Warren, Iowa	42.9	25.0
Crawford, Iowa	40.0	26.1
Hamilton, Iowa	56.0	28.1
Union, Iowa	52.9	30.2
Blooming Grove, Wisconsin[a]	55.6	39.6
Chelsea, Vermont	—	39.0

Note: Dash indicates not available.
[a] Michael Conzen attributes the high rate of persistence in Blooming Grove to its proximity to the Madison urban market; see *Frontier Farming in an Urban Shadow* (Madison, Wis., 1971).
Source: Trempeleau County: Merle Curti, *The Making of an American Community* (Stanford, 1959), 70; Kansas: James C. Malin, "The Turnover of Farm Population in Kansas," *Kansas Historical Quarterly* 4 (1935): 365–6; Iowa townships: Allan G. Bogue, *From Prairie to Corn Belt* (Chicago, 1968), 26; Blooming Grove: Michael Conzen, *Frontier Farming in an Urban Shadow* (Madison, Wis., 1971), 127.

The relatively high level of persistence in Chelsea becomes more pronounced once the crude rates are corrected for mortality.[4] Once the effect of death is accounted for, almost half the males in Chelsea, two-thirds of the household heads, and fully three-fourths of the farm operators do not leave the township during the second half of the nineteenth century (Tables 5.3, 5.4, and 5.5).

In large part, this high level of persistence in Chelsea was a function of the selective nature of migration. In Chelsea and the other rural communities that have been studied, migration was a selective phenomenon whose frequency varied widely according to different characteristics of the population. Although the rate of out-migration differed, the patterns of selectivity were virtually the same from place to place; and, in Chelsea at least, they remained almost constant over time. Decades of repeated selective out-migration from Chelsea coupled with declining in-migration altered the composition of the township's population. As a result, the people least likely to leave formed a much larger percentage of the local population than was the case in the Midwest. Rather than reflecting any absolute difference in the behavior of individuals, then, the higher persistence measured in Chelsea resulted from the changing structure of the community.

Age was one of the most important factors in selective out-migration. It is clear that the younger age groups were much less persistent than those over thirty and that their rate of departure varied little during this period (Table 5.3). This continuous exit, combined with a decrease in the number of young in-migrants, declining fertility, and improving mortality, caused the age structure in Chelsea to become progressively older. Thus, the larger proportion of older and more sedentary inhabitants in Chelsea accounts for some of the higher level of persistence, and the increase in Chelsea's own persistence rates during the second half of the nineteenth century was due largely to the aging of the township's population.[5]

Among adult males, out-migration from Chelsea was also selective according to economic ties to the community. As is already evident from the higher overall persistence of farm operators, property ownership was a distinguishing feature of those who remained. Almost half the male farm owners between the ages of twenty and forty-nine listed in the 1860 Census stayed to 1880, whereas only 31 percent of their contemporaries who did not have farms remained. In a more general sense, any wealth, whether it was a farm, other real estate, or personal property, was associated with greater persistence. Except for the richest group, persistence rates increased as the level of wealth went up (Table 5.6). These relative differences did not change very much during the course of the century. Between 1880 and 1900, 56 percent of the farm owners between the ages of twenty and forty-nine stayed, in contrast to 39 percent of those without farms. Controlling for age also has little effect in either period. Propertied men in their twenties, for example, were consistently more likely to stay than their contemporaries with no assets.[6]

Of the different occupational groups, farmers and merchants were the most stable, whereas artisans and laborers were the least. The relative stability of the different occupational groups also changed little between 1860 and 1900 (Table 5.7). Farmers and merchants were, of course, more likely to own substantial property and thus be tied to the community; but this pattern also reflects the varied economic fortunes of local merchandising and small-scale manufacturing. Throughout the period, the few small shops in Chelsea and a number of local artisans were displaced by the rise of larger factories and the development of mass-production industries in southern New England. Chelsea merchants, in turn, filled the economic gap created by this change as they augmented their own operations by retailing the new centrally manufactured goods.[7]

Persistence in Chelsea was associated with noneconomic charac-

Table 5.3. *Persistence by age group, all males*

			1860–80			
Age (1860)	N (1860)	Survival rate[a]	Estimated survivors N (1880)	No. of persisters	Unadjusted rate (%)	Adjusted rate (%)[b]
0–9	171	.885[c]	151	40	23.4	26.5
10–19	169	.892	151	45	26.6	29.8
20–29	133	.848	113	42	31.6	37.2
30–39	85	.771	65	39	45.9	60.0
40–49	100	.623	62	38	38.0	61.3
50–59	89	.385	34	33	37.1	97.1
60–69	58	.126	7	3	5.2	42.8
70+	37	—	—	—	—	—
Total	842	—	583	240	28.5	41.2

1880–1900

Age (1880)	N (1880)	Survival rate[d]	Estimated survivors N (1900)	No. of persisters	Unadjusted rate (%)	Adjusted rate (%)
0–9	117	.911	107	28	23.9	26.2
10–19	131	.914	120	36	27.5	30.0
20–29	102	.877	89	37	36.3	41.6
30–39	91	.804	73	54	59.3	74.0
40–49	77	.658	51	30	39.0	58.8
50–59	76	.416	32	18	23.7	56.2
60–69	56	.144	8	9	14.3	100.0+
70+	60	—	—	1	1.7	100.0+
Total	710		480	213	30.0	44.4

Note: Dash indicates not available.

[a] Using Model West, level 14 life tables, the survival rate is computed according to the standard formula: rate = $L_{(age\ 186C + 20)}/L_{(age\ 1860)}$.

[b] Adjusted rate = N persisters/N estimated survivors.

[c] Survival rate for the youngest age group is computed according to: rate = $L_{(20-29)}/L_{(0)} + L_{(1-4)} + L_{(5-9)}$.

[d] Using Model West, level 16 life tables, the survival rate is computed according to the standard formula: rate = $L_{(age\ 1880 + 20)}/L_{(age\ 1880)}$.

[e] The occasional rates above 100% are statistical artifacts and are due to the approximate nature of the mortality estimates and the small numbers involved in the older age groups. In no case does the number of persisters exceed the estimated number of survivors by more than two.

Source: Manuscript Schedules, U.S. Census of Population, 1860, 1880, and 1900; Ansley Coale and Paul Demeny, *Regional Model Life Tables and Stable Populations* (Princeton, 1966).

Table 5.4. *Persistence by age group, male household heads*

			1840–60			
Age (1840)	N (1840)	Survival rate[a]	Estimated survivors N (1860)	No. of persisters	Unadjusted rate (%)	Adjusted rate (%)
20–29	35	.816	29	14	40.0	48.3
30–39	107	.733	78	47	42.7	60.3
40–49	72	.583	42	29	40.3	69.0
50–59	64	.351	22	16	25.0	72.7
60–69	36	.109	4	3	8.3	75.0
70+	29	—	4	1	3.6	100.0+
Total	343	—	175	110	32.1	62.9

			1860–80			
Age (1860)	N (1860)	Survival rate[b]	Estimated survivors N (1880)	No. of persisters	Unadjusted rate (%)	Adjusted rate (%)
20–29	45	.848	38	18	40.0	47.4
30–39	70	.771	54	32	45.7	59.2
40–49	85	.623	53	35	41.2	66.0
50–59	83	.385	32	32	38.5	100.0
60–69	46	.126	6	3	6.5	50.0
70+	21	—	—	—	—	—
Total	350	—	183	120	34.3	65.6

1880–1900

Age (1880)	N (1880)	Survival rate	Estimated survivors N (1900)	No. of persisters	Unadjusted rate (%)	Adjusted rate (%)
20–29	27	.877	24	12	44.4	50.0
30–39	60	.804	48	37	61.7	77.1
40–49	63	.658	41	28	44.4	68.3
50–59	72	.416	30	17	23.6	56.7
60–69	54	.144	8	9	16.7	100.0+
70+	47	—	—	1	2.1	100.0+
Total	323		151	104	32.2	68.9

Note: Dash indicates not available.

[a] Based on Model West, level 12 life table. See Table 5.3 for computational formula and substitute 1840 for 1860.
[b] Based on Model West, level 14 life table. See Table 5.3.
[c] Based on Model West, level 16 life table. See Table 5.3.

Source: Manuscript Schedules, U.S. Census of Population, 1840, 1860, 1880, and 1900; Ansley Coale and Paul Demeny, *Regional Model Life Tables and Stable Populations* (Princeton, 1966).

Table 5.5. Persistence by age group, male farm operators

1860–80

Age (1860)	N (1860)	Survival rate[a]	Estimated survivors N (1880)	No. of persisters	Unadjusted rate (%)	Adjusted rate (%)
20–29	29	.848	25	16	55.1	64.0
30–39	43	.771	33	24	55.8	72.7
40–49	46	.623	29	17	36.9	58.6
50–59	48	.385	18	20	41.7	100.0+
60–69	29	.126	4	3	10.3	75.0
70+	10	—	—	—	—	—
Total	205	—	109	80	39.0	73.4

1880–1900

Age (1880)	N (1880)	Survival rate[b]	Estimated survivors N (1900)	No. of persisters	Unadjusted rate (%)	Adjusted rate (%)
20–29	15	.877	13	9	60.0	69.2
30–39	40	.804	32	28	70.0	87.5
40–49	42	.658	28	17	40.5	60.7
50–59	50	.416	21	18	36.0	85.7
60–69	33	.144	5	7	21.2	100.0+
70+	25	—	—	1	4.0	100.0+
Total	205	—	99	80	39.0	80.8

Note: Dash indicates not available.
[a] Based on Model West, level 14 life table. See Table 5.3.
[b] Based on Model West, level 16 life table. See Table 5.3.
Source: Manuscript Schedules, U.S. Census of Population, 1860, 1880, and 1900, and U.S. Census of Agriculture, 1860 and 1880; Ansley Coale and Paul Demeny, Regional Model Life Tables and Stable Populations (Princeton, 1966).

Table 5.6. *Persistence by wealth, males 20–49,ᵃ 1860–1880*

Value ($)	N	Persistence rate (%)ᵇ
	Real estate	
0	156	30.1
1–999	44	40.9
1000–2999	93	50.5
3000+	24	29.2
	Personal estate	
0	92	23.9
1–249	44	25.0
250–749	75	38.7
750–2499	85	56.5
2500+	21	42.8
	Total wealth	
0	91	23.1
1–499	49	26.5
500–999	30	43.3
1000–2999	84	52.4
3000+	63	44.4

ᵃ Persistence rate for all males 20–49 = 37.6% (N = 317).
ᵇ Not adjusted for mortality.
Source: Manuscript Schedules, U.S. Census of Population, 1860 and 1880.

teristics as well. From 1860 to 1900, persons born in Vermont stayed more often than those who migrated to Chelsea from another state. The handful of Irish immigrants, however, was more persistent than any other nativity group (Table 5.8). Single men in every age group were more footloose than were married men, and those who were the heads of households or related to the head remained with greater frequency than nonkin. Although not a factor between 1860 and 1880, the few heads of extended families were more sedentary between 1880 and 1900 than were nuclear family heads, and household heads with several children remained more often than those with one or no children (Table 5.9). In addition to economic considerations, then, social connections to the community and family ties were also important correlates of nonmigration.[8]

In addition to the cumulative effect of decades of selective out-migration, persistence rates in Chelsea were made higher by the overall decline in population. Obviously, this population decline was

Table 5.7. *Persistence by occupation, males 20–49*

Occupation	1860–80		1880–1900	
	N	Persistence rate (%)	N	Persistence rate (%)
Farmer	112	50.0	89	57.3
Merchant	19	57.9	17	52.9
Professional	13	46.1	16	37.5
Craftsman	47	29.8	34	38.2
Farmer without farm[a]	77	32.5	37	62.2
Laborer	14	7.1	42	19.0
Works out, etc.[b]	—	—	16	43.7
No occupation	34	17.6	18	22.2
Total	316	37.6	269	45.0

[a] The farmer without farm category refers to those listed as farmers with no corresponding farm found in the agricultural census schedules. Apparently the composition of this category changed from census to census. The group appears to include farm laborers in 1860 but does not include them in 1880. Conversely, the use of laborer does not include farm laborers in 1860 but does include them in 1880.
[b] This category usually described sons living in their father's household but working elsewhere in the township.
Source: Manuscript Schedules, U.S. Census of Population, 1860, 1880, and 1900, and U.S. Census of Agriculture, 1860 and 1880.

not caused by excessive out-migration. Instead, it was primarily the result of lessened in-migration as Chelsea's stagnant economy failed to attract enough newcomers to replace those who left. Computing the number of in-migrants as a percentage of those who left shows that the newcomers replaced just under half the number of locals who migrated or died between 1860 and 1880. Between 1880 and 1900, this replacement ratio declined even further to 34 percent (Table 5.10). These less persistent newcomers also formed a smaller portion of the township's population and accounted for 48 percent of the adult males in 1880 but only 39 percent by 1900. Thus, the decreasing number of in-migrants made the more persistent who remained an even larger part of the total population.[9]

As individuals, then, middle-aged farm owners in Chelsea in 1880 were probably no more persistent than their midwestern counterparts. As a community, however, Chelsea was much more stable, much less subject to the constant turnover and flux that characterized nineteenth-century society. Yet none of the processes that led to

Table 5.8. *Persistence by place of birth, males 20–49*

	1860–80		1880–1900	
Place of birth	N	Persistence rate (%)	N	Persistence rate (%)
Vermont	263	40.3	234	45.7
Other U.S.	42	21.4	18	38.9
Ireland	7	57.1	4	50.0
Other foreign	5	0.0	14	35.7
Total	317	37.6	270	45.0

Source: Manuscript Schedules, U.S. Census of Population, 1860, 1880, and 1900.

Table 5.9. *Persistence by household type and number of children, male household heads 20–49*

	1860–80		1880–1900	
	N	Persistence rate (%)	N	Persistence rate (%)
Household type				
Solitaire	2	0.0	4	50.0
Nuclear	179	43.0	125	47.2
Extended	19	42.1	21	76.2
Total	200	42.5	150	51.3
Number of children				
0	42	42.9	36	41.7
1	58	41.4	33	36.4
2–3	65	49.2	55	58.2
4+	35	31.4	26	69.2
Total	200	42.5	150	51.3

Source: Manuscript Schedules, U.S. Census of Population, 1860, 1880, and 1900.

Chelsea's stability was peculiar to that township or region. What distinguished Chelsea from the newer rural areas was primarily the longer duration of those processes and, in some cases, their degree. Migration throughout rural America was selective according to age and social and economic ties to the community; but whereas in the Midwest this selectivity spanned only one or two generations by

Table 5.10. *In-migration*

Age (1860)	N (1860)	No. of persisters	Age (1880)	1860–80				
				N (1880)	No. of new[a]	New/N (1880) (%)[b]	Adjusted new[c]	Replacement ratio (%)[d]
0–9	171	40	20–29	102	62	60.8	65	49.6
10–19	169	45	30–39	91	46	50.5	49	39.5
20–29	133	42	40–49	77	35	45.4	39	42.9
30–39	85	39	50–59	76	37	48.7	43	93.5
40–49	100	38	60–69	56	18	32.1	25	40.3
50–59	89	33	70–79	53	20	37.7	38	67.9
60+	95	3	80+	7	4	57.1	17	18.5
Total	842	240		462	222	48.0	276	45.8

1880–1900

Age (1880)	N (1880)	No. of persisters	Age (1900)	N (1900)	No. of new	New/N (1900) (%)	Adjusted new[c]	Replacement ratio (%)
0–9	117	28	20–29	58	30	51.7	31	34.8
10–19	131	36	30–39	61	25	41.0	26	27.4
20–29	102	37	40–49	62	25	40.3	27	41.5
30–39	91	54	50–59	78	24	30.8	28	75.7
40–49	77	30	60–69	48	18	37.5	24	51.1
50–59	76	18	70–79	33	15	45.4	27	46.5
60+	116	10	80+	12	2	16.7	8	7.5
Total	710	213		352	139	39.5	171	34.4

[a] No. of new = N (1880) – No. of persisters.

[b] This is the percentage of newcomers in each age group.

[c] The number of newcomers is adjusted upward to account for those who moved into Chelsea and died before the 1880 Census. The assumption is that the in-migrants moved into town in the middle of the intercensal period, so ten-year survival rates were calculated based on age in 1870 using the Model West, level 14 life table, and the number of newcomers was multiplied by the reciprocal of that survival rate.

[d] This is the adjusted number of newcomers as a percentage of those who left the township or died.

[e] Uses Model West, level 16 life table. See note c.

Source: Manuscript Schedules, U.S. Census of Population, 1860, 1880, and 1900.

1880, in Chelsea it had been occurring for almost one hundred years. Similarly, as another study indicates, the amount of in-migration to the Midwest also decreased progressively after the initial settlement period. There appears to be, as one historian has suggested, a built-in "natural history" or life cycle of rural community development in the United States, going from the settlement phase through a period of rapid growth to a leveling off or ultimate decline in population. It is probable that other older rural communities also became more stable and homogeneous as overall growth slowed and an increasing percentage of the local population was influenced by extensive bonds of economy and kinship.[10]

The ties that bind kept most adult men in Chelsea and other older rural communities from moving on, but not everyone established those ties. It is clear from the much lower persistence rates for those under twenty that many young men were either not able or chose not to fashion a stake in their hometown. But what distinguished these young men from their siblings or schoolmates? Although the census data is helpful in delineating the static characteristics of these important connections to the community, they give very little sense of how such ties developed and how they influenced the numerous individual decisions that underlay broader structural change.

To deal with these questions in greater depth, the career patterns of all males between the ages of thirty and thirty-nine listed in the 1880 Census were reconstructed from a number of sources. These 90 men have been linked backward to the 1860 Census and forward to the 1887 directory in *Child's Orange County Gazette* and the 1900 Census. Their wealth and property ownership were indicated by the tax lists for 1880 and 1895, and their numerous real estate transactions were traced through the local land records over the second half of the nineteenth century. Finally, marriage records, published genealogical information, and local maps provided more data on cohort members and their family connections.[11]

Of the 90 men, 46 were found in the 1860 Census and were born and/or raised in the township. Of these 46, 31 stayed to 1900: 23 farmers and 8 in nonagricultural occupations. The other 44 in the cohort moved into town between 1860 and 1880, and 20 farmers and 4 village residents in this group remained to 1900. As might be expected in a farming community, property ownership was the strongest determinant of persistence for the whole cohort, and the in-migrants who stayed were just as likely to own land as were the native sons. More than 80 percent of the 30 men who owned farms

Table 5.11. *Wealth and land mobility, 1880–1895, persisting males 30–39 (N = 54)*

Wealth (1880)	Wealth (1895)			
	$0	$1–499	$500–999	$1000+
$0	8	4	4	3
$1–499	0	8	1	5
$500–999	0	3	3	6
$1000+	0	1	4	4

Change in landholdings 1880–95 (acres)	N	%
−100+	3	5.6
−50–99	1	1.8
−1–49	4	7.4
no change	19	35.2
+1–49	15	27.8
+50–99	3	5.6
+100+	9	16.7
Total		100.0

Note: Wealth levels are those recorded in the tax lists and represent only a fraction of the true value of an individual's property and capital.
Source: Manuscript Grand List of Taxes for Chelsea, Vermont, 1880 and 1895.

in 1880 remained, and most of the propertyless farmers who did stay also eventually owned land by 1895. Although more than one-half of the cohort did not have any assets in 1880, only 8 of the 54 who remained, primarily village residents, failed to accumulate any taxable wealth. Those who stayed either owned land or expected to, and they experienced little adversity or dramatic changes (Table 5.11). In contrast to the roller coaster of urban and frontier mobility, the pattern in Chelsea was much less dynamic and much more stable.[12]

Although acquiring land was the key to persistence and security in rural communities like Chelsea, the process of getting a farm in such settled rural areas has not been studied in detail. In contrast to the numerous studies of inheritance in early modern Europe or colonial America, historians have paid little attention to the nineteenth-century farm family's strategies for transferring its land to the next generation and providing for those children who did not take over the home farm.[13]

The average Chelsea farmer at midcentury had five children and a farm that was not large enough to support more than one completed family. Geographical and technological constraints also precluded a shift to more intensive forms of agriculture, so the farmer transmitted his farm as a whole to only one heir, and typically that heir was the youngest son. Nineteen of the twenty-three farmers in the cohort who spent their entire lives in the township took over their fathers' farms, and most of them were either the youngest or one of the younger children.[14]

Chelsea farmers favored one of their youngest sons because they came of age precisely when the older farmer was ready to retire or cut down the scope of his activity. Holton Annis, Horace Moxley, Benson Sanborn, Wilbur Dewey, and Marshall Gates, to cite a few examples, were all younger sons who received all or part of their fathers' farms when they were in their midtwenties and their fathers were between sixty and seventy. These patterns of land transfer seem to have been the norm earlier in the century as well. Holton Annis's father was also a younger son in his twenties when he took over his father's farm, which was cleared in 1789, and Marshall Gates's grandfather, Jonas, was sixty-nine when he deeded the familial domain to his twenty-nine-year-old youngest in 1833.[15]

This pattern was not an immutable custom, however. When the father married late in life, it was not necessarily the youngest who stood in line to succeed him. Azariah Barnes, the firstborn, bought his family's farm in 1867 at the age of twenty-five when his father was seventy. Although most Chelsea farmers relinquished at least partial control when their successor was in his twenties, a few remind one of the authoritarian colonists evoked by Philip Greven. George Bacon held off the inevitable until he was seventy-six and his youngest son was thirty-eight, and Cal Goodwin had to wait until he was forty-seven and his father had died before claiming title to his family's land. But these were exceptional cases. Chelsea's fathers usually transferred title to their land while they were still alive, and Chelsea's sons, older and younger, typically bought their first farm and made their start in life between the ages of twenty-five and thirty.[16]

As the price of this guaranteed legacy, the younger son incurred considerable responsibility that bound him to his family and his community. In several cases, the details of such obligations were spelled out in the deed as conditions for the initial sale of the family farm. First, the younger son had to agree to continue working the land with his father in the customary fashion and not to sell or dispose of his share without parental consent as long as either of his parents was alive. He also usually assumed his father's debts and liabilities, including any mortgages on the farm, although father and son split the burden of local taxes equally.[17]

Mostly, however, the younger son promised to take care of his folks. The timing and nature of the transfer ensured not only a continuous level of farm activity but also care for the elderly farm couple in their remaining years. For the privilege of buying his father's 110-acre farm, Marshall Gates committed himself to do the following for his parents, Alanson and Ruby Gates:

> to provide for and furnish to the said Alanson and Ruby Gates his wife, for and during their and each of their natural lives, convenient rooms and privileges in the house upon the premises above conveyed, and now occupied by them or elsewhere, as the parties may agree. Also provide and furnish . . . clothing, bedding, food, drink and medicines suitable and necessary . . . according to their degree and state in life, and to nurse, doctor, take care of and support them . . . in such manner as the infirmities of their declining years shall require, and give them . . . a decent Christian burial . . . and furnish and set up suitable grave stones . . . further to furnish . . . with sufficient and reasonable spending from time as they may require for such reasonable journeyings as they may desire to make, and to provide for themselves such necessaries and comforts as they may desire; to furnish for their use a suitable horse and carriage from time to time they or either of them may require.[18]

In cases where an unmarried daughter still lived at home, the younger son was also obligated to care for her. To buy one-half of the 180-acre homestead in 1868, Wilbur Dewey promised to provide maintenance and a home on the family farm for his parents and his sister, Adelia Maria, as long as she remained single. If his father was no longer alive for her wedding, Wilbur was responsible for the $500 dowry. Benson Sanborn had the same duty, although his sister's dowry amounted to only $100. Typically, the heir was also required to distribute a previously determined sum of money to each of the daughters, married or single, after the death of both parents. In several instances where the younger son bought only half the family farm, he bought the other half after his father's death, paying a small sum – usually $100 – to his mother and his brothers and sisters.[19]

Although there are only a half-dozen of these conditional deeds for this particular cohort, there is considerable evidence that the pattern of responsibilities was widespread. Many of those who stayed in the township from 1860 to 1900 were still sons in their fathers'

The ties that bind: Mrs. Horace Moxley, Mrs. Don Ballou, Horace Moxley, and Guy Moxley in front of the Moxley homestead around the turn of the century. Horace was a younger son who took over his father's farm and married Jane Gates, his neighbor's daughter. Guy, their youngest son, also stayed at home and took over the family farm. Mrs. Ballou was a good friend and neighbor. [Reprinted from W. S. Gilman, *Chelsea Album* (Chelsea, Vt., 1980).]

households in 1880 when they were in their thirties, but those who were already the heads of households usually housed their widowed parent or spinster sister. By 1900, most of the parents had died, but those that were still alive continued to live with their sons and their families. Certain architectural accommodations had to be made. As a distinguished historian of New England rural life recently pointed out, an ell was a typical feature of the region's farmhouses and was added to the original dwelling to "house the family of the son who would eventually take over." According to the conditional deeds, as the son assumed the primary role on the farm, he and his family traded places with the older couple. The most succinct and telling testimony to the duration and commonness of these obligations throughout the region comes from an observer in western Massachusetts during the 1850s. Writing from Wendell Township in Franklin County, he noted that all the sons were sure to move on, "except for the youngest, perhaps, who remained to inherit a worn-out farm – and the worn-out parents."[20]

This strategy for passing the farm intact to one heir, as well as the various conditions intended to provide for other family members, was a continuation of older traditions in rural New England. As recent social historians of the region have argued, such concern for the family was the central feature of the *mentalité* of preindustrial rural Americans. In her recent analysis of what she labels the corporate family economy during the first half of the nineteenth century, Mary Ryan notes the reluctance to split up the family farm and finds a similar array of obligations attached to the transfer of farm property among the Yankee settlers in Oneida County, New York. The goal, of course, was to provide a competence or an independence for all of one's children, preferably next door or nearby. In Chelsea during the second half of the nineteenth century, however, that goal posed an increasingly difficult challenge because of the fixed number of local economic opportunities.[21]

As a result, the older brothers usually left town in their twenties, and only four brothers of the permanent farmers in the cohort also stayed in Chelsea to 1900. George H. Bacon, for example, bought a farm that was next door to his father's place from a man who had no sons and was moving out of the township. His younger brother, Erdix, continued to work with their father and eventually gained title eighteen years later. Although Benson Sanborn carried on his family's farm, his older brother bought a small piece of land near the village and specialized in breeding and raising Morgan horses. Other older sons tried their hands at local nonagricultural occupations. Elgin Barnes, who went from being a butcher to peddling fish and fruit, wound up as the proprietor of the Orange County Hotel and dabbled in village real estate investments.[22]

Although the majority of sons from farm families migrated out of Chelsea, a good number probably did not move very far. A few from the 1880 cohort who did not stay to 1900 only moved to neighboring townships and farmed there. From the newspapers, it is evident that those who did move great distances in the late nineteenth century were usually not farmers but professionals and businessmen. J. J. Keyes embarked for Byron, Minnesota, in 1885 to visit his brother who was a physician. From Byron, he planned to go to Antigo,

Wisconsin, to practice law, and he eventually became a judge. Similarly, William Carpenter went away at the age of twenty-six and opened a hardware store in Andover, Dakota Territory, whereas his younger brother stayed on the family farm in Chelsea.[23]

The records of the local Congregational Church give a better indication of out-migrant destinations. Between 1840 and 1880, 110 members of the church left Chelsea and letters of recommendation were forwarded to their new congregations whether they were Congregational or some other denomination. Before 1840, thirty-six such moves were recorded. Although these church members are not necessarily a representative sample of Chelsea's out-migrants, the distribution of their destinations is instructive. Most moves were within Vermont and New Hampshire, and the overwhelming majority did not leave New England. More than three-fourths of the earliest out-migrants moved to communities in these two states, and a total of six letters were sent to New York, Ohio, and Michigan. Between 1840 and 1860, more than half the letters were sent to other rural towns in Vermont ($N = 31$) and New Hampshire ($N = 6$). Only sixteen out-migrants moved to the West, and the remainder went to either New York or Massachusetts. Between 1860 and 1880, of forty-four letters, only four were sent west of New York. Again, more than half moved within Vermont ($N = 14$) or New Hampshire ($N = 9$), and the rest went elsewhere in New England. Urban destinations, however, were more common than in the earliest periods, and Lowell and Boston and Concord, New Hampshire, and Burlington, Vermont, received a total of ten migrants.[24]

The township's militia list from the Civil War gives additional representative evidence of the regional character of migration from Chelsea and the relative stability of the local population. Of the approximately 350 men between the ages of eighteen and forty-five listed in 1864, more than 100 were either dead, in the military, or already discharged from military service, and 44 men were subsequently stricken from the rolls because they moved out of the township between 1864 and 1867. More than half these migrants moved to other rural townships in Vermont. Only 4 moved to the Midwest, 5 moved to cities in the Northeast, and the remainder mostly scattered between rural New Hampshire, Massachusetts, and New York. Of the out-migrants, 33 were listed in the 1860 Census, and 29 were members of families in the community. Of the 29, 12 were older brothers whose younger brothers remained in Chelsea in 1880, and three-fourths of the older brothers moved only to nearby townships. Five other migrants had older brothers or cousins who stayed at home, and 7 others returned to Chelsea by 1880. Thus, only 5 of the 29 families either disappeared or had no sons from the younger generation in town in 1880.[25]

Those who wrote letters of greetings to Chelsea's first Old Home Week celebration in the summer of 1901 were also concentrated in New England. Of course, most of those who attended from out of town were from the region, but of the 58 letters sent to the fete, 22 were from ex-Chelseans in other Vermont townships, 11 were from Massachusetts, and only 13 were from the former frontier states west of the Adirondacks.[26]

Given the choice between a farm in the township or a nearby community and a farm in the West, it appears that a surprising number of Chelsea's sons preferred to stay close at hand. Those who stood to take over the home farm remained in spite of the sizable burden of family obligations that went with it. Those who searched for other agricultural opportunities often found them nearby, either in Chelsea or in a neighboring township.

One of the most important reasons Chelsea farm children stayed close to home was the critical role that the family played in providing long-term economic assistance. All sons of farm families with some resources received capital, typically the amount of a down payment on a farm, with which to make their start in life in Chelsea or elsewhere. Similarly, daughters got a comparable dowry for their marriage – effectively a down payment on a farm if they married a farmer. But throughout one's life, family connections also aided significantly by providing loans with generous terms and other forms of support.[27]

Eugene Thorne, for example, got married and made his start in life in 1880 at the age of twenty-nine when he bought his father's old farm. Fortunately, he left a diary and a detailed financial account that recorded this transaction and the sources of his capital. The entry for Tuesday, 30 March 1880, reads: "I go down to the village and father deeds the farm to me, price $2,800. $400 down and balance due in two years $200 and Int. Notes all written in on before so that I can pay them at any time." From the land records, it is clear that Eugene bought the farm from his father and then mortgaged it back to him, agreeing to pay twelve promissory notes of $200 each – "payable serially on or before the first day of April 1882, 1884, 1886, 1888, 1890, 1892, 1893, 1894, 1895, 1896, 1897 and 1898 with interest annually."[28]

Mortgaging the farm to his father had definite advantages. Eugene made the down payment easily by cashing $427.25 in government bonds, which he either got from his family or his wife's dowry. But he was also able to borrow that money back from his father to buy livestock and implements. He also did not have to make his first payment until two years after the sale, and the interest his father charged was well below the going rate. In his 1884 ledger of accounts, Eugene indicated that he paid $6 interest on the $200 promissory note that was due by April first. Assuming that he paid interest annually, his rate was 3 percent, or about half the conventional rate on New England farm mortgages during the decade. If we assume that $6 was the total interest due on the note, the annual rate of interest was actually much lower. Finally, after the old man died in 1893, Eugene, as administrator of his father's estate, simply discharged the remainder of his obligation as well as another mortgage that his father held from Eugene's sister and her husband.[29]

Such arrangements were common among those who continued to farm in their hometown. Fewer than one-half of the permanent farmers in the cohort never recorded a mortgage on their farms, but those that did got loans from their parents, some other relative, or their neighbor. Typically, whoever sold the farm also took a mortgage on it and allowed payments in installments over a long period of time. One might reasonably assume that the rate of interest was also lower than that charged by the village merchants. Milo Camp's mortgage to his parents, for example, does not even mention an interest charge. Of the twenty-three farmers, only two took sizable initial mortgages with merchants in the village, and in both cases the terms were less generous. Instead of a two- or three-year grace period followed by a schedule of gradual payments, only one note was written and the entire sum plus interest was due on demand after only one year.[30]

Although local farmers turned to the merchants more often for smaller loans, family and friends were also instrumental in providing ongoing financial assistance. Parents continued to help out while they were alive. Neighbors, in addition to the customary swapping of labor, sold each other land and underwrote loans and mortgages. Relatives by marriage were important resources and in many cases lived on adjacent farms. Frank Gilman, Calvin Goodwin, Lewis Lucas, and others helped, and were helped by, their wives' families. Of the nineteen men in the group who married, eleven wed Chelsea women and three took brides from just across the township lines. Six of these men literally married the girl next door. Moreover, at least twelve of the sisters of the permanent farmers married locally, so several of the permanent farmers lived next door to their brothers-in-law. Frank Hemmenway was the youngest of six sons and twelve children of Jonathan W. Hemmenway. Although he was the only son to stay in Chelsea, three of his sisters married and lived in town. Two of them were his neighbors and the other was just down the road. Thus, although only one son usually stayed in the community, the kinship network was still well developed and important. In addition to the initial transmission of farm property from father to son, lateral connections between brothers-in-law and other relatives also ensured economic stability. Those who stayed were bound by ties within the generations as well as those between them.[31]

In a recent study of kinship in nineteenth-century Londonderry, Vermont, a community much like Chelsea, an anthropologist notes many of the same patterns. As in Chelsea, an increase in residential continuity in Londonderry was coupled with the growing prevalence of family ties through land transfers between relatives and marriage to other families in the community. Almost half of the first and last land transfers of a sample of all individuals in the township were between relatives. After focusing on fifteen representative families over the course of the nineteenth century, the study finds that of the total number of offspring who married and remained in the community, more than 70 percent married local spouses, causing ninety different families to become related to the sample family groups. "Residential continuity . . . tended to reinforce an increasingly encompassing network of relatives," the author wrote, causing him to see Londonderry as a "series of linked, overlapping kinship groups."[32]

Family connections continued to be important to the children who moved out of the township and farmed nearby. It is difficult, however, to follow the careers of sons who left Chelsea for neighboring farm communities.[33] Just as most of Chelsea's out-migrants moved nearby, most of the in-migrants were also from adjacent townships. Thus, focusing on those from the cohort who moved into Chelsea between 1860 and 1880 and continued to farm there through 1900 will approximate the experiences of some of Chelsea's own departed native sons.

Chelsea during the late nineteenth century was not an island in any migratory stream. Instead, those who trickled in usually came only a short way. According to the 1880 Census, 95 percent of the township's population was born in Vermont or a neighboring state, and immigrants from Canada, Ireland, and Europe accounted for only 4 percent. Between 1840 and 1880 the Congregational Church received eighty-eight letters of recommendation for new members from out of town. Half were from nearby rural communities in Vermont, and fourteen moved in from rural New Hampshire. In-migration or return migration from either the West or urban Massachusetts accounted for a total of nine letters between 1840 and 1860 and thirteen from 1860 to 1880. In each period the congregation accepted a single immigrant family from the Presbyterian Church of Raphoe, County Donegal, Ireland. Unlike the destinations of local out-migrants, the sources of Chelsea's in-migration remained almost constant over time. As the church membership list suggests, many of the new settlers in the 1880 cohort actually moved from neighboring townships. As a young man, George Goodrich bought a farm in Chelsea that bordered on his home township of Brookfield. Edward Smith was from nearby West Fairlee, Fernando Perkins from neighboring Washington, and John Ballou came from Tunbridge, the next township south of Chelsea. Only Richard Kennedy and Joseph McConnell moved in from any great distance, being immigrants from Canada and Ireland, respectively.[34]

A handful of the twenty newcomer farmers did not need to take out mortgages when they bought their land in Chelsea, but this proportion was much lower than among their contemporaries who were born in the township. Instead, a greater number had to rely on loans from local merchants. In-migrants, however, often continued to get help from their families and had mortgages that involved relatives from outside the community. John Ballou took out his initial mortgage with a Chelsea merchant but got more money later when he sold or mortgaged a smaller part of the farm to his father back in Tunbridge. When Carleton Slack bought his farm in town in 1865, his loan was sponsored by his father in Lebanon, New Hampshire. Andrew Woodruff, who did not stay until 1900, married a Chelsea woman, lived in Brookfield for a while, and moved into town in 1875. Although his Chelsea in-laws were well off, he continued to rely on his hometown bank and his father in Woodstock, Vermont, for financial assistance.[35]

A number of in-migrants were actually a part of a larger family migration. A key factor that distinguished those who moved to Chelsea and stayed from those who eventually left was the simultaneous arrival of other family members. William E. Bacon moved to town with his older brother's household and worked for his brother until he bought his own farm. Similarly, several Moulton brothers crossed over from Tunbridge, and Charles Rich moved in from Northfield with two of his siblings. Although three of the seven family migrations involved the older generation, most of the family's members usually remained in the hometown. When John Ballou made his move, his brother Walter came to help and also settled in Chelsea. Their father, two other brothers, and two sisters stayed in Tunbridge, however, and a third sister lived with her husband in another nearby community. Thus, in addition to continued reliance on the home family, many of the successful in-migrants moved in with a ready-made network of kin-based support.[36]

The new farmers, especially those who moved into Chelsea alone, also established their own connections in the community. Church membership was one possibility, but few in this group appear to have joined the Congregational fold. For Lyman Haywood, however, that affiliation may have helped him get favorable terms on a sale and mortgage from another member of the congregation. Marriage was another route, though only two cases of marital in-migration emerge from the data. Willis Scales moved in and lived with his wife in her father's household. Because the older farmer had no sons, Scales eventually carried on the farm and cared for him in his retirement. In-migrants who were not family members sometimes acted as such for neighbors who had no one else to turn to. In 1869 Roxanne Estabrook became a widow and had already lost her youngest son in the Civil War. Warren Stearns moved in from West Windsor and made a sizable down payment on the farm, and the subsequent mortgage payments continued to provide for the widow and her daughters over the next fifteen years. Newcomer Scott George also became a surrogate son when he agreed to care for and maintain his elderly widowed neighbor after buying some of her farmland.[37]

Locating near home had definite financial advantages. The costs of searching for a new farm were less because one was more likely to hear of good land for sale by some childless widow in a neighboring community than a thousand miles away. More important, farm families and kin networks in nineteenth-century Vermont were instrumental in providing continuous aid and support to their members, whether they were next door or in the next township. Technically, monetary assistance could be mailed anywhere in the country, though not without some risks. Face-to-face relationships and long-standing ties of familiarity were equally important, albeit more subtle and subjective determinants of credit, and these were much less transferable.

Certainly the ties that bind had their economic dimensions, but they were also important in a more general way. As one social scientist recently put it, with that flair for words that only sociologists seem to have, there is the need to consider the noneconomic determinants of nonmigration. The advice of a nineteenth-century New

Hampshire farmer who urged his neighbors not to move West makes the same point more lyrically and stresses the cultural amenities of settled life:

> Farmers of New Hampshire, if you will live in huts instead of houses, work like slaves the year in and out, never allow yourself to look up at the sun or into a book . . . you can make more money than does any Western farmer . . . Had you not better be content to keep and improve the old homestead, so near the school house, where you can hear the church bell, and where you can enjoy the association of good neighbors? I have decided on this course for myself, and let those do better who can.[38]

Other evidence also indicates the psychic importance of certainty and familiarity in the decision to stay put. A regional folk song from the period plays a Vermont farmer's western fever against his wife's more sober assessment of the disadvantages of moving to Wisconsin and emphasizes the virtues of the familiar over the hazards of new fortunes. The husband begins by singing:

> Since times are so hard, I've thought, my true heart,
> Of leaving my oxen, my plough and my cart
> And away to Wisconsin, a journey we'd go
> To double our fortune as other folks do.
> While here I must labor each day in the field
> And the winter consumes all the summer doth yield.

To which his wife responds:

> Oh, husband, I've noticed with sorrowful heart
> You've neglected your oxen, your plough and your cart,
> And your sheep are disordered; at random they run
> And your new Sunday suit is now everyday on.
> Oh, stay on your farm and you'll suffer no loss.
> For the stone that keeps rolling will gather no moss.

The debate ensues over several verses as the husband promises his wife riches and dreams of being governor. She, in turn, points out:

> Oh, husband, remember that land is to clear
> Which will cost you the labor of many a year,
> Where horses, sheep, cattle and hogs are to buy
> And you'll scarcely get settled before you must die.

Finally, it is not the cost of developing a new farm but the specter of Indians, that metaphor for uncertainty, that convinces the farmer to stay in Vermont, and he ends by singing:

> We'll stay on the farm and we'll suffer no loss.
> For the stone that keeps rolling will gather no moss.[39]

In a figurative sense, farmers gathered moss in many older rural areas during the late nineteenth and early twentieth centuries. Increasingly, their communities came to consist primarily of people born locally or nearby. One early sociological study traced the careers of 2,445 rural men and women from Ellisburg Township in Jefferson County, New York, who had attended the local academy in Belleville between 1824 and 1920. Even though the population of the township declined by 30 percent between 1860 and 1900, 1,123 of the 2,445 students settled in the immediate vicinity of their homes, an area that contained 928 farms, and 500 others lived elsewhere in the county. To quote the author of the study: "Those who chose farming, for the most part remained in the home community, and usually upon the home farm or upon a farm in close proximity to it." Moreover, students often met their spouses at school, and the academy "proved to be an instrument for weaving family lines into a close community texture." In 1920 Belleville itself contained 307 farms, yet only 66 of the farm families had been in the community for only one generation.[40]

The social surveys of older rural communities conducted during the first decades of the twentieth century paint a similar picture with broader strokes. Of the farmers in several rural New York communities in 1921, 44 percent were born in the same township and an additional 17 percent came from other townships in the same county. A later study of rural Genesee County found that more than half the farm owners and 45 percent of the tenants came from the same or a bordering township and that 66 percent of the men living in the township of their birth married local spouses. Commenting on his findings, the author noted that rural families "do not move often, nor do they move far." Similar surveys of farm communities in Ohio, Illinois, Iowa, and Minnesota found more or less the same results: About one-half the farmers were natives of their townships and almost three-fourths were born in the same county. On the other side of the coin, farm children who left home typically lived nearby. Data from eight different Ohio townships during the twenties show that 62 percent of all adult sons and 57 percent of all adult daughters lived within twenty miles of their parental homes, and more than 80 percent of the children who lived on farms were within that radius.[41]

As in Chelsea, this demographic stability was linked to the transfer of farm property and other forms of family assistance. In Dryden Township, New York, more than 60 percent of the farmers in 1918 with farms larger than 100 acres were related to the previous owner.

Farm sons typically worked for their fathers without receiving wages until they married and started out for themselves. To quote from the study: "If the farm is of good size and the family not too large, there is usually room for the son at home, either as a partner or as a tenant. If the father is able, he usually gives the son his financial support, either directly or by signing notes or by lending him money." In Ohio, 39 percent of the sons of farmers from eight different townships had also become farmers by 1927, and "at least 80 percent of this group received parental aid in the form of either money or land . . . Most of those who could not find a place as owners or renters on farms owned by their fathers, or who received no financial assistance, went into other occupations."[42]

To the farmers in Chelsea and other older rural communities, the traditional goal of settling all their children close at hand was beyond reach. Still, farmers strove to help their children and to get them started in life. Although not all of the next generation stayed near home, those that did became linked by marriage to a wider kinship network, which compensated for their siblings who had moved on. This concern for the family line and the central role that the family continued to play in older rural communities resemble the earlier *mentalité* described by several recent authors. But to assume, as they do, that such rural familism was ultimately incompatible with commercial agriculture and a capitalist market economy is questionable, for the evidence from Chelsea and other older rural areas strongly suggests otherwise.[43]

 In contrast to farmers, Chelsea's sons who followed nonagricultural pursuits were less likely to stay at home or nearby. As the number of local industrial opportunities diminished, displaced artisans found their ways to larger centers. Older farm children also left to work in factories in Manchester, Lowell, and Boston. A disproportionate number of older sons from rural New England families moved to Boston during the nineteenth century according to a recent analysis of migration to that city, and another study notes an analogous pattern among the Yankee women who worked in the Lowell mills.[44]

Opportunities for professionals in Chelsea were also limited. Numerous young men studied medicine or read law in Chelsea but wound up practicing elsewhere, and few sons continued in their fathers' offices. Dr. George K. Bagley's son started in his father's practice in the early 1860s but soon moved to Topsham, Vermont. Another local physician taught more than half a dozen medical students, including two of his sons, from 1870 to the turn of the century, but not one remained to practice in the township. Similarly, of the thirty-plus members of the Orange County Bar from Chelsea during the nineteenth century, only one turned over his practice to his son.[45]

Some, no doubt, found the situation in Chelsea stifling. Levi Vilas, an attorney who was active in Chelsea politics, was already on the rise at a relatively young age. He was elected as the township's representative to the state legislature in 1840 at the age of twenty-nine and became judge of probate in 1843 and the state senator from Orange County in 1845. Because of his efforts, Chelsea became a stronghold of the Vermont Democratic party, and twice Vilas was the Democratic candidate for national office – the House in 1844 and the Senate in 1848. Defeated both times by the more numerous Whigs and seeing little future for his minority party in state politics, he packed up his young family and moved to Madison, Wisconsin, in 1851. There he served as a state legislator and was elected mayor without opposition in 1861. His son, William F. Vilas, later achieved the goal that had eluded his father when he became U.S. senator from Wisconsin and served as postmaster general and secretary of the interior in Grover Cleveland's cabinet. Other young Chelsea attorneys also sought broader, if less illustrious, horizons in Boston, Chicago, Texas, Alabama, and Minnesota.[46]

Some, however, regretted the need to move on. George H. Steele, a contemporary of Vilas, was a young Dartmouth graduate who was reading law in his father's office in Chelsea in 1846. He wrote to his friend, another hometown son starting out as a merchant in the larger town of Brattleboro, about his impending move to Troy, New York:

> Dr. Hendrick you know is very decidedly of the opinion that New York is a much better place than Vermont (if not the best place in the world) for everybody, and particularly for Lawyers. And I believe Father is of pretty much the same opinion. It seems to be a fancy of them both that I shall "settle" there. But I, by no means, determine *now* to do so. I shall probably remain there a year or more, and then do what I have a mind to. I do not yet give up Vermont. "A little farm well tilled" [etc.] answers my vision of happiness and I believe I locate *that* in Vermont.[47]

We do not know whether young Steele eventually found such happiness, but he never returned to Chelsea.

Steele's friend, William B. Hale, was typical of Chelsea's sons who went into business. Although his father was a wealthy merchant in Chelsea, Hale moved to Brattleboro to start his career. According to the R. G. Dun & Company records between 1850 and 1890, none of the village's larger mercantile concerns spanned more than one generation, and only a few of the smaller businesses experienced that continuity. Rufus Hyde and Elihu Hyde were the two richest merchants in 1860 with extensive investments in local real estate, and each admitted one of his sons as a partner in their respective firms. In both cases, however, the sons sold their interests and moved out of town to pursue larger ventures.[48]

Sons of local businessmen rarely clerked in their fathers' stores; instead, they went elsewhere for their training. Although it was no advantage for young farmers to learn how to farm in a different township, for aspiring merchants this wider commercial experience was invaluable. A few came back to the family enterprise in Chelsea; however, most, especially those who went to the larger centers of Lowell and Boston, did not return.[49]

As with the professions, business opportunities in Chelsea were either too few in number or too limited in scope to hold onto its more worldly-wise and ambitious progeny. Daniel T. Tarbell quit marketing local agricultural commodities and left town when he saw that the railroad would be coming through a nearby township. In his memoirs, he recalled the events of 1848, a year of revolution:

> Having had some experience in the effects of railroads in matters of commerce and feeling that necessity of all communities conforming to the revolution that railways must make, I saw clearly the importance of a point being made there to favor the demands of the public. All that spring my mind dwelt upon the subject of locating on the road of business.

Tarbell made his move and was one of the founders of the railroad town of South Royalton. Whereas he gained riches and notoriety, his brother, a tailor, stayed in Chelsea and lapsed into insolvency.[50]

Charles I. Hood left town in 1861 at the age of fifteen to apprentice with an apothecary in Lowell, Massachusetts. Rather than returning to help his father, whom the R. G. Dun & Company records describe as "honest but of poor business talents," Charles opened his own business in Lowell. He made millions manufacturing Hood's Sarsaparilla and pioneered in the use of mass advertising. In contrast, his brother also apprenticed as a druggist in Lowell during the 1860s but returned to help in the family drugstore; he had to be satisfied with only small gains and a business that R. G. Dun & Company assessed as "not very sharp."[51]

Even though young professionals and merchants usually left Chelsea, family and hometown connections were still helpful in paving their ways in the outside world. When Adelbert Carpenter went to

William Hood, Charles's brother, in front of the Hood store in Chelsea village around 1890. [Reprinted from W. S. Gilman, *Chelsea Album* (Chelsea, Vt., 1980).]

clerk in Boston in 1887, it was for the firm of Halley and Corwin, Corwin being a transplanted Chelsean. Similarly, Corwin's own relative went off in 1886 to be a bookkeeper for C. I. Hood's sarsaparilla company in Lowell. The patent medicine king himself owed part of his success to the timely intercessions of hometown connections. After the prospects of a partnership following his apprenticeship evaporated when his employer unexpectedly sold the business, another Chelsea migrant helped him obtain a position with a larger wholesale and retail drug firm in Boston. In the same vein, he later tapped fellow Vermonters for the capital to start his own enterprise.[52]

Those who did stay in Chelsea to work in village occupations were not the offspring of local professionals or merchants. All but one of the eight nonfarmers in the 1880 cohort who lived in Chelsea all of their lives were the sons of local farmers and craftsmen. Thus the village merchants, professionals, and artisans were not a separate and self-perpetuating clique. Instead, they were like the lifelong farmers, part of local kinship networks that extended into the countryside. Several in the cohort were brothers and cousins of farmers in the township and had various dealings with them. Moreover, the few who moved into the village and stayed established comparable ties in the community. Willard Townsend came to Chelsea from Williamstown in 1867 at the age of eighteen to clerk for a local merchant. He was, according to R. G. Dun & Company, an "industrious close young man," and his employer took him in as his partner in 1873. Although the owner, J. B. Bacon, was quite wealthy, Townsend was never worth much outside of his interest in the business. As a single man, he did not maintain his own home but boarded in the Orange County Hotel. His marriage in 1881, however, linked him to two established local families with members who farmed and were involved in village commerce. By 1886 he was a full-fledged member of the community, a homeowner, and a township selectman.[53]

In contrast to the men who settled permanently in Chelsea, whether native sons or in-migrants, those who came to town but did not stay had little hope or desire for establishing the ties that bind. They were the propertyless laborers like Sam Tramp, sons of poor families who did not have enough capital to make a down payment and get credit for a mortgage. They were artisans like Charles Robinson, a printer who found too little demand for his skills to support himself, his wife, and young son. They were the immigrants from Sweden and Canada who did not blend into the Congregational membership quite as easily as the devout Ulstermen from Raphoe. They were the brothers, like Alvah Little and Edgar Rich, who helped their brothers set up their farms but found none available for themselves. They were the clerks and businessmen who were either not industrious or "close" enough or had ambitions too large for a Vermont country town. Only five of the twenty in the cohort who moved in and out of Chelsea were farm owners, and the reasons for their departure are not known.[54]

During the course of the second half of the nineteenth century, however, fewer and fewer such strangers found their way into town. Instead, those who lived in Chelsea knew each other very well, bound together in a myriad web of economic and family ties, which spread from neighbor to neighbor and from village to countryside. To the sons that stayed, the trade-off between the restrictions of familial obligations and the security of financial stability was sufficiently attractive to keep them from seeking larger fortunes elsewhere. Those who did move into Chelsea and settled there came with the means to establish themselves and were not really strangers, for they resembled no one so much as the township's own departed sons who farmed in adjacent communities. Young men with higher aspirations or a more cosmopolitan perspective, such as the sons of village merchants and professionals, left town. But filling their places were other native sons whose world view was, no doubt, more narrowly focused, paralleling that of their brothers and cousins in the field.

The overall effect of such pervasive and long-standing ties made Chelsea a much different sort of community than is usually envisioned in late-nineteenth-century America. Removed from the processes of growth with their concomitant diversity, turnover, and flux, Chelsea's populace became more homogeneous and intertwined. Nor were such changes limited to Chelsea or northern New England. In varying degree, increasing stability and homogeneity occurred throughout the rural North, as former frontier regions evolved beyond the initial conditions of settlement and rapid growth and as those who lived there became enmeshed in the ties that bind.

6   *Their town: the emergence of consensus and homogeneity in a settled rural community*

On 28 May 1892, Lyman R. Dennison, an elderly Chelsea farmer, celebrated the fifteenth anniversary of his second marriage, and a circle of friends and kinfolk gathered to wish the couple well and commemorate the occasion. The local newspaper reported the event and published a guest list that included other farmers, a day laborer, a carpenter, a lawyer, a teamster, and a salesman. Guests came from the village as well as different parts of the countryside. Some were Congregationalists, some were Methodists, and some belonged to no church. A few were from families who had lived in Chelsea for many years, whereas others had moved in much more recently. In a large city or a newer rural community, perhaps, these differences might have been more important, even divisive, but not in Chelsea, Vermont, in 1892.[1]

Chelsea at the turn of the century was a remarkably homogeneous and like-minded community. Its inhabitants embodied a settled rural respectability. They were overwhelmingly Protestant, Republican, God-fearing if not churchgoing, and steadfastly opposed to liquor. Local voluntary associations, which ranged from fraternal orders to baseball and debating clubs, sponsored an unending series of events and sociables that involved much of the community. On a less formal and more individual basis, Chelseans spent a good deal of time visiting with each other as in the case of the Dennisons' anniversary. Few class, ethnic, or ideological conflicts divided them, and the turmoil so prevalent in the larger society had little impact on the placidity of local life.

This bucolic consensus bore little relationship to the nature of community in Chelsea earlier in its history, however. Chelsea in the 1890s was not a covenanted city on a hill that had been meticulously preserved since its founding. The ideal of a consensual community was present from the very beginning, but the different settlers had competing visions of what that community would entail. Consequently, life in the township during the first half century after settlement was fraught with division and conflict. The random and rapid process of settlement, the social differentiation resulting from economic development, and the religious and political tempests that

112

eddied about New England created numerous local factions. Calvinist and Arminian, villager and farmer, Mason and Antimason, Democrat and Whig – each added a different facet to the character of community life.

Eventually, however, local differences declined, conflicts abated, and a single (but not singular) point of view prevailed. Changes in the structure of the local economy and the stagnation of Chelsea's economic development lessened local occupational diversity and precluded any significant in-migration, especially by the foreign-born. Family strategies for inheritance and subsequent patterns of migration and persistence defused potential conflicts over land and led to an increasing homogeneity among the township's population. The village became more tightly intertwined with the countryside as more local merchants and professionals came from farm families and as a growing number of retired farmers, farm widows, and spinster daughters also resided there. Moreover, much of the emerging common viewpoint stemmed from the simple passage of time and the growing familiarity of lives spent together in the same place.

In addition to economic and demographic adjustments, and interrelated with them, new attitudes and social institutions further contributed to growing homogeneity and like-mindedness in the community. The 1840s and 1850s were critical years in this process, and many of the building blocks of consensus began as responses to the challenges of lessened growth and limited opportunities that became apparent during this period. The Second Great Awakening and the temperance crusade introduced new codes of behavior during uncertain times, which gradually became the most important criteria for inclusion in community life. The formation of the Republican party facilitated political unity in Chelsea, and the proliferation of voluntary associations during the second half of the nineteenth century instituted a new and different form of community that ameliorated older conflicts.

Evangelical Protestantism was an important component of consensus in Chelsea, and the Second Great Awakening reached the community in full force during the 1830s and 1840s. Local Congregationalists had experienced revivals in 1809 and 1819, but the religious excitements of 1831 and 1842 brought in more than twice as many new members. The 1831 revival was actually more of a continuation of those previous experiences rather than a new departure. It was part of a larger movement that began as a series of spontaneous awakenings in Caledonia County but was promoted in a deliberate and organized fashion throughout eastern Vermont. From a theological perspective, Vermont Congregationalists retained their notions of predestination in a modified form and did not embrace the more radical doctrines of Charles Grandison Finney and other prominent evangelists. In Chelsea, the Reverend Calvin Noble led the 1831 revival just as he had in 1809 and 1819, and as a result, the seventy-three new believers were drawn from the same constituencies as in the earlier awakenings. Most were from established Congregational farm families, unmarried women accounted for almost half the converts, and married and single women together formed two-thirds of the new membership.[2]

Although there is no direct evidence of revivals in the other denominations in Chelsea, they also made advances during the 1830s. The Methodists built their own church in the village in 1837. Members of different denominations who lived on the West Hill cooperated and formed the West Hill Union Meeting House in 1833. Fifty-two pews, one for each Sunday of the year, were auctioned to the residents of that neighborhood, and as of 1844 the pews were divided among eighteen Methodists, eleven Freewill Baptists, ten Universalists, six Calvinist Baptists, six Christians, and one Congregationalist.[3]

The biggest awakening in Chelsea's history occurred in 1842, and in contrast to the 1831 Congregational revival, it was a more spontaneous phenomenon and reached a larger number and a wider variety of local inhabitants. Inspired by the preachings of an outside evangelist named Parker, ninety-one converts professed their faith and joined the Congregational Church during the July communion, and fifteen others were received in September. This excitement affected previously unawakened elements of the community. About half the new members were men and a significant proportion of them were village artisans and merchants instead of farmers. For the first time, sizable numbers came from families who did not already have ties to the local Congregational Church, although this was much more the case for the male enthusiasts than for the women.[4]

Coming in the wake of the economic depression of the late 1830s and at a time when opportunities in Chelsea were no longer expanding, the 1842 revival held particular attractions for those who faced an uncertain future as a result of lessened local opportunities or increased involvement in the larger market economy. More than three-fourths of the men who professed their new faith were not proprietors or were only young household heads in their twenties, and twenty-eight of the forty-six women converts were single. Their doubts about the future were probably compounded by the realization that they would have to leave the township to make their homes because only eight of the young men and five of the unmarried women who converted were still living in Chelsea twenty years later. In addition to spiritual rewards, church membership afforded those who left another advantage: The letters of recommendation that were forwarded by the church to their new congregations eased that transition whether they moved nearby, to the city, or to the western frontier.[5]

Established residents, especially those who were most involved in the market economy and had experienced the economic troubles of the late 1830s most directly, were also drawn to the church for the first time in 1842. Amplius Blake, the wealthiest merchant and the heaviest investor in Chelsea, saw the light when he was in his sixties. The other older converts were also merchants or landlords, including Joshua Dickinson, a former Mason, and Nathan Hale who owned a local tavern. Mechanics and artisans figured prominently in the revival, and more than two-thirds of the male converts who stayed in Chelsea to 1860 were engaged in nonagricultural occupations. For these men, the growing fellowship of evangelical faith provided more security in business dealings by subjecting economic transactions to religious as well as secular sanctions. According to the second item of the moral code of the Congregational Church from 1848, "we abhor all attempts to deal unjustly or oppressively or to take advantage of others . . . or to withhold from any their due or to evade any civil obligation but will honestly provide for the Liquidation of debts to the extent of our ability."[6]

More important, the revival inculcated a spirit of self-discipline that was increasingly felt to be necessary during this period of economic uncertainty. The church's 1848 moral code explicitly forbade frivolities such as balls, dancing schools, circuses, and theaters for the first time. Liquor was also forbidden: "We deem the use of intoxicating Liquors as a beverage injurious and wrong and thus their Manufacture and Sale for this purpose is Wrong, Even if Sanctioned by Civil law and that we Cannot consistently use it or furnish it for others. Therefore pledge ourselves to total abstinence." And when self-discipline lapsed, a standing committee inquired into the conduct of any member "whose course is disorderly, or gives occasion of public scandal."[7]

Even after their revivals the Congregationalists comprised only a minority of Chelsea's inhabitants, but the self-discipline that they promulgated became more widespread in the community during the temperance crusade. Although temperance had been discussed in New England since the beginning of the century, the first indication of the issue in Chelsea does not occur until 1839. Responding to "certain individuals" who "have got up a grate [sic] excitement on temperance and intemperance . . . a thing heretofore unknown in this town," the town meeting directed the selectmen to convene two days later and "approbate all such persons as shall make applicants as said [crowd?] shall deem suitable and proper." The fact that this meeting was to be held at Jacob Perkins's tavern suggests that a strict licensing policy and the temperance issue in general had limited support.[8]

After the economic depression of the late 1830s and the revival of 1842, however, temperance developed a broader local constituency. On 22 January 1844, 16 men from Chelsea signed a pledge of total abstinence and formed the Chelsea Washington Total Abstinence Society, part of the larger Washingtonian temperance movement. During the following ten months, 191 other men and 170 women also signed the pledge and joined the society, which, according to its records, met weekly except in the summer until the spring of 1845.[9]

As might be expected, temperance appealed to every religious denomination in Chelsea. Of the 207 male abstainers, more than 50 were listed as members in Chelsea Congregational Church records, and most of these were received during the 1842 revival. Although no membership lists survive from either the Methodist Church or the West Hill Union Meeting House, at least 15 pledged teetotalers can be linked to these congregations through other sources. Even a former Masonic master, Daniel Wyman, was one of the earliest to swear off drinking, along with six other ex-Masons. Although temperance was a Whig political issue, numerous Democrats also favored abstinence, and Levi Vilas, the local party leader, was the sixth man to sign the pledge.[10]

Ninety of the male pledge signers can be found in either the 1840 or the 1850 census returns, and from this data it is clear that the initiative for temperance reform came from the village, not the countryside. The overwhelming majority of those who founded the society were artisans, merchants, and professionals, as were the bulk of the earlier signers; and just over half of all the abstainers were engaged in nonagricultural occupations. Most of the farmers who took the pledge did not do so until almost two months after the society's organization.[11]

Like the converts in the 1842 revival, local craftsmen, professionals, and merchants were probably the first to rally behind the cause of temperance because they were the most directly linked to larger social and economic developments. As other historians have suggested, temperance reform was integrally related to the basic transformation of the time, the rise of free wage labor and a market economy. Sobriety was attractive because it promised necessary efficiency and greater capital accumulation for both the abstemious worker and his capitalist employer; and according to another study, urban workingmen pledged abstinence in order to "assert their independence and self-worth in the face of a threatening economy." The most intriguing hypothesis argues that temperance and evangelical religion in general offered a substitute for the traditional social bonds that had been destroyed by the emergence of free wage labor and translocal economic relationships. By emphasizing both the possibility of individual perfectability and salvation and the practice of self-discipline, this impulse simultaneously legitimized new free-market relationships while providing a guide for behavior in uncertain times. Thus, the self-disciplining character of abstinence probably held particular attractions for the numerous Chelsea craftsmen and merchants who took the pledge as they faced the vagaries of the market economy.[12]

Some temperance reformers were also concerned with the nature of their community as a whole in addition to individual self-discipline. Whereas many who took the pledge in Chelsea were single young men and women who would probably have to move out of the township, family men and women in their thirties and forties who had a greater stake in the community also swore off liquor. In contrast to the mobility of the younger converts and cold-water advocates, these older teetotalers were more stable. More than two-thirds of the fifty-six older pledge-takers who were listed in the 1840 Census were in the 1850 Census and almost half persisted until 1860.

Because it drew support from different local factions, then, temperance had the potential for being the basis of a new social order in Chelsea, which would transcend older divisions and establish the consensus that had eluded the first settlers. In general, early temperance activism was assimilative as reformers attempted to persuade others to join them under the common aegis of sobriety, and the Washingtonian movement in particular recruited members from a wide variety of backgrounds and sponsored many different activities designed to foster a new sense of community as well as to reinforce abstention.[13]

Abstinence had widespread appeal in Chelsea as an individual strategy for coping with uncertain times, but efforts to impose it on the community as a whole met substantial local opposition. At the insistence of the teetotalers, the March 1844 town meeting passed a resolution stating "that the use of intoxicating drinks as an ordinary beverage are injurious and that being so the use and traffick in them ought to be discouraged." However, they rejected two stronger-proof measures that would have actually mandated action by local and county officials to curtail the sale and use of liquor.[14]

The fight continued throughout the late 1840s in a series of votes on local licensing, which split Chelsea's voters. The Vermont legislature enacted a law allowing local restrictions on liquor in 1845, but opponents to that policy held the edge in Chelsea, so no such measures were adopted. The young lawyer George H. Steele, a pledged abstainer, wrote his friend and fellow teetotaler W. B. Hale in 1846 and noted that "we are awfully *rum* in this county . . . You are not surprised, are you?" In 1852, however, after demands for liquor control became more widespread, Vermont townships passed a prohibitory measure modeled on Maine's influential law of 1851. Statewide, the measure won by only a small majority, and in Chelsea, townsmen opposed it with a vote of 250 to 142.[15]

Drinkers and nondrinkers formed two different camps in Chelsea during the middle of the nineteenth century, but the split over prohibition entailed other dimensions as well. Some temperance advocates opposed the measure, especially teetotaling Democrats who felt comfortable with moral suasion but rejected attempts to codify morality for the community as a whole. In part, their vote reflected partisan loyalties, but at a deeper level it expressed a different vision of society that had its roots in earlier republican traditions of individual freedom and opposition to the standing order.

Aided by the new law, however, prohibitionists actively worked to eliminate local divisions over liquor and to institute abstinence as a social boundary of community life. During the 1850s, a group of "friends of the law" formed the Orange County Temperance Society to ensure proper enforcement. Actually, the statute allowed some liquor to be sold by a town agent, who was appointed by an elected county commissioner, as long as it was to be used for "medical, chemical and mechanical purposes only." The determination of what exactly constituted appropriate or legitimate uses under the law, however, ultimately rested with the town agent and the county commissioner who appointed him.[16]

This gray zone between the intent of the law and its enforcement was, according to the resolutions adopted by the Temperance Society, the source of much abuse. Troubled by an increase in the sale of liquor under one county commissioner, the society urged in 1859 "that all friends of humanity should strive to secure the absolute friends of the law as Commissioners and agents." At the previous year's convention in Chelsea, they voted that town agents be advised "to sell for chemical purposes only to those well known as scientific and practical chemists, nor to mechanics except those whose business [requires?] the article and for medical purposes only in small doses such as Doctors administer to their patients."[17]

In addition to lobbying for their candidates for county commissioner and town agent, Chelsea prohibitionists also went after clandestine local taverns. A resolution adopted at the 1862 town meeting expressed concern that Chelsea's reputation as "a low place filled with rum shops while drunkards staggered through the streets" was scaring away many "good citizens who would otherwise become members of our community." Fifty-four townsmen signed a pledge to put an end to this by "moral suasion if possible and by enforcing the law if necessary," and a few years later, two signers actually led a raid on a local grocery store in search of illicit cider.[18]

Gradually, the advocates of legally enforced temperance gained the upper hand. Early elections for county commissioner were essentially contests between supporters and opponents of state prohibition, which divided Chelsea's voters. By the 1870s, however, the Temperance Society's candidate typically ran unopposed, and the laws were enforced. Moses King, for example, had been a traveling vendor of "essences, liniment, camphor gum and yankee notions," as well as illegal liquor, in and around Chelsea for more than fifteen years when he was finally arrested, convicted, and fined in 1876. Thus, in contrast to their urgent and anxious resolutions of the 1850s and 1860s, the 1883 convention of the Temperance Society calmly admonished its supporters to practice "continued vigilance and activity in this important cause that this is no time for inaction or indifference."[19]

Active drinkers became an increasingly insignificant and ostracized element of town life. When one young clerk who was new to Chelsea shot and killed a drunken townsman who was throwing chairs about the store in 1870, the local jury found him innocent by reason of self-defense. One local physician was a drinker, according to the R. G. Dun & Company reports; although respected during the 1860s, he saw his practice and credit rating erode during the 1870s because of liquor. By the 1880s, incidents of public intoxication were so infrequent as to be newsworthy items. Of the twenty-three persons incarcerated in the Orange County jail in Chelsea between 1877 and 1899, only three were arrested for either being drunk or selling liquor.[20]

The experiences of one of these individuals, Richard Kennedy, perhaps best illustrates prevailing attitudes toward drink and drinkers. An Irish immigrant from Canada, Kennedy was something of a social pariah in Chelsea, and more than any other individual in the community he was continuously involved in some kind of altercation throughout the last decades of the nineteenth century. He was arrested for illicit distilling and selling liquor on at least four occasions and jailed several times. Kennedy was involved in at least as many civil lawsuits and was in trouble repeatedly for assault, in one instance for striking a woman and her daughter with his fists. According to the records of his trial in 1892, Kennedy sold liquor to the same twelve people on every other day between 7 June 1889 and 7 June 1892. Like himself, his regular customers were also on the fringes of Chelsea's society, and in the face of such active legal and social sanctions, their numbers were shrinking rather than increasing.[21]

Thus, when the issue of prohibition came up for a statewide referendum in 1903, Chelsea voters rejected its repeal by a vote of 184 to 57. In contrast to the 1852 balloting, more than three-fourths of the local freemen now favored the strictest liquor controls. Although the state adopted a more liberal local license option as a result of the 1903 vote, Chelseans repeatedly rejected allowing any local sales by a margin of more than 3 to 1. Finally, in 1914, Guy Back received the first liquor license allowed in the township, but it was only a fifth-class license that permitted the sale of alcohol solely by a doctor's prescription.[22]

Temperance reform began in Chelsea during the 1830s and 1840s as an individual strategy for coping with economic uncertainties, but during the course of the century it became a means for defining the local community with sobriety as the most visible social boundary. Although some temperance advocates, especially among the Congregationalists, subscribed to such a goal from the very beginning, others rejected it as being too coercive and at odds with their vision of society. By the end of the century, however, that split had disappeared.

In part, political developments weakened the partisan basis of this division and reinforced the trend toward like-mindedness and homogeneity when the formation of the Republican party changed Chelsea into a one-party town. Between 1845 and 1854, party politics in Vermont were in a state of disarray. State Democrats opposed slavery and formed several alliances with Vermont's Free-Soilers, much to the consternation of national Democratic leaders. On the other hand, the 1848 presidential candidacy of Whig slave owner Zachary Taylor created a problem for Vermont Whigs and began that party's disintegration. Throughout these years, Chelsea voters split between Whigs, regular Democrats, and various antislavery, Free-Soil, and Barnburner Democratic candidates.[23]

The inadequacy of both parties became apparent during the Kansas-Nebraska crisis in 1854, and Vermonters abandoned their traditional allegiances. Mass meetings and conventions were held throughout the state, including a "Republican" convention in Orange County, in an appeal to all persons "opposed to the aggressions of the slave power." In addition to antislavery, temperance was the initial bond that rallied Whigs, temperance Free-Soilers, and teetotaling Democrats under one political banner. The Republican party became a permanent organization in Vermont in 1855, and it regularly garnered between 75 and 85 percent of Chelsea's votes for the rest of the century.[24]

The ideology of the Republican party before the Civil War was not yet the creed of big corporations or wealthy entrepreneurs that it would become later in the century. Instead, according to its leading historian, "it was its identification with the aspirations of the farmers, small entrepreneurs, and craftsmen of northern society which gave the Republican ideology much of its dynamic, progressive, and optimistic quality." Republicans aspired to the competence, modest independence, or small capital that were the hallmarks of what they called free labor, and they were suspicious of wage earners, wealthy speculators, and slave owners who did not embody such an ethic. These attitudes were already familiar to the farmers in Chelsea through their own attempts to provide for their children and through the writings of mid-nineteenth-century agriculturalists, and in the Republican party they found their most enduring political expression.[25]

The Civil War probably also contributed to the emergence of consensus in Chelsea. Throughout the North, Protestants of all denominations came to regard the war as a millennial event, the climactic test and confirmation of America as the redeemer nation, the new Israel. As one historian puts it: "In baptizing the Civil War with the bloody urgency of the Apocalypse, Protestants were fighting for more than the political integrity of the Union; the issue was no less than the survival of corporate identity and purpose." This mission transcended denominational differences and created a new unity of spirit among northern Protestants. From their pulpits, northern clergymen also attacked Jeffersonian notions of individual freedom, which they blamed for the excess of democracy that had led to the war. Yet in Chelsea and in many other northern communities, Jeffersonian ideals of democracy were the source of opposition to the evangelical vision of community and contributed to local divisions and conflict.[26]

More than other developments, the rise of voluntary associations in Chelsea ameliorated the divisions between these different views of society by instituting a new form of social organization that facilitated a compromise – a collective consensus based on individual voluntarism rather than on coercion. The first major voluntary association in Chelsea began, like the emergence of the temperance crusade, as a response to the problems of lessened growth when Chelseans attempted to meet the challenges of limited opportunities in a more collective manner and founded the Orange County Agricultural Society in 1846. The society sponsored an annual fair and awarded prizes, and, as mentioned earlier, it was part of a broader movement in the region that received publicity and support from the agricultural press as well as the state government.[27]

Agricultural reform in Chelsea mostly attracted local inhabitants who were older, established, and stable. The membership of the society (in the late 1840s) included 107 Chelsea men and 1 woman, of whom almost two-thirds were already household heads in 1840 and more than half were still in Chelsea in 1860. Society members came from every religious denomination, political party, and occupation in the community. Although these dividing lines had already been crossed during the 1842 Congregational revival and the temperance crusade, and although many converts and teetotalers also became agricultural reformers, membership in the Orange County Agricultural Society comprised an even wider cross section of the local community.[28]

In contrast to religion, temperance, or politics, agricultural reform was a less divisive issue. The need for such reform was apparent, and the promotion of better farming practices threatened neither individual freedom nor any larger vision of society. The Orange County Agricultural Society was dedicated to a fairly specific form of voluntary self-improvement, and membership entailed a narrower and more limited commitment that implied little about fundamental values. Consequently, although the common bond provided by the society was relatively superficial, it encompassed a greater variety of Chelsea's permanent population than any other affiliation.

After the Civil War, a plethora of voluntary associations developed in Chelsea as in other rural communities and small towns and established additional common grounds among the local inhabitants. Local chapters of national temperance societies – the International Order of Good Templars, the Sons of Temperance, the WCTU, and the YWCTU (Women's and Young Women's Christian Temperance Unions) – helped to institutionalize the local code against drinking. Each church organized a women's benevolent society and a young people's mission circle, which sponsored social and educational activities. The Grand Army of the Republic, the Sons of Veterans, and the Ladies' Aid Society of the Sons of Veterans all had local chapters. Even the Masons rechartered a lodge in Chelsea in 1860. More strictly local groups included a drama club, the Chelsea Cornet Band, two volunteer fire companies, the Chelsea Baseball Club and other athletic groups, various sewing circles, the "TP" Club, and the Chelsea Debating Club.

Like the Agricultural Society and in contrast to the social networks and secret societies of an earlier period, the new organizations involved a wide cross section of the community. The Vulture Engine Company drew volunteers from every walk of life, and the baseball club's teams brought together farmers and doctors and Methodists and Congregationalists. Leadership as well as membership was broadly based. When the H. E. K. Hall Camp of the Sons of Union Veterans was chartered in 1883, its founding officers consisted of three farmers, one tenant farmer, one farm laborer, a salesman, and a lawyer. Even the Masons no longer constituted a distinct or elite society. Unlike their fraternal forebears, late-nineteenth-century Masons in Chelsea were from the countryside as well as the village, often belonged to either the Methodist or Congregational church, and were little different from anybody else.[29]

Organized events, activities, and public sociables were the mainstays of these societies' existence, and one cannot help but be impressed by the array of goings-on touted in the local newspapers, even though one's desire actually to attend may be far less compelling. From the 1870s through the 1890s, there seemed to be an unending series of oyster suppers, popcorn sociables, literary exercises, dramatic presentations, promenade concerts, and fancy-dress parties, which were open to all comers. Most often, the entertainment was local, with music furnished by the Chelsea Cornet Band or Moore's Orchestra and recitations by Chelsea residents. But occasionally outsiders such as the Dartmouth College Glee Club, Miss Flora H. Averill, a graduate of the Boston Conservatory of Elocution, two traveling women evangelists, or the neighboring West Randolph Dramatic Club provided the principal attraction. Sporting events such as the baseball games or velocipede races drew big crowds, as did demonstrations of the latest gadgetry such as the phonograph exhibition in 1891.[30]

Not all adults in Chelsea belonged to voluntary associations, but the events sponsored by such organizations attracted large audiences. More than one hundred couples turned out for the annual ball at the Orange County Hotel in Chelsea in 1874, and at least that many came to a fancy-dress party in the same hall in 1891 to look at thirty couples in costumes representing the thirty days of the month. Local

The Chelsea Brass Band (formerly the Chelsea Cornet Band) at the turn of the century. [Reprinted from W. S. Gilman, *Chelsea Album* (Chelsea, Vt., 1980).]

sports and dramatic clubs competed and exchanged performances with neighboring towns' organizations and added a new dimension to Chelseans' conception of their community. When the Chelsea nines were victorious or the local thespians gave a particularly stirring rendition of a temperance play, it reflected on the township as a whole. Indeed, rivalry with other nearby communities was a principal cause of the proliferation of local organizations after the Civil War.[31]

Voluntary associations provided a nexus for community life in Chelsea that subsumed earlier conflicts and reinforced consensus. All the organizations, even those that were not related to the temperance movement or the church, upheld the local code against drinking. The Vulture Engine Company explicitly prohibited liquor in "the engine houses, at fires or at any parade of the company," and the other groups adopted similar restrictions.[32]

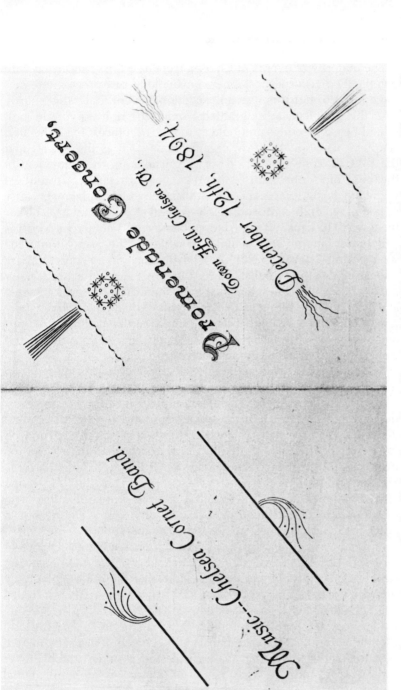

Promenade concert program for the Chelsea Cornet Band. [Reprinted from W. S. Gilman, *Chelsea Album* (Chelsea, Vt., 1980).]

The majority of events in Chelsea were also little concerned with potentially divisive issues. One woman did lecture on women's suffrage in 1886, but this was an exceptional event that came shortly after the state legislature granted women the right to vote in local school-board meetings and hold school-board offices. Even the local chapters of national reform organizations such as the WCTU and the YWCTU concentrated on social functions for the enjoyment of the township's inhabitants rather than on reform politics. In contrast to the heyday of temperance and antislavery reform, the main cause in late-nineteenth-century Chelsea was an effort to buy a piano for the town to be kept and rented for public use, and numerous sociables and presentations were actually benefits for the piano fund. The young adults' debating club occasionally considered contemporary issues such as the Populist call for the direct election of senators or public control of utilities, but their more immediate concerns emerged at a mock town meeting in 1898 when they voted for a "place where ginger teas and a Bellows Falls evaporator can be had" and to "put an awning over Mrs. Mattoon's freestone steps to keep those who stand there from being moonstruck."[33]

It is ironic that these activities, which were most respectable in the 1890s, were just the sort of frivolities that the Congregational Church forbade in 1848. By the late nineteenth century, however, the church had ceased to be the principal source and arbiter of moral discipline and authority. In contrast to the first half of the century, for example, the records of the Congregational Church show no instances of disciplinary action after the Civil War. In large part, the vigilance of former years was unnecessary because the burgeoning of associational life had instituted a different but compatible form of community. Local voluntary associations were certainly not at odds with the churches in Chelsea. On the contrary, they often sponsored events of a semireligious nature or raised money for church-related causes. Rather, churches became part of a mutually reinforcing network of voluntary associations, and, like the other clubs, they initiated greater numbers of social and educational activities. In this vein, denominational lines also blurred. The West Hill Union Meeting House became a regular Methodist church in the 1870s, and the local Methodists and Congregationalists joined together to promote temperance, sponsor visiting evangelists, and conduct union prayer meetings. In addition, they began an annual nondenominational "week of Prayer" after Christmas in 1870.[34]

The social and ideological consensus that emerged from the web of voluntary associations in Chelsea was a compromise between older and competing ideals. On the one hand, the sense of community in late-nineteenth-century Chelsea was more artificial and less visceral than that envisioned by the earliest settlers or the evangelical revivalists. Yet that very superficiality allowed for more widespread voluntary participation. This was a compromise that well suited the tenor of life in Chelsea in the 1890s. The young debaters who snickered about sparking on Mrs. Mattoon's porch steps were far removed from the anxious teenagers who professed their newfound faith during the 1842 revival. The fires of earlier excitements and convictions had been blanketed by too many Vermont winters, and the larger economic tensions that gave them their particular urgency and appeal had long since been resolved by family strategies and broader structural change.

This social and ideological consensus also permeated the less formal interactions among Chelsea residents that were an important aspect of community life. Visiting was common, and typically Saturday and Sunday were given to making social calls or receiving guests. As might be expected, visiting often cut across denominational, occupational, and geographical lines. According to two farmers' diaries from 1880, relatives and neighbors did the most socializing, although it was not unusual to travel to the village or the other side of the township to visit with friends. Both diarists were from farm families who had been in Chelsea since the beginning of the century, yet their visits included many new families as well as more established townsmen. One of the diarists, Alvah Carpenter, belonged to the West Hill Union Meeting House. His wife, however, joined the Congregational Church in 1867, and they got together with members of all three local congregations. The same held true for the other diarist, Eugene Thorne, and his new bride who were both members of the Methodist Church in the village and also regular attendants of the union prayer meetings in the Congregational Church.[35]

Work and business transactions also provided opportunities for informal social interaction. Both farmers often went to the village to trade and talk with local merchants and artisans, as well as to all parts of the township to swap livestock or implements with other farmers. Neighbors were particularly important with respect to work as well as leisure. Both diarists exchanged labor and skills in addition to casual visits with those nearby. Alvah Carpenter and his neighbor, Charles Moulton, worked on each other's farms during busy harvest periods. Carpenter also took his team of oxen over to help B. F. Smith, a near neighbor and distant cousin; and when it came time to butcher his hog, another neighbor, George Goodrich, lent a hand.

Hired help was usually a neighbor's son, and there was little social distance between employer and employee other than age.[36]

Just as Chelsea organizations shunned national reform issues for more local concerns, private lives were also oriented predominantly around the immediate community. According to Collamer Abbott's perceptive summary of his grandfather's diaries, "Gramp" Abbott rarely traveled beyond Chelsea and its environs during his adult life. As a youth, he worked in a cotton mill in Nashua, New Hampshire, and saw distant action in the Civil War, but after settling on a farm in Chelsea, "Gramp" ventured as far as Boston only once in 1890. Similarly, the two diarists from 1880 made journeys to neighboring townships to market produce or purchase wares, but never beyond. Eugene Thorne's brother and sister-in-law visited several times from Boston, and his subscriptions to the *Rural New Yorker* and the *Boston Journal* no doubt kept him abreast of larger developments. His primary frame of reference, however, was local, continuously memorialized by GAR (Grand Army of the Republic) dramatics in the village, Sunday dinners at his aunt's, and reaping the fields with his neighbor.[37]

Perhaps the best way to sum up the nature of community in late-nineteenth-century Chelsea with its shared attitudes is with a story. The scene is the second meeting of the Chelsea Debating Club on 8 November 1897, and the topic for consideration was: "Resolved that New England farms can be made to pay." The debate must have been a contentious one, because the three judges turned in a split decision – two in favor of the affirmative and one for the negative. When the question was then turned over to the audience for a vote, however, they voted unanimously, 21 to 0, that New England farms could be made to pay. Quickly the debaters who argued the opposite position moved for adjournment, but the motion did not carry. Instead, the other club members all stood up and sang "Hurrah for Old New England." There is a postscript: Neither Edward Bicknell nor Richard Emanuel who argued against the viability of local farming were still in town three years later for the 1900 Census. In contrast, their opponents continued to live in Chelsea and farmed their fathers' land.[38]

The change from social conflict to social consensus occurred in other older rural communities as well. Initial turmoil was endemic to the settlement process throughout the nineteenth-century North as disparate groups of people found themselves cast together in new communities. An early sociological study of Waterville in Oneida County, New York, for example, sees factions and quarrels as the most pervasive aspects of the early history of that community. Early settlers sued each other frequently and fought denominational, Antimasonic, and temperance battles similar to those in Chelsea. In contrast to its early contentiousness, however, Waterville was much less acrimonious by the end of the nineteenth century. The development of more widespread kinship networks broke down the older barriers between families and neighborhoods, and the rise of new voluntary associations and the decreasing rigidity of denominational affiliation facilitated a broader sense of community.[39]

Later sociological studies of rural communities in New York find similar patterns. After the Civil War, local churches developed a series of auxiliary organizations that sponsored social activities, and the number of other clubs and associations increased markedly between 1870 and 1900. To quote a study of Marathon, New York, a township slightly larger than Chelsea, those years "were marked by intense activity in the social and recreational life of the village." In 1895, for example, Marathon was the setting for thirty-seven socials, nine visiting dramatic or concert companies, five local talent plays, three fairs and field days, and three excursions. Membership and participation included farmers and villagers, and the older sense of neighborhood loyalty broke down and was replaced by a community-wide orientation.[40]

Rural surveys from the 1920s and 1930s give a more detailed account of the degree of involvement in associational life. Only 13 percent of almost 3,000 New York farmers surveyed in 1934 never belonged to any organization and about the same number belonged only to the church, so almost three-fourths were members of two or more organizations. A comparable study of Madison and Union counties in Ohio found that fewer than 10 percent of the local farm owners did not participate in a church, lodge, grange, or farm bureau chapter. Typically, villages of about 500 people like Chelsea were the main point of contact for rural dwellers. At least half the members in these village organizations were farmers, and "those farmers who attended the meetings were considered on the same social plane as were the town members." In larger villages and towns of more than 1,000, however, farmers formed a smaller percentage of the local membership, and social distinctions were more pronounced.[41]

In addition to voluntary associations, temperance reform and prohibitionism helped to establish a local consensus and to define social boundaries in many rural areas that were predominantly Protestant and pietistic. According to one historian, this commitment to temperance served as a substitute for the social covenant that was lacking in communities settled randomly by diverse groups of people. Various reminiscences from northern New England recall the local code against drinking. The journalist R. L. Duffus remembered some of the lessons in his elementary school in Williamstown, Vermont, around the turn of the century: "They tried by putting the evils of alcohol into our school curriculum. Indeed, they poured them in . . . The teacher also told us of certain diseases that came from excessive use of alcohol in any form. We had an elementary textbook in physiology that had pictures to prove this point." Whereas older boys and younger men engaged in such illicit rustic pleasures as sap beer and hard cider, abstinence remained the most visible yardstick of respectability in settled rural life.[42]

It is wrong, of course, to overstate the universality of social consensus in older rural communities. Williamstown, Vermont, for example, had a number of stone quarries and, consequently, a small Italian population, which held very different views about liquor. Relatively little is known, however, about the scope and dimensions of ethnicity in older rural areas and about how interethnic relations changed over time. Moreover, voluntary associations can institutionalize social differences as well as transcend them, and this was indeed the case in the larger towns surveyed by rural sociologists where social classes and distinctions were more marked.[43]

Splits occurred within common social boundaries as well. Settlements that began as communal or covenanted colonies sometimes experienced their own versions of declension as new social and economic realities altered and eroded initial religious and ideological unity. When the new Congregational minister in Williamstown, Vermont, urged the Ladies' Aid Society to put on a play strictly for the fun of it, some of the more old-fashioned members were offended and the congregation argued about the issue. Elsewhere, images of vicious gossip and enduring quarrels permeate literary depictions of settled rural life, albeit by authors who usually chose to leave town rather than those who stayed.[44]

Nevertheless, settled rural life during the late nineteenth century was characterized by a degree of homogeneity and inertia that distinguished it from the volatility of the frontier or the city. Incisive and unromanticized reminiscences of life during the period in a Maine hamlet, several rural towns in central Vermont, and on farms in Ohio and Illinois paint pictures similar to the life-style in Chelsea. Life was filled with family, church, and community activities. Social divisions were not pronounced, and those that did exist were static, rather than dynamic, aspects of local society. Potentially disrupting forces from the larger society such as economic pressures or looser urban moral values were mitigated to a large degree by the stability and constancy of family and social ties and by the localism that continued to predominate in the world view of settled rural inhabitants.[45]

In Chelsea, the rapid demographic and economic development of the early years fueled local divisions and tensions. By the end of the nineteenth century after an extended period of lessened growth, however, the nature of community life was much more staid and uneventful. For those who lived in Chelsea and places like it, this emerging social and ideological consensus represented a significant departure from their own historical experiences. More important, it diverged considerably from the prevailing tenor of contemporary urban and industrial society.

Conclusion: those who stayed behind

At the second Old Home Week celebration in Chelsea in 1902, local inhabitants and former residents visiting the community heard two addresses by native sons who had gone on to bigger and better things in the urban centers of southern New England. One of the speakers, Charles I. Hood, the son of the local druggist, had become a multimillionaire by manufacturing Hood's Sarsaparilla in Lowell, Massachusetts. The other orator, also a son of a local merchant, was the Reverend William H. Davis, D.D., pastor of the Eliot Church in the fashionable Boston suburb of Newton, Massachusetts.[1]

Charles I. Hood gave a talk in the tradition of Andrew Carnegie, Russell Conwell, and other apostles of the gospel of success. After recounting the story of his own climb from an apprenticeship in a Lowell apothecary to the helm of an industrial concern that spent more than $5 million on newspaper advertising alone, Hood offered some advice to his former townsmen. He offered them not acres of diamonds but acres of gold:

> A few years ago everyone was interested in the stories that reached us of the fabulous amounts of gold found in the Klondike country . . . But when the prospectors arrived, they found it necessary to work, and work hard too, in order to find the gold. It is just the same the world over. It is so here in Chelsea. You have a Klondike right at your door, if you realize it, and are willing to work hard enough to secure it.

The biggest failure in Chelsea according to Hood was a failure to make the most of local opportunities: "You need not sit down and wonder when your opportunities will come. They are around you now. Each one faithfully fulfilled will open the way for others. If you make the most of those within your reach others will surely follow."[2]

Dr. Davis's speech was more scholarly. He began by applauding the recent institution of Old Home Week celebrations throughout New England and New York and paid homage to the proud history of the Green Mountain Boys and the American Revolution. Then, like Charles Hood, he also sounded a theme that was heard often in late-nineteenth-century America: "Fifty years ago the city was the great objective . . . But now the objective is changed, and the 'country town' is the social study and problem of the twentieth century." Davis offered a different kind of advice to his former townsmen and preached the gospel of Progressive reform:

> But this week must be supplemented by a local public spirit, that generous sense of the common weal and needs, if it is to do its largest service in our communities. This spirit must show itself in its public schools, in its loyal support of its churches, in the making of good roads, and in that assimilation of its alien population which shall Americanize the foreign born among us. For in these ways, in its revived and expanded industries, will come the real prosperity of the old towns, which have been and will continue to be the sources of supply in stock and character, as in population, for the centres of trade and industry.[3]

In these two speakers, the people of Chelsea had spokesmen for the two major configurations of values that emerged from the great social and economic transformations of the second half of the nineteenth century: laissez-faire individualism and the spirit of progressive reform. Yet even though both speakers were native sons speaking in their hometown, their ideas and proposals were out of step with the experiences and beliefs of their friends, kinfolk, and former neighbors.

In contrast to the rapid growth, social diversity, and flux so prevalent in the nation's cities, life in late-nineteenth-century Chelsea was bounded by the familiar and the familial, and Charles I. Hood's promises of riches ill-fitted Chelseans' own expectations for themselves. Market-oriented, Chelsea farmers adopted new technologies and better techniques in order to make the most from their farms. But they also made other choices and enjoyed rewards that derived more from their forebears' belief in the virtues of a competence and the importance of kinship ties than from the profit-maximizing entrepreneurial ethic so prevalent in the larger towns and cities. Even Dr. Davis recognized this when he condescendingly paid homage to those who stayed by the farms and carried on the business of the village:

> We realize that it is sometimes easier to go than to stay at home, for those who seek their fortunes in the great West and in the intenser life of the cities have the zest of their adventures and the novelty of new scenes and successes to spur them on; but those who tarry in familiar places and do the routine duties are held to their labors and fidelities by the sheer sense of obligation and necessity. To do this and to keep sweet and brave in the

doing of it makes a heavy call upon patience and faith, and yet
it is just this brave and commonplace thing that so many of you
have done![4]

However flattered by this portrayal, the commonplace heroes of
Chelsea probably did not share Dr. Davis's assessment of the problems
of the country town or his larger vision of a country life restructured
by Progressive reformers according to criteria of professionalism and
social efficiency. Ironically, much of what they did in Chelsea – the
abundance of associational activity and the movement toward interdenominational cooperation – often paralleled the programs es-
poused by the Country Life Movement. But in Chelsea, the impetus
and perspective that informed these developments were local and
had little to do with any plans for broader societal change. Instead,
they stemmed from the community's own history of social divisions
and its desires and attempts to institute a social and ideological
consensus. Competing values and beliefs led to numerous conflicts
in Chelsea's early history between Congregationalists and dissenters,
Masons and Antimasons, Whigs and Democrats, and drinkers and
teetotalers. The proliferation of voluntary associations after the Civil
War finally ameliorated local divisions, but the nature of the community
embodied by that consensus was a far cry from that envisioned and
experienced by urban middle-class reformers.

Those who stayed behind in Chelsea, Vermont, experienced the
great transformations of the nineteenth century in ways profoundly
different from those of their urban and western contemporaries.
Their society was characterized by lessened growth but by increasing
economic, demographic, and social stability. The number of farms
in the community became more or less fixed, and the rise of centralized
manufacturing forced a series of adjustments that precluded expansion
in other parts of the local economy. The limited number of available
opportunities and the relative attractiveness of outside opportunities
led fewer people to move to Chelsea, and family strategies for providing for the next generation resulted in a population that was
homogeneous, intertwined, and persistent. Social institutions and
relationships in the town embodied an emerging consensus that
paralleled and reinforced these economic and demographic developments, a consensus that was most visible in the wide range of
associational activities and the community's steadfast opposition to
liquor. As a result, Chelseans experienced few of the disruptions so
prevalent in newer rural areas or the nation's cities and managed
to continue and adapt older values in spite of increasing involvement
with the larger society. Consequently, rural Chelsea represented an

enigmatic combination of attributes: kinship ties and social interactions reminiscent of a preindustrial village coupled with the economic links and organizational structure characteristic of modern society.

In a more general sense, the pattern of lessened economic and demographic growth and their social consequences found in Chelsea was repeated in other settled rural communities throughout the North. In contrast to rapidly expanding cities and frontiers, older rural communities like Chelsea became increasingly staid, uniform, and uneventful. More than elsewhere, society there was characterized by a pervasive equilibrium between economic opportunities, the size and composition of the local population, familial and individual expectations, and local institutions and social life. Those who lived in the older rural North were not searching for order in the late nineteenth century – they had found it.

An understanding of the social characteristics of settled rural life, especially the experiences of stability and lessened economic and demographic growth, points out the degree to which urban and rural America diverged during the late nineteenth century. These differences found their voice in a series of political and cultural conflicts that pitted city against countryside, and perhaps the most significant and far-reaching of these battles was fought over liquor. Although historians have been quick to echo H. L. Mencken's disparaging appraisals of rural narrow-mindedness and provincialism, few have examined the social bases of prohibitionism in the late-nineteenth-century countryside. In Chelsea, the temperance appeal represented more than simply a reaction to the threat posed by urban and immigrant cultures. It was also a central fixture in the social and ideological consensus that had ameliorated long-standing local conflicts and divisions.

Older settled rural life also differed markedly from conditions in newer rural areas. Populism, for example, was not a significant movement in the Northeast and many parts of the Old Northwest. Farmers there raised less vulnerable crops, but they also had less room to speculate and were not as overextended when the depression hit during the 1890s. The tensions between the countryside and the market town, which students of the Populist movement have found, were probably less heartfelt in more established rural areas where kinship ties and other long-standing connections linked villagers and farmers more closely. Moreover, family networks and other social bonds in older rural communities provided additional buffers against the vicissitudes of the market economy.[5]

Finally, the history of Chelsea during the second half of the nineteenth century illustrates the continuing importance of local life in settled rural America. Whereas the new urban middle classes sought order in bureaucratic organizations and other translocal institutions, Chelsea and places like it were, to play on Robert Wiebe's famous phrase, island communities against the stream. Farmers there were at once tied to larger national markets and also entwined in a face-to-face local life that remained central. An understanding of this underscores the inadequacy of the categories used in developmental theories as well as the fallacious assumption that they are mutually exclusive. Whereas the transitions from feudal to bourgeois, from traditional to modern, or from *Gemeinschaft* to *Gesellschaft* may characterize the broad path traveled by nation-states, they do not reflect accurately changes in smaller rural communities during the nineteenth century.[6]

Those who stayed behind in older rural America were not necessarily left there by the progressive advance of an urban and industrial society. Many chose to stay and experienced a sense of stability that eluded a good number of their contemporaries. But that order had its price. Although society in Chelsea became more homogeneous and although life within the boundaries of community was rarely marred by social conflict, those boundaries eventually became rigid and anachronistic and excluded new people and outside ideas. Perhaps this is a basic paradox in American life: that the experience of harmony and equality is often predicated on just such an exclusion. As Americans today also face an all-too-ominous future of limited opportunities and expectations, perhaps we should ponder Chelsea's history of lessened growth. For us, as for the hardscrabble farmers of nineteenth-century Vermont, the coming situation will pose new challenges, and its blessings will be mixed.

Notes

1. After the frontier

1 See Stephan Thernstrom, *Poverty and Progress: Social Mobility in a Nineteenth-Century City* (Cambridge, Mass., 1964), for the earliest example of these trends.

2 Clarence Danhoff's *Change in Agriculture: The Northern United States, 1820–1870* (Cambridge, Mass., 1969) provides the best overview of the commercialization of agriculture.

3 Robert Swierenga, "Towards the 'New Rural History': A Review Essay," *Historical Methods Newsletter* 6 (1972): 112. For Swierenga's recently suggested theoretical perspective for rural history, see his "Theoretical Perspectives on the New Rural History: From Environmentalism to Modernism," *Agricultural History* 56 (1982): 495–502. This is only a preliminary attempt, however, and Swierenga accepts modernization theory too uncritically.

4 Frederick Jackson Turner, *The Frontier in American History* (New York, 1920). Turner's work on sectionalism does deal with rural society after the frontier, but it does not discuss social and economic change and it treats sections as a constant in American history.

5 Richard Hofstadter, *The Progressive Historians: Turner, Beard, Parrington* (New York, 1968).

6 See especially the collected essays of Paul Gates, *Landlords and Tenants on the Prairie Frontier* (Ithaca, N.Y., 1970); Richard Wade, *The Urban Frontier: The Rise of Western Cities, 1790–1830* (Cambridge, Mass., 1959); T. Scott Miyakawa, *Protestants and Pioneers: Individualism and Conformity on the American Frontier* (Chicago, 1964); and the collection of essays edited by Richard Hofstadter and Seymour Martin Lipset, *Turner and the Sociology of the Frontier* (New York, 1968).

7 Ellen von Nardroff, "The American Frontier as Safety Valve – The Life, Death, Reincarnation and Justification of a Theory," *Agricultural History* 36 (1962): 123–42; and Allan Dawley, *Class and Community: The Industrial Revolution in Lynn* (Cambridge, Mass., 1976), 214–41.

8 An exception might be James C. Malin's work except for its idiosyncratic nature. See Robert Malen Bell, "James C. Malin and the Grasslands of North America," *Agricultural History* 46 (1972): 414–24; and Thomas H. LeDuc, "An Ecological Interpretation of Grassland History: The Work of James C. Malin as Historian and as Critic of Historians," *Nebraska History* 31 (1950): 226–33.

9   William Parker, "Agriculture," in Lance Davis et al., *American Economic Growth: An Economist's History of the United States* (New York, 1972): 369–417.

10 Danhoff, *Change in Agriculture*; Allan Bogue, *From Prairie to Corn Belt: Farming on the Ilinois and Iowa Prairies in the Nineteenth Century* (Chicago, 1968); and Eric E. Lampard, *The Rise of the Dairy Industry in Wisconsin: A Study in Agricultural Change, 1820–1920* (Madison, Wis., 1963).

11 For recent discussions of the use of theory by historians, see James A. Henretta, "The Study of Social Mobility: Ideological Assumptions and Conceptual Bias," *Labor History* 18 (1977): 166–78; James A. Henretta, "Social History as Lived and Written," *American Historical Review* 84 (1979): 1293–1322; and Elizabeth Fox-Genovese and Eugene Genovese, "The Political Crisis of Social History: A Marxian Perspective," *Journal of Social History* 10 (1976): 205–20.

12 The French *Annalistes*, scholars associated with the journal *Annales: Économies, Sociétés, Civilisations*, emphasize the interrelationships between social, economic, and demographic history in order to grasp the totality of the intellectual and psychological climate of the past. For a discussion of their approach, see Henretta, "Social History," 1295–1301. James A. Henretta, "Families and Farms: *Mentalité* in Pre-Industrial America," *William and Mary Quarterly*, 3rd ser., 25 (1978): 3–32. For a recent attempt to fuse Turnerian theory with an *Annales* perspective, see Walter T. K. Nugent, *The Structures of American Social History* (Bloomington, Ind., 1981).

13 Michael Merrill, "Cash Is Good to Eat: Self-Sufficiency and Exchange in the Rural Economy of the United States," *Radical History Review* 3 (1977): 42–71; Christopher Clark, "The Household Mode of Production – A Comment," *Radical History Review* 18 (1978): 166–71; and Christopher Clark, "The Household Economy: Market Exchange and the Rise of Capitalism in the Connecticut Valley, 1800–1860," *Journal of Social History* 13 (1979): 169–89. For Winnifred Rothenberg's criticism of this view of preindustrial rural attitudes, see "The Market and Massachusetts Farmers, 1750–1855," *Journal of Economic History* 41 (1981): 283–314.

14 Dawley, *Class and Community*; Henretta, "Social History."

15 Clark, "Household Economy"; Henretta, "Families and Farms."

16 Howard Newby and Frederick H. Buttel, "Toward a Critical Rural Sociology," in Buttel and Newby, eds., *The Rural Sociology of the Advanced Societies: Critical Perspectives* (Montclair, N.J., 1980), 1–35, esp. 5.

17 Ibid.

18 Ibid.

19 Danhoff, *Change in Agriculture*; Bogue, *From Prairie to Corn Belt*; Margaret B. Bogue, *Patterns from the Sod: Land Use and Tenure in the Grand Prairie, 1850–1900* (Springfield, Ill., 1959); LaWanda C. Cox, "The American Agricultural Wage Earner, 1865–1900: The Emergence of a Modern Labor Problem," *Agricultural History* 22 (1948): 95–114; and LaWanda C. Cox,

"Tenancy in the United States, 1865–1900: A Consideration of the Agricultural Ladder Hypothesis," *Agricultural History* 18 (1944): 97–105.

20 Gates, *Landlords and Tenants*; John T. Schlebecker, *Whereby We Thrive: A History of American Farming, 1607–1972* (Ames, Iowa, 1975).

21 Parker, "Agriculture," 393–402; Alfred D. Chandler, *The Visible Hand: The Managerial Revolution in American Business* (Cambridge, Mass., 1978), 242. For the same point made in terms of Marxist theory, see S. A. Mann and J. M. Dickinson, "Obstacles to the Development of a Capitalist Agriculture," *Journal of Peasant Studies* 5 (1978): 466–81.

22 Donald L. Winters, *Farmers Without Farms: Agricultural Tenancy in Nineteenth-Century Iowa* (Westport, Conn., 1978), 3–11, 78–91; and David E. Schob, *Hired Hands and Plowboys: Farm Labor in the Midwest, 1815–1860* (Urbana, Ill., 1975), 209–33. A problem with studying social mobility in rural communities is the fact that upward social mobility often meant geographical mobility out of the community.

23 Lewis Atherton, *Main Street on the Middle Border* (Bloomington, Ind., 1954); Wayne E. Fuller, *RFD: The Changing Face of Rural America* (Bloomington, Ind., 1964); Danhoff, *Change in Agriculture*; and Bogue, *From Prarie to Corn Belt*.

24 Robert R. Dykstra, "Town-Country Conflict: A Hidden Dimension in American Social History," *Agricultural History* 38 (1964): 195–204; Stanley Parsons, *The Populist Context: Rural versus Urban Power on a Great Plains Frontier* (Westport, Conn., 1973); Anne Mayhew, "A Reappraisal of the Causes of Farm Protest in the United States, 1870–1900," *Journal of Economic History* 32 (1972): 464–75; Don S. Kirschner, *City and Country: Rural Responses to Urbanization in the 1920s* (Westport, Conn., 1970).

25 Jane Jacobs, *The Economy of Cities* (New York, 1969); Allan Pred, "American Metropolitan Growth: 1860–1914, Industrialization, Initial Advantage," in Pred, *The Spatial Dynamics of U.S. Urban-Industrial Growth, 1800–1914* (Cambridge, Mass., 1966), 12–85.

26 Parker, "Agriculture," 369–79; Robert Higgs, *The Transformation of the American Economy, 1865–1914: An Essay in Interpretation* (New York, 1971), 80.

27 Parker, "Agriculture," 369–79, 393–402.

28 Ibid., 379–93; for a discussion of stabilizing economic growth rates after the settlement phase, see Richard A. Easterlin, "Population Change and Farm Settlement in the Northern United States," *Journal of Economic History* 36 (1976): 45–75.

29 Pred, "American Metropolitan Growth."

30 Wilbur Zelinsky, "Changes in the Geographic Patterns of Rural Population in the United States, 1790–1960," *Geographical Review* 52 (1962): 492–524.

31 Calvin L. Beale, "Rural Depopulation in the United States: Some Demographic Consequences of Agricultural Adjustments," *Demography* 1 (1964): 264–72; Calvin L. Beale and Donald J. Bogue, "Recent Population

Trends in the United States and Their Causes," in James H. Copp, ed., *Our Changing Rural Society: Perspectives and Trends* (Ames, Iowa, 1964), 71–126; John Saville, *Rural Depopulation in England and Wales, 1851–1951* (London, 1957); Ward W. Bauder, *The Impact of Population Change in Rural Community Life: The Economic System* (Ames, Iowa, 1963); Easterlin, "Population Change"; Richard A. Easterlin, "Factors in the Decline of Farm Fertility in the United States: Some Preliminary Research Results," *Journal of American History* 63 (1976): 600–14; and David Lowenthal and Lambros Comitas, "Emigration and Depopulation: Some Neglected Aspects of Population Geography," *Geographical Review* 52 (1962): 193–210.

32 Anthony C. Hilfer, *The Revolt from the Village, 1915–1930* (Chapel Hill, N.C., 1969), 3–63; Blanche H. Gelfant, *The American City Novel* (Norman, Okla., 1954), 3–41.

2. The storm before the calm

1 In a certain sense, lessened growth was nothing new to rural New England in the nineteenth century. Recent studies of colonial communities document the economic saturation that occurred in Puritan farm villages only three generations after their founding. New generations and new settlers led to increasing population pressure and land hunger, and only migration to relatively unsettled areas in the region alleviated these conditions. The most influential of these studies is Philip J. Greven, *Four Generations: Population, Land, and Family in Colonial Andover, Massachusetts* (Ithaca, N.Y., 1970). See also Darrett B. Rutman, "People in Process: The New Hampshire Towns of the Eighteenth Century," *Journal of Urban History* 1 (1975): 268–92; and Daniel Scott Smith, "A Malthusian-Frontier Interpretation of United States History Before c. 1815," in Woodrow Borah et al., eds., *Urbanization in the Americas: The Background in Comparative Perspective* (Ottawa, Ontario, Canada, 1980), 15–23.

Although the townships of northern New England began as a response to the same pressures that spawned their colonial antecedents, by the early nineteenth century there were significant differences that altered the patterns of development in these communities and changed their relationship to the rest of American society. Unlike earlier covenanted settlements, New England townships founded after the Revolution did not begin with the ideal of a village settlement but were divided checkerboard-style into farm lots. The transition from Puritan to Yankee had already been made and a much wider spectrum of conflicting religious and political views circulated throughout the region. At a more personal level, parental authority began to decline and freer attitudes toward marriage and migration prevailed. See Charles E. Clark, *The Eastern Frontier: The Settlement of Northern New England, 1610–1763* (New York, 1970), 352–59; Daniel Scott Smith, "Parental Power and Marriage Patterns: An Analysis of Historical Trends in Hingham, Massachusetts," *Journal of Marriage and the Family* 35 (1973): 419–28; Robert A. Gross, *The Minutemen and Their World* (New York, 1976), 68–108; and Douglas Lamar Jones, *Village and Seaport: Migration and Society in Eighteenth-Century Massachusetts* (Hanover, N.H., 1981), 103–21.

Most important, patterns of economic development changed. The rise of commercialized agriculture and the growth of small rural factories in the early nineteenth century at first permitted greater local economic growth than the semisubsistence agricultural economy of the colonial period, but those larger economic connections also made northern New England more vulnerable to fluctuations and changing conditions outside the region. Unlike the first and second generations of New England villages, which contended primarily with the problems of subsistence and increased population, early-nineteenth-century rural communities were buffeted by much larger forces, and the disparity between their experiences and those of the rest of society became quite marked.

2 Chelsea was chosen from all Vermont townships that lost at least one-fourth of their population during the second half of the nineteenth century. In terms of its settlement history and patterns of development, Chelsea is much like the other townships in the area, but more records were available for Chelsea than for the other communities. See John M. Comstock, *Chelsea, Vermont* (n.p., 1944); and Paul W. Gates, "Two Hundred Years of Farming in Gilsum," *Historical New Hampshire* 33 (1978): 1–24.

3 Comstock, *Chelsea*; Manuscript Schedules, U.S. Census of Population, 1800. For other regional fertility statistics, see Mary P. Ryan, *Cradle of the Middle Class: The Family in Oneida County, New York, 1790–1865* (New York, 1981), 249, Table A.6; and Randolph A. Roth, "Whence This Strange Fire? Religious and Reform Movements in the Connecticut River Valley of Vermont, 1791–1843" (Ph.D. diss., Yale University, 1981), 229, Table 3.1.

4 Manuscript Town Records, Chelsea, Vermont, vol. 1, Vermont State Division of Public Records, microfilm, hereafter cited as Chelsea Town Records. For descriptions of agriculture in the region, see Howard S. Russell, *A Long, Deep Furrow: Three Centuries of Farming in New England* (Hanover, N.H., 1976), 233–44, 276–9; and Percy W. Bidwell, "Rural Economy in New England at the Beginning of the Nineteenth Century," *Transactions of the Connecticut Academy of Arts and Sciences* 20 (1916): 319–53.

5 Page Smith, *As a City Upon a Hill: The Town in American History* (New York, 1966), 17–36.

6 Comstock, *Chelsea*, 8–10, 28–9, 50–2; also, *Manual of the Chelsea, Vermont Congregational Church* (n.p., 1888), 32–63, contains a complete record of church membership through 1887, hereafter cited as *Manual*.

7 David Ludlum, *Social Ferment in Vermont, 1791–1850* (New York, 1939), 25–62.

8 On the growth of Methodism and Universalism in the 1780s and 1790s, see Roth, "Whence This Strange Fire?" 64–81.

9   Chelsea Town Records, vol. 1.

10 Comstock, *Chelsea*, 16–18.

11 William A. Robinson, *Jeffersonian Democracy in New England* (New Haven, Conn., 1916), 76–94; Donald B. Cole, *Jacksonian Democracy in New Hampshire, 1800–1851* (Cambridge, Mass., 1970), 16–46; and Roth, "Whence This Strange Fire?" 81–94.

12 Hamilton Child, *Child's Orange County Gazette, 1762–1888* (Syracuse, N.Y., 1888), 242–3; *Manual*, 53–5; and manuscript records, Chelsea, Vermont, Congregational Church, 1789–1857, Vermont Historical Society.

13 Comstock, *Chelsea*, 29–30.

14 Ludlum, *Social Ferment*, 3–62; manuscript Grand List of Taxes, 1837, Office of the Town Clerk, Chelsea, Vermont, hereafter cited as Manuscript Tax List; Roth, "Whence This Strange Fire?" 97–8, Tables 1.3 and 1.4.

15 Roth, "Whence This Strange Fire?" 18–35, 81–94.

16 Manuscript Schedules, U.S. Census of Population, 1820; Zadock Thompson, *A Gazetteer of the State of Vermont* (Montpelier, Vt., 1824), 100–1; Noah J. T. George, *Gazetteer of the State of Vermont* (Haverhill, N.H., 1823), 45.

17 Samuel F. Barry and C. Benton, *A Statistical View of the Number of Sheep in the Several Towns and Counties in Maine, New Hampshire, Vermont, etc. . . . in 1836* (Cambridge, Mass., 1837), 28; 1840 statistics quoted in Zadock Thompson, *Thompson's History of Vermont* (Burlington, 1842), Part III, 52.

18 Robert A. Gross, "Culture and Cultivation: Agriculture and Society in Thoreau's Concord," *Journal of American History* 69 (1982): 42–61; Lewis D. Stilwell, *Migration from Vermont* (Montpelier, Vt., 1948), 159–61.

19 Manuscript Schedules, U.S. Census of Population, 1840; Abby M. Hemenway, *The Vermont Historical Gazetteer* (Burlington, 1871), vol. II, 980; Barry and Benton, *A Statistical View*, 110; Thompson, *History of Vermont*, Part III, 52.

20 Manuscript Tax List, 1837.

21 Comstock, *Chelsea*, 34–6; Ludlum, *Social Ferment*, 86–133. Freemasonry provided an alternative network to the church; consequently, Masons were typically not church members or were non-Calvinists; see Dorothy A. Lipson, *Freemasonry in Federalist Connecticut* (Princeton, N.J., 1977); and Roth, "Whence This Strange Fire?" 125, 171, Table 2.15.

22 Manuscript Tax List, 1837; Lipson, *Freemasonry*, 354–5, Tables 7–10; Comstock, *Chelsea*, 44–54, contains a list of all national, state, county, and township officials from Chelsea between 1788 and 1944.

23 One indication of the number of non-church members in Chelsea is the dramatic increase in the number of local inhabitants taking the Freeman's Oath in 1808 immediately after disestablishment. Sixty-nine men took the oath that year as opposed to the usual eight or ten in the preceding years. These inhabitants could not qualify for tax exemption under the older laws because they did not belong to a dissenting congregation

and were reluctant to have their names entered on the poll lists. Robinson, *Jeffersonian Democracy*, 76–94; local voting information is from Chelsea Town Records, vol. 1.

24 Ludlum, *Social Ferment*, 86–133.

25 Child, *Child's Orange County Gazette*, 87–8; Chelsea Town Records, vol. 1; Comstock, *Chelsea*, 44–54.

26 Chelsea Town Records, vol. 1 and vol. 2.

27 Ludlum, *Social Ferment*, 86–133; Roth, "Whence This Strange Fire?" 246–72; Whitney Cross, *The Burned-Over District: The Social and Intellectual History of Enthusiastic Religion in Western New York, 1800–1850* (New York, 1965), 113–25; Paul Johnson, *A Shopkeeper's Millennium: Society and Revivals in Rochester, New York, 1815–1837* (New York, 1978), 66–71.

28 Chelsea Town Records, vol. 2; Walter Hill Crockett, *A History of Vermont*, 4 vols. (Burlington, 1938), vol. 3, 226–415.

29 Manuscript Schedules, U.S. Census of Population, 1840.

30 Manuscript Tax List, 1837; U.S. Census, 1840.

31 Thelma M. Kistler, "The Rise of Railroads in the Connecticut River Valley," *Smith College Studies in History* 23 (1937–8): 217–18; Edward C. Kirkland, *Men, Cities, and Transportation: A Study in New England History, 1820–1900*, 2 vols. (Cambridge, Mass., 1948), vol. 1, 166–91; T. D. Seymour Bassett, "500 Miles of Trouble and Excitement: Vermont Railroads, 1848–1861," *Vermont History* 49 (1981): 138; George H. Steele to William B. Hale, January 9, 1846, George H. Steele Papers, Vermont Historical Society.

32 U.S. Census of Population, 1840, 1850, 1860, 1870, 1880, 1890, and 1900.

33 Stilwell, *Migration*; James W. Goldthwait, "A Town That Has Gone Downhill," *Geographical Review* 17 (1927): 527–52; Harold Fisher Wilson, *The Hill Country of Northern New England: Its Social and Economic History, 1790–1930* (New York, 1936).

34 One example of these methodological problems is the changing census definition of improved farmland between 1860 and 1900. Because this definition was more restrictive during the last quarter of the century, the amount of land recorded as improved declined, whereas actual land-use patterns changed much less. See John D. Black, *The Rural Economy of New England* (Cambridge, Mass., 1950), 137–61, for a discussion of this problem. Other authors estimate past population by counting the number of abandoned cellar holes in their communities; see Goldthwait, "A Town That Has Gone Downhill."

35 Wilson, *Hill Country*, 79.

36 Margaret Pabst, "Agricultural Trends in the Connecticut River Valley Region of Massachusetts, 1800–1900," *Smith College Studies in History* 26 (1940–1): 1–138, esp. 80.

37 Robert A. Riley, "Kinship Patterns in Londonderry, Vermont, 1772–1900: An Intergenerational Perspective of Changing Family Relationships," (Ph.D. diss., University of Massachusetts-Amherst, 1980), 55–74; Paul

G. Munyon, *A Reassessment of New England Agriculture in the Last Thirty Years of the Nineteenth Century: New Hampshire, A Case Study* (New York, 1978).

3. The different meanings of rural decline in nineteenth-century America

1 For good bibliographies of late-nineteenth-century expressions of concern, see G. T. Nesmith, "The Problem of the Rural Community, with Special Reference to the Rural Church," *American Journal of Sociology* 8 (1903): 835–7; and Harold Fisher Wilson, *The Hill Country of Northern New England* (New York, 1936), 403–37. For references on the literature of the Country Life Movement, see William L. Bowers, *The Country Life Movement in America, 1900–1920* (Port Washington, N.Y., 1974), 167–83.
2 Wilson, *Hill Country*, 56–74.
3 Ibid., 64–6, 117; Lewis D. Stilwell, *Migration from Vermont* (Montpelier, Vt., 1948), 183, 214–30.
4 *Maine Farmer*, August 5, 1843; "Better Stay at Home," *Country Gentleman*, May 28, 1857.
5 Henry F. French, "Stick to the Farm," *Country Gentleman*, April 27, 1854.
6 These agricultural societies occurred throughout the North but were most prevalent in New England; see Wayne C. Neely, *The Agricultural Fair* (New York, 1935), 72–109; Wilson, *Hill Country*, 174–83; and Stilwell, *Migration from Vermont*, 199.
7 Manuscript records, Orange County Agricultural Society, 1846–61, Chelsea Historical Society, hereafter cited as Agricultural Society records.
8 Ibid.; *Aurora of the Valley* (Newbury, Vt.), October 13, 1849.
9 S. C. Charles, "New England Emigration," *American Agriculturalist* 4 (1845): 145–6, reprinted in *New England Farmer*, July 2, 1845. For legislative support of agriculture, see the following three selections by Edwin C. Rozwenc: "The Evolution of the Vermont State Department of Agriculture," *Vermont Quarterly* 14 (1946): 163–83; "Agriculture and Politics in the Vermont Tradition," *Vermont History*, n.s. 17 (1949): 81–96; and "The Group Basis of Vermont Farm Politics, 1870–1945," *Vermont History* 25 (1957): 268–87. Heath quoted in Vermont State Board of Agriculture, *Report* (Montpelier, Vt., 1872), 42, hereafter cited as *Report* (1872).
10 "Our Worn-Out New England Soils," *New England Farmer*, July 9, 1845.
11 Spear's address is reprinted in *Aurora of the Valley*, October 13, 1849. The first winner of the essay competition in 1847 was Justin S. Morrill, who later became senator from Vermont. See Vermont State Board of Agriculture Reports, 1872–1900, especially J. H. Putnam, "The Depopulation of Our Rural Districts: Cause and Some Suggestions in Regard to a Remedy," *Fifth Report* (Montpelier, Vt., 1878), 132–9.
12 Heath, *Report* (1872), 42–3; Z. E. Jameson, "Vermont as a Home," *Report* (1872), 553–67; "Emigration from New England," *New Genesee Farmer* 4 (1843): 46; George Perkins Marsh, "Address Delivered Before the Ag-

ricultural Society of Rutland County" (1848), reprinted in Barbara Gutman Rosenkrantz and William A. Koelsch, *American Habitat* (New York, 1973), 359–60; L. D. Mason, "Comments on Western Emigration," New Hampshire Board of Agriculture, *Report* (Concord, N.H., 1873), 185–99.

13   *Aurora of the Valley*, October 13, 1849.
14   Wilbur Zelinsky, "Changes in the Geographical Patterns of Rural Population in the United States, 1790–1960," *Geographical Review* 52 (1962): 492–524; Henry U. Fletcher, "The Doom of the Small Town," *Forum* 19 (1895): 214–23.
15   Josiah Strong, *The New Era* (New York, 1893), 164.
16   William D. Hyde, "Impending Paganism in New England," *Forum* 13 (1892): 528. These ideas were also expressed by Strong, *New Era*, 177.
17   Rodney Welch, "The Farmer's Changed Condition," *Forum* 10 (1891): 696–7.
18   Strong, *New Era*, 170–3.
19   Amos N. Currier, "The Decline of Rural New England," *Popular Science Monthly* 38 (1891): 388–9.
20   Hyde, "Impending Paganism"; *Andover Review* cited by Strong, *New Era*, 169.
21   Fletcher, "Doom," 214.
22   Strong, *New Era*, 173; Rollin Lynde Hartt, "A New England Hill Town," *Atlantic Monthly* 83 (1899): 561–74 and 712–20; Charles B. Davenport, "The Nams: The Feeble-minded as Country Dwellers," *Survey* 27 (1912): 1844–5; and with Florence H. Danielson, "The Hill Folk – Report on a Rural Community of Hereditary Defectives," *Eugenics Record Office Memoir* 1 (1912); Edward A. Ross, "Folk Depletion as a Cause of Rural Decline," in "The Sociology of Rural Life," *Publications of the American Sociological Society* 11 (1917): 21–30; it is interesting that most of the commentators at the conference rejected Ross's portrayal of rural decline. For a discussion of contemporary northern middle-class attitudes toward the mountain south, see Henry D. Shapiro, *Appalachia on Our Mind: The Southern Mountains and Mountaineers in the American Consciousness, 1870–1920* (Chapel Hill, N.C., 1977).
23   Welch, "Changed Condition," 695, 698; Strong, *New Era*, 174.
24   T. H. Hoskins, "New England Agriculture," *Popular Science Monthly* 38 (1891): 700; Alvan F. Sanborn, "The Future of Rural New England," *Atlantic Monthly* 80 (1897): 74–83; James E. Boyle, "The Passing of the Country Church," *Outlook* 77 (1904): 230–4.
25   Hoskins, "New England Agriculture," 700; Phillip Morgan, "The Problems of Rural New England: A Remote Village," *Atlantic Monthly* 79 (1897): 580.
26   Robert H. Wiebe, *The Search for Order, 1877–1920* (New York, 1967), 44.
27   Roy V. Scott, *The Reluctant Farmer: The Rise of Agricultural Extension to 1914* (Urbana, Ill., 1970); Charles E. Rosenberg, "The Adams Act: Politics and the Cause of Scientific Research," *Agricultural History* 38 (1964): 3–12.

28 Bowers, *Country Life Movement*, 30–5. Bowers's sample of Country Life reformers ignores some key figures and includes others who were comparatively marginal to the movement.

29 For urban trends, see Robert H. Bremner, *From the Depths: The Discovery of Poverty in the United States* (New York, 1956), 67–85 and 140–63.

30 Wilbert L. Anderson, *The Country Town: A Study of Rural Evolution* (New York, 1906), 3.

31 Ibid., 45–6, 76.

32 Ibid., 147.

33 Ibid., 260–1, 273.

34 Thomas L. Haskell, *The Emergence of Professional Social Science: The American Social Science Association and the Nineteenth-Century Crisis of Authority* (Urbana, Ill., 1977), 24–47; Anderson, *Country Town*, 11.

35 Paul L. Vogt, "Discussion," in "The Sociology of Rural Life," *Publications of the American Sociological Society* 11 (1917): 38.

36 For a bibliography of the Rural Church Movement, see Nelson R. Burr, *A Critical Bibliography of Religion in America* (Princeton, N.J., 1961), vol. 2, 743–50.

37 Charles Otis Gill and Gifford Pinchot, *The Country Church: The Decline of Its Influence and the Remedy* (New York, 1913); and Gill and Pinchot, *Six Thousand Country Churches* (New York, 1920).

38 On Warren Wilson, see Seth William Hester, "The Life and Works of Warren H. Wilson and Their Significance in the Beginnings of the Rural Church Movement in America" (M.A. thesis, Drew Theological Seminary, 1946). See also Edmund deS. Brunner, *The Growth of a Science* (New York, 1957), 1–10; Paul L. Vogt, ed., *The Church and Country Life* (New York, 1916); Anton T. Boisen, "Factors Which Have to Do with the Decline of the Country Church," *American Journal of Sociology* 22 (1916): 177–92; Hermann Nelson Morse and Edmund deS. Brunner, *The Town and Country Church in the United States as Illustrated by Data from One Hundred and Seventy-nine Counties and by Intensive Studies of Twenty-five* (New York, 1923); and Charles Luther Fry, *Diagnosing the Rural Church: A Study in Method* (New York, 1924).

39 George F. Wells, "The Country Church and Its Social Problems," *Outlook* 83 (1906): 895; Edwin L. Earp, *The Rural Church Movement* (New York, 1914), 77–80.

40 Ellwood P. Cubberly, *Rural Life and Education: A Study of the Rural-School Problem as a Phase of the Rural-Life Problem* (Boston, 1914); David B. Tyack, *The One Best System: A History of American Urban Education* (Cambridge, Mass., 1974), 13–27; David B. Danbom, "Rural Education Reform and the Country Life Movement, 1900–1920," *Agricultural History* 53 (1979): 462–74; Wayne E. Fuller, *The Old Country School: The Story of Rural Education in the Middle West* (Chicago, 1982), 218–45.

41 Gill and Pinchot, *Country Church*, 37–53; Danbom, "Rural Education Reform," 471; Tyack, *One Best System*, 23.

42 G. Walter Fiske, "The Development of Rural Leadership," in "The So-

ciology of Rural Life," *Publications of the American Sociological Society* 11 (1917): 56–7; also Fiske, *The Challenge of the Country: A Study of Country Life Opportunity* (New York, 1913).

43 Warren H. Wilson, "Social Life in the Country," in "Country Life," American Academy of Political and Social Science, *Annals* 40 (1912): 119–30, esp. 123; also Myron T. Scudder, "Rural Recreation: A Socializing Factor," in ibid., 175–90.

44 For a discussion of the role of the Arcadian myth in urban reforms, see Peter J. Schmitt, *Back to Nature: The Arcadian Myth in Urban America* (New York, 1969). For a similar interpretation of the attitudes of the Country Life Movement toward the city, see R. Richard Wohl, "The 'Country Boy' Myth and Its Place in the American Urban Culture: The Nineteenth-Century Contribution," *Perspectives in American History* 3 (1969): 148–53.

45 "Country Life," American Academy of Political and Social Science, *Annals* 40 (1912); and "The Sociology of Rural Life," *Publications of the American Sociological Society* 11 (1917).

46 Brunner, *Growth of a Science*; Charles R. Hoffer, "The Development of Rural Sociology," *Rural Sociology* 26 (1961): 1–14; Dwight L. Sanderson, "The Teaching of Rural Sociology, Particularly in the Land-Grant Colleges and Universities," in "The Sociology of Rural Life," *Publications of the American Sociological Society* 11 (1917): 163–214; and Bowers, *Country Life Movement*, 86–101, 128–34. The best history of the discipline of rural sociology is Lowry Nelson, *Rural Sociology: Its Origins and Growth in the United States* (Minneapolis, Minn., 1969).

47 Bowers, *Country Life Movement*; Scott, *Reluctant Farmer*; and Wayne E. Fuller, *RFD: The Changing Face of Rural America* (Bloomington, Ind., 1964).

48 *U.S. Census of Religious Bodies, 1926* (Washington, D.C., 1930), vol. 2, 589–92.

49 Ruth Zinar, "Educational Problems in Rural Vermont, 1875–1900: A Not So Distant Mirror," *Vermont History* 51 (1983): 197–220, esp. 197; Manuscript Town Records, Chelsea, Vermont, vol. 2, Vermont State Division of Public Records, microfilm; and Tyack, *One Best System*, 25.

50 Danbom, "Rural Education Reform," 473; and Clayton S. Ellsworth, "The Coming of Rural Consolidated Schools to the Ohio Valley, 1892–1912," *Agricultural History* 30 (1956): 119–28.

51 Bowers, *Country Life Movement*, 102–27.

4. Quitting the farm and closing the shop

1 John B. Mead, "Opportunities for Young Farmers," Vermont State Board of Agriculture, *Third Report* (Rutland, Vt., 1876), 516–32.

2 Of the young males listed in the 1880 Census, 73% were gone by 1900. For both periods, this rate of out-migration was much higher than that for older age groups. Whereas depopulation was actually the compound

result of net out-migration (the amount of out-migration less the amount of in-migration), fertility decline, and increased mortality, net out-migration was the most important factor in Chelsea and affected the other two trends. Because the selective character of migration altered the age structure of the community, the percentage of young adults in the family-forming years decreased, and the percentage of the old who were more likely to die increased. For an analogous contemporary situation, see Gordon DeJong, *Appalachian Fertility Decline* (Lexington, Ky., 1968).

3 Simon Kuznets et al., *Population Redistribution and Economic Growth, United States 1870–1950*, 3 vols. (Philadelphia, 1957–64), vol. 1, 1–7; vol. 3, xxiii–xxxv.

4 Harold Fisher Wilson, *The Hill Country of Northern New England: Its Social and Economic History, 1790–1930* (New York, 1936); also, Lewis D. Stilwell, *Migration from Vermont* (Montpelier,Vt., 1948), focuses on migration before 1860. Studies of specific communities include: James W. Goldthwait, "A Town That Has Gone Downhill," *Geographical Review* 17 (1927): 527–52; Harold Fisher Wilson, "The Roads of Windsor," *Geographical Review* 21 (1931): 379–97; H. C. Woodworth, "Nute Ridge: The Problem of a Typical Backtown Community," University of New Hampshire Extension Service, *Circular* 68 (1927); and H. C. Woodworth, "A Century of Adjustments in a New Hampshire Back Area," *Agricultural History* 11 (1937): 223–36.

5 In "Nute Ridge," Woodworth presents a detailed picture of local agricultural change based on local interviews but examines a community in which the inhabitants made their living from shoemaking, not farming. Holman B. Jordan uses manuscript census data and challenges the traditional view in "Ten Vermont Towns: Social and Economic Characteristics, 1850–1870" (Ph.D. diss., University of Alabama, 1966). Unfortunately, Jordan does not base his analysis on the township level but on aggregates of several townships from different parts of the state within four categories: hill towns, isolated towns, railroad towns, and one exceptional town. The townships he aggregates display uncharacteristic or divergent trends. For instance, the aggregate population of the four hill towns is increasing during this period rather than declining; and, under the category of isolated towns, he merges data from Chelsea where population declined with data from Cornwall where population increased.

6 Chelsea was the shire town, or county seat, of Orange County. However, county government in Vermont during the nineteenth century was a relatively insignificant affair and did not distinguish Chelsea from other villages of comparable size. Court was only in session for a few weeks in June and December, and the county clerk's only functions were to probate wills for the eastern half of the county and to register and license preachers, peddlers, and stud horses.

7 Zadock Thompson, *A Gazetteer of the State of Vermont* (Montpelier, Vt., 1824), 100–1; Zadock Thompson, *Thompson's History of Vermont* (Burlington, Vt., 1842), Part III, 52; "Conditions in Orange County," Vermont State Board of Agriculture, *Twelfth Report* (Montpelier, Vt., 1892), 134–6. Also, Robert O. Sinclair and Frederick S. Tefft, "Off-Farm Migration and Farm Consolidation in Central Vermont, 1953–1963," University of Vermont Agricultural Experiment Station, *Bulletin* 642 (1965), 11, 16.

8 1840 Census statistics reported in Thompson, *Thompson's History of Vermont*, Part III, 52; manuscript records, Orange County Agricultural Society, 1846–61, Chelsea Historical Society, hereafter cited as Agricultural Society records.

9 Farm data from the Manuscript Schedules, U.S. Census of Agriculture, 1860, Vermont Division of Public Records, microfilm; prices from Thurston M. Adams, "Prices Paid by Vermont Farmers for Goods and Services and Received by Them for Farm Products, 1790–1940; Wages of Vermont Farm Labor, 1780–1940," University of Vermont Agricultural Experiment Station, *Bulletin* 507 (1944); Agricultural Society records.

10 Diary of Alvah Carpenter, 1861–1863, in the possession of Carroll Carpenter, Chelsea, Vermont, is the source for the description of Carpenter's farm operation.

11 On haying in nineteenth-century New England, see William R. Baron and Anne F. Bridges, "Making Hay in Northern New England: Maine as a Case Study, 1800–1850," *Agricultural History* 57 (1983): 165–80.

12 Unless otherwise noted, the quantitative data for this book come from the Manuscript Schedules, U.S. Census of Population for 1840, 1860, 1880, and 1900, National Archives, microfilm; the Manuscript Schedules, U.S. Census of Agriculture for 1860 and 1880, Vermont Division of Public Records, microfilm; and the manuscript Grand List of Taxes for 1837, 1855, 1865, 1875, 1885, and 1895, Office of the Town Clerk, Chelsea, Vermont.

13 H. F. Wallings, *Map of Orange County Vermont* (New York, 1858); and F. W. Beers, *Atlas of Orange County Vermont* (New York, 1877).

14 Diary of Alvah Carpenter, 1880, in the possession of Carroll Carpenter, Chelsea, Vermont.

15 Livestock population figures are from F. C. Williams, "Census of Livestock," Vermont State Board of Agriculture, *Seventeenth Report* (Montpelier, Vt., 1897), 198. The Orange County Creamery Company at Chelsea is listed in Vermont State Board of Agriculture, *Fourteenth Report* (Montpelier, Vt., 1894), 334, and in Vermont Dairymen's Association, *Twenty-Ninth Annual Report* (Montpelier, Vt., 1899), 120. Lists of abandoned farms were published semiannually by the Vermont State Board of Agriculture under various titles: for example, *The Resources and Attractions of Vermont with a List of Desirable Homes for Sale* (Montpelier, Vt., 1891), and *A List of Desirable Farms and Summer Homes in Vermont* (Montpelier, Vt., 1895).

16 Adams, "Prices Paid by Vermont Farmers," 154.

17 These estimates of consumption and yields come from "Cows or Sheep," *Rural Vermonter*, August 6, 1886, and D. E. Salmon, ed., *Special Report on the History and Present Condition of the Sheep Industry of the United States* (Washington, D.C., 1892), 328–9.

18 Sheep were raised in both Lyme, New Hampshire, and West Windsor, Vermont, until the close of the century; see Goldthwait, "Town That Has Gone Downhill," and Wilson, "Roads of Windsor." County-level census statistics show conclusively, the ecological fallacy notwithstanding, that those counties that suffered the most population decline also continued to produce constant amounts of wool between 1850 and 1890 and did not shift into dairying.

19 James M. Sykes, "Trends in Vermont Agriculture," Vermont Resources Center, *Report 7* (1964), 14; and U.S. Geological Survey, *15' Series Map* for Barre, East Barre, Randolph, and Strafford, Vermont (Washington, D.C., n.d.).

20 Manuscript Schedules, U.S. Census of Agriculture, 1880.

21 Alvah Carpenter diary, 1880; Diary of Eugene Thorne, 1880, in the possession of Sid Gilman, Chelsea, Vermont; from 1878 on, the *Herald and News*, the *White River Valley Herald*, and the *Chelsea Herald* occasionally reported the prices paid by local merchants for farm products.

22 Agricultural Society records; F. D. Douglas, "Butter-Making," Vermont State Board of Agriculture, *Second Report* (Montpelier, Vt., 1874), 63–89; *Eighth Report* (1884), 46–7; *Tenth Report* (1892), 60–1; *Eighth Report* (1884), 19.

23 For a discussion of correlation coefficients, see Hubert M. Blalock, *Social Statistics* (New York, 1972), 361–400.

24 John Lynde, "The Interests of Agriculture in Orange County," Vermont State Board of Agriculture, *Second Report* (Montpelier, Vt., 1874), 609–10.

25 Adams also points out that between 1840 and 1914 Vermont farm wages did not rise as fast as industrial wages; see "Prices Paid by Vermont Farmers," 92.

26 The good showing at the fairs should not be taken as evidence of any atypical emphasis on sheep raising in Chelsea. Rather, because the fair was held in town, the sweep by local farmers so irked farmers from other townships that they quit the county society and formed a splinter group, the Union Agricultural Society, which continues to this day. County fair information is from Agricultural Society records, especially the Entry Book of the Orange County Agricultural Society. Hybrid corn: Zvi Griliches, "Hybrid Corn and the Economics of Innovation," in Robert Fogel and Stanley Engerman, eds., *The Reinterpretation of American Economic History* (New York, 1971), 207–13. Carman is quoted in Salmon, *Special Report*, 320.

27 E. R. Skinner, "The Butter Dairy," Vermont State Board of Agriculture, *Fifth Report* (Montpelier, Vt., 1878), 69. Examples of other dairying advice include the following articles from the Vermont State Board of Agriculture: "Butter Making in Competition with the West," *Second Report* (1874),

120–8; E. H. Cleveland, "Feeding Grain to Milch Cows," *Third Report* (1876), 70–3; and E. R. Towle, "Winter Care of Stock," *Tenth Report* (1888), 171–7.

28 Fred Bateman, "Labor Inputs and Productivity in American Dairy Agriculture, 1850–1910," *Journal of Economic History* 29 (1969): 206–29. See also Fred Bateman, "Improvement in American Dairy Farming, 1850–1910: A Quantitative Analysis," *Journal of Economic History* 28 (1968): 255–73; and Fred Bateman, "The Marketable Surplus in Northern Dairy Farming: New Evidence by Size of Farm in 1860," *Agricultural History* 52 (1978): 345–63.

29 For a discussion of partial correlation coefficients, see Blalock, *Social Statistics*, 433–7, and Norman H. Nie et al., *SPSS: Statistical Package for the Social Sciences* (New York, 1975), 301–5. All correlations are significant at the .05 level or better.

30 The constant production of maple sugar also underscores the importance of the supply of labor. Even though sugar prices did not rise, farmers continued making large amounts of maple sugar because: (a) sugar trees represented a long-term fixed capital investment, (b) the land they were on was probably not suitable for other forms of agriculture, (c) the cost of removing the trees to clear new fields would have been prohibitive, and (d) sugaring required labor only during the early spring, when there were little other demands on farm labor.

31 Manuscript Schedules, U.S. Census of Manufactures, 1870, Vermont State Library; Densmore, *Argus and Patriot* (Montpelier, Vt.), April 17, 1873.

32 Samuel F. Barry and C. Benton, *A Statistical View of the Number of Sheep in the Several Towns and Counties in Maine, New Hampshire, Vermont, etc. . . . in 1836* (Cambridge, Mass., 1837), 110; also manuscript Grand List of Taxes, 1837.

33 Manuscript Schedules, U.S. Census of Manufactures, 1850, Vermont State Library; also manuscript Grand List of Taxes, 1855, 1860.

34 Manuscript Schedules, U.S. Census of Manufactures, 1850; also manuscript credit ledgers, R. G. Dun & Co., Orange County, Vermont, vol. 16, Baker Library, Harvard University School of Business Administration.

35 Town Records, Chelsea, vol. 2; *Argus and Patriot*, March 19, 1868; Town Records, Chelsea, vol. 3; *White River Valley Herald* (Randolph, Vt.), April 7, 1892, and October 27, 1892.

36 Alan Dawley, *Class and Community: The Industrial Revolution in Lynn* (Cambridge, Mass., 1976); also manuscript credit ledgers, R. G. Dun & Co., vol. 16; Agricultural Society records.

37 Hamilton Child, *Child's Orange County Gazette, 1762–1888* (Syracuse, N.Y., 1888), 33–43; also manuscript credit ledgers, R. G. Dun & Co., vol. 16.

38 Ward W. Bauder, *The Impact of Population Change on Rural Community Life: The Economic System* (Ames, Iowa, 1963); also Manuscript Schedules, U.S. Census of Manufactures, 1850, 1870.

39 Child, *Child's Orange County Gazette.*
40 Manuscript credit ledgers, R. G. Dun & Co., vol. 16; Manuscript Schedules, U.S. Census of Manufactures, 1880; also Child, *Child's Orange County Gazette.*
41 Manuscript Schedules, U.S. Census of Agriculture, 1860, 1880.
42 Paul G. Munyon, *A Reassessment of New England Agriculture in the Last Thirty Years of the Nineteenth Century: New Hampshire, A Case Study* (New York, 1978); Robert A. Riley, "Kinship Patterns in Londonderry, Vermont, 1772–1900: An Intergenerational Perspective of Changing Family Relationships" (Ph.D. diss., University of Massachusetts-Amherst, 1980), 55–74; and Bruce Melvin, "The Sociology of a Village and the Surrounding Territory," Cornell University Agricultural Experiment Station, *Bulletin* 523 (1931).
43 James M. Williams, *An American Town* (New York, 1906); Melvin, "Sociology of a Village"; Gladys Kensler and Bruce L. Melvin, "A Partial Sociological Study of Dryden, New York, with Special Emphasis on Its Historical Development," Cornell University Agricultural Experiment Station, *Bulletin* 504 (1930); and Riley, "Kinship Patterns," 63.

5. The ties that bind

1 Stephan Thernstrom, *The Other Bostonians: Poverty and Progress in an American Metropolis, 1880–1970* (Cambridge, Mass., 1973), 9–44; Allan G. Bogue, *From Prairie to Corn Belt: Farming on the Illinois and Iowa Prairies in the Nineteenth Century* (Chicago, 1968), 8–28; and Stephan Thernstrom and Peter R. Knights, "Men in Motion: Some Data and Speculations about Urban Population Mobility in Nineteenth-Century America," *Journal of Interdisciplinary History* 1 (1970): 17–47.
2 A persistence rate is, quite simply, the percentage of the population listed in one census that remains and is found again in a subsequent census. Demographically, it is not an accurate measure of migration because it does not distinguish between death and out-migration as the cause of an individual's disappearance. Persistence rates also do not measure any migration and return migration that might occur between the two censuses. It is, however, the best indicator of individual migration readily available to American historians, and ever since the pioneering work of James C. Malin, it has been used extensively by students of midwestern frontier development and, more recently, by the new urban historians. See James C. Malin, "The Turnover of Farm Population in Kansas," *Kansas Historical Quarterly* 4 (1935): 339–72; Thernstrom, *Other Bostonians*; Michael B. Katz, Michael J. Doucet, and Mark J. Stern, "Migration and the Social Order in Erie County, New York: 1855," *Journal of Interdisciplinary History* 8 (1978): 669–701.
    To compute persistence rates, the population schedules for Chelsea were linked nominally over three time periods: 1840–60, 1860–80, and 1880–1900. Because Chelsea was a comparatively small community,

many of the methodological problems associated with the repetition of common names and variations in spelling from one census to the next were easily dealt with by hand; there is good reason to be confident as to the accuracy and completeness of the census enumeration because the census taker was a local official and long-standing resident of the community rather than an outsider. Local tax lists, directories, and genealogical information provided additional verification when particular links were obscure.

The twenty-year rates represent a departure from the usual intercensal measurement. Twenty-year intervals, however, allow one to cover more time and permit intergenerational analysis while still effectively distinguishing between permanent residents and the more transient local inhabitants. The rates for 1840–60 refer only to household heads in the 1840 Census. Rates for the other two periods are based on all male inhabitants. Regretfully, female inhabitants were not linked because of the difficulties involved in tracing name changes after marriage. For a statement of the importance of including women in studies of social mobility and a delineation of linkage methods appropriate for urban-industrial situations, see Thomas Dublin, "Women Workers and the Study of Social Mobility," *Journal of Interdisciplinary History* 9 (1979): 647–65.

3   See Table 9.1 in Thernstrom, *Other Bostonians*, 222–3; and Merle Curti, *The Making of an American Community* (Stanford, Calif., 1959).

4   To estimate the effect of mortality, the probable number of survivors of each age group for each of the three time periods was calculated using the model life tables devised by Ansley Coale and Paul Demeny. The corrected persistence rates, then, are the number of those who stay as a percentage only of the number who are likely to survive. Following the example of Michael Katz's recent study, Model West, level 12 is used for the period 1840–60. To approximate the general improvement in mortality rates throughout the nineteenth century, level 14 for 1860–80 and level 16 for 1880–1900 are used. The increase in male life expectancy that this range of tables implies (from 44.5 years to 54.1 years at birth) parallels the amount of increase that Jacobsen found in his study of cohort survival after 1840. The actual level of mortality that is used is lower, however, because of the recent criticism that Jacobsen overestimated the level of mortality. The use of model life tables represents only an approximation of the effect of mortality. Chelsea's population amd most U.S. populations did not meet the criteria of stable populations that these model tables assume. For historians, however, they remain a useful, if rough, shortcut for imputing mortality. See Katz, Doucet, and Stern, "Migration and the Social Order." On the computation of model life tables, see Ansley Coale and Paul Demeny, *Regional Model Life Tables and Stable Populations* (Princeton, N.J., 1966). On nineteenth-century life expectancy, see Paul H. Jacobsen, "Cohort Survival for Generations Since 1840," *Milbank Memorial Fund Quarterly* 42 (1964): 36–

53; and Maris Vinovskis, "The Jacobsen Life Table of 1850: A Critical Reexamination from a Massachusetts Perspective," *Journal of Interdisciplinary History* 8 (1978): 703–24. See also Michael Haines, "The Use of Model Life Tables to Estimate Mortality for the United States in the Late Nineteenth Century," *Demography* 16 (1979): 289–312, which criticizes this technique.

Again, the adjusted twenty-year figures for Chelsea are much higher than the twenty-year rates (also adjusted for mortality) implicit in Katz's Buffalo data. The twenty-year rates for male household heads in Buffalo between 1845 and 1865 are:

Age	Rate (%)
20–29	46.6
30–39	36.5
40–49	39.1
50–59	48.9
60+	—

Source: Computed from data of Michael B. Katz, Michael J. Doucet, and Mark J. Stern, "Migration and the Social Order in Erie County, New York: 1855," *Journal of Interdisciplinary History* 8 (1978): 669–701.

5 By standardizing the persistence rates in Chelsea by the younger age structure of Trempeleau County (1860) and Buffalo (1845), the effect of the older age structure on overall persistence can be approximated. Standardization is a common demographic technique used to eliminate differences in rates that are due to the particular age structure (or sex, race, nativity, etc.) of the population. In both cases, the younger age distributions lower Chelsea's general persistence rate by about 4%, narrowing the gap but by no means eliminating it. Once Chelsea persistence between 1880 and 1900 is standardized by Chelsea's earlier and younger age structure in 1860, the persistence rates for the two periods are almost identical. This implies that almost all the increase in Chelsea's persistence rates is due to the changing age structure of the community. On standardization of crude rates, see Henry S. Shryock and Jacob S. Siegel, *The Methods and Materials of Demography* (Washington, D.C., 1975), vol. 1: 289–91; vol. 2: 418–24.

6 Curti also finds higher persistence among the propertied; see Curti, *Making of an American Community*. See also Katz's discussion of rural Erie County in "Migration and the Social Order" and some of the older frontier studies such as William L. Bowers, "Crawford Township, 1850–1870: A Population Study of a Pioneer Community," *Iowa Journal of History* 58 (1960): 1–30; and Mildred Throne, "A Population Study of an Iowa County in 1850," *Iowa Journal of History* 57 (1959): 305–30.

7   As with property, the other persistence studies found occupation to be
    a distinguishing factor. See especially Michael Conzen, *Frontier Farming
    in an Urban Shadow* (Madison, Wis., 1971), 44–51. Katz, however, found
    no significant effect of occupation once the other variables were controlled
    for. Unfortunately, the small size of Chelsea's population does not
    permit the use of enough controls to eliminate the effect of multicollin-
    earity. In a large sense, however, Katz argues that the explanatory
    strength of a particular variable is not very important because it was
    the "accumulation of differences rather than any one specific factor"
    that accounted for variation in persistence. See Katz, "Migration and
    the Social Order," 692.

8   For a recent theoretical discussion of the importance of social connections
    to the community, see Peter Uhlenberg, "Non-Economic Determinants
    of Non-Migration: Sociological Considerations for Migration Theory,"
    Rural Sociology 38 (1973): 296–311. The traditional historians also em-
    phasized military service in the Civil War as a cause for out-migration
    from northern New England. Those who broadened their awareness
    of the outside world were much less likely to return and stay in their
    hometowns. Yet data from Chelsea show no difference in the persistence
    rates of young men who fought and survived ($N = 59$) and those who
    did not join up. Military service is recorded in John Moore Comstock,
    Chelsea, Vermont (n.p., 1944), 56–61.

9   High persistence rates are not uncommon in present-day rural com-
    munities that lose population as a result of decreased in-migration. See
    Calvin L. Beale, "Rural Depopulation in the United States: Some De-
    mographic Consequences of Agricultural Adjustments," *Demography* 1
    (1964): 264–72.

10 Malin, "Turnover of Farm Population"; Daniel Scott Smith, "A Perspective
    on Demographic Methods and Effects in Social History," *The Newberry
    Papers in Family and Community History*, No. 77-4K (1977): 11–13. Beale
    points out that decade out-migration rates for middle-aged farmers
    rarely exceed 10% in present-day rural areas that are declining in size
    (Beale, "Rural Depopulation," 269). Finally, fertility decline (which led
    to an older age structure) occurred in all parts of the rural north after
    the settlement stage was completed. See Richard A. Easterlin, "Population
    Change and Farm Settlement in the Northern United States," *Journal
    of Economic History* 36 (1976): 45–75; Richard A. Easterlin, "Factors in
    the Decline of Farm Fertility in the United States: Some Preliminary
    Research Results," *Journal of American History* 63 (1976): 600–14; Richard
    A. Easterlin, George Alter, and Gretchen Condran, "Farms and Farm
    Families in Old and New Areas: The Northern States in 1860," in Tamara
    K. Hareven and Maris A. Vinovskis, eds., *Family and Population in Nine-
    teenth-Century America* (Princeton, N.J., 1978), 22–84.

11 Genealogical information and directory for 1887 is published in Hamilton
    Child, *Child's Orange County Gazette, 1762–1888* (Syracuse, N.Y., 1888);
    manuscript Grand List of Taxes, 1880 and 1895, Office of the Town

Clerk, Chelsea, Vt.; manuscript Land Records and Vital Records for Chelsea, Vermont, Vermont State Division of Public Records, microfilm, hereafter cited as Chelsea Land Records; maps of Chelsea are from H. F. Wallings, *Map of Orange County Vermont* (New York, 1858), and F. W. Beers, *Atlas of Orange County Vermont* (New York, 1877). The 30–39 age group was selected because these men lived in the township throughout the entire period of this study.

12 See Thernstrom, *Other Bostonians*, on urban social mobility.

13 See Jack Goody, Joan Thirsk, and E. P. Thompson, eds., *Family and Inheritance: Rural Society in Western Europe 1200–1800* (Cambridge, 1976); and Philip J. Greven, *Four Generations: Population, Land, and Family in Colonial Andover, Massachusetts* (Ithaca, N.Y., 1970). See also James D. Tarver, "Intra-Family Farm Succession Practices," *Rural Sociology* 17 (1952): 266–71, for a study of Wisconsin farms that stayed in the same family for a century or more. More recent scholarship is beginning to remedy the lack of attention to nineteenth-century inheritance. See Robert A. Riley, "Kinship Patterns in Londonderry, Vermont, 1772–1900: An Intergenerational Perspective of Changing Family Relationships" (Ph.D. diss., University of Massachusetts-Amherst, 1980); David P. Gagan, "The Indivisibility of Land: A Micro-analysis of the System of Inheritance in Nineteenth-Century Ontario," *Journal of Economic History* 36 (1976): 126–41; and Marvin McInnis, "Comment," *Journal of Economic History* 36 (1976): 142–6.

14 The number of children is estimated from data on household size for all married farmers in their forties listed in the 1840 Census. Riley also finds an average of five births for Vermont farm wives during the middle of the nineteenth century ("Kinship Patterns," 100, Table 21). These twenty-three farmers came from only twenty families because the cohort includes three pairs of brothers.

15 According to Riley, nineteenth-century Vermont men married at age 24 or 25. Their wives were typically 21 and bore their last child at 37 or 38 when the husband was over 40. See Riley, "Kinship Patterns," 85, Table 18. Chelsea Land Records: Annis: vol. 17, 163; Moxley: vol. 16, 164; Sanborn: vol. 17, 19; Dewey: vol. 17, 133; Gates: vol. 18, 310.

16 Chelsea Land Records: Barnes: vol. 17, 11; Bacon: vol. 19, 374; Goodwin: vol. 20, 223. Premortem land transfers were common elsewhere in the region. See Riley, "Kinship Patterns," 162; and Mary P. Ryan, *Cradle of the Middle Class: The Family in Oneida County, New York, 1790–1865* (New York, 1981), 27–31.

17 Chelsea Land Records: Annis: vol. 17, 163; Dewey: vol. 17, 133; Gates: vol. 18, 310; Sanborn: vol. 15, 485; Goodwin: vol. 20, 427; Lucas: vol. 21, 336.

18 Chelsea Land Records: Gates: vol. 18, 310.

19 Chelsea Land Records: Dewey: vol. 17, 133; Sanborn: vol. 15, 485.

20 Howard S. Russell, *A Long, Deep Furrow: Three Centuries of Farming in*

New England (Hanover, N.H., 1976), 411; Massachusetts quotation from Lester Klimm, "The Relation between Certain Population Changes and the Physical Environment in Hampden, Hampshire and Franklin Counties, Massachusetts, 1790–1925" (Ph.D. diss., University of Pennsylvania, 1933), 44. See also Riley, "Kinship Patterns," and Ryan, *Cradle of the Middle Class*, 27–31.

21 James A. Henretta, "Families and Farms: *Mentalité* in Pre-Industrial America," *William and Mary Quarterly*, 3rd ser., 25 (1978): 3–32; Ryan, *Cradle of the Middle Class*, 27–31; Christopher Clark, "The Household Economy: Market Exchange and the Rise of Capitalism in the Connecticut Valley, 1800–1860," *Journal of Social History* 13 (1979): 169–89.

22 Because the cohort of permanent farmers is biased toward younger sons, an extra effort was made to identify and gather data on their older brothers and sisters using all available sources. Chelsea Land Records: Bacon: vol. 16, 271; Sanborn: vol. 19, 187; Barnes: vol. 20, 77. Also Beers, *Atlas*; Child, *Child's Orange County Gazette*; and the manuscript credit ledgers, R. G. Dun & Co., Orange County, Vermont, vol. 16, Baker Library, Harvard University School of Business Administration.

23 Keyes: *Herald and News* (Randolph, Vt.), April 9, 1885, and Child, *Child's Orange County Gazette*. Carpenter: *Rural Vermonter* (Montpelier, Vt.), December 24, 1886.

24 *Manual of the Chelsea, Vermont Congregational Church*, 32–63. In her study of Massachusetts hill towns, in which she uses similar church records to indicate out-migration destinations, Margaret Pabst also finds a predominant pattern of local or regional migration. See Pabst, "Agricultural Trends in the Connecticut Valley Region of Massachusetts, 1800–1900," *Smith College Studies in History* 26 (1940–1): 44–6.

25 Manuscript List of Enrolled Militia, 1864–1867, Chelsea, Vermont, Vermont State Division of Public Records, microfilm, Office of the Town Clerk.

26 *Old Home Week Celebration, Chelsea, Vermont: 1901* (Lowell, Mass., 1901).

27 On the practice of providing a start in life, see Easterlin, Alter, and Condran, "Farms and Farm Families," 72–3.

28 Diary of Eugene Thorne, 1880, in the possession of Sid Gilman, Chelsea, Vermont; Chelsea Land Records: vol. 19, 163.

29 Diary of Eugene Thorne, 1880 and 1884, in the possession of Sid Gilman, Chelsea, Vermont; Chelsea Land Records: vol. 19, 163, and vol. 20, 297. Lance E. Davis, "The Investment Market, 1870–1914: The Evolution of a National Market," *Journal of Economic History* 25 (1965): 375.

30 Chelsea Land Records: Camp: vol. 18, 214; Barnes: vol. 17, 10; Robbins: vol. 19, 165.

31 Based on local marriage records, maps, and land records, as well as the genealogical entries in Child, *Child's Orange County Gazette*.

32 Riley, "Kinship Patterns," 126–39. Riley, however, does not trace the career patterns of individuals or calculate persistence rates.

33   A feasible, though tedious, strategy for following those who leave has been suggested by Charles Stephenson, "Tracing Those Who Left: Mobility Studies and the Soundex Indexes to the U.S. Census," *Journal of Urban History* 1 (1974): 73–84.

34   Manuscript records, Chelsea, Vermont, Congregational Church, Vermont Historical Society; Chelsea Land Records: Goodrich: vol. 18, 433; Ballou: vol. 17, 446. Chelsea Vital Records: Smith: vol. 2, 5. Perkins: Child, *Child's Orange County Gazette*. Although the church records are obviously biased toward Yankee in-migrants, the very low percentage of foreign immigrants in Chelsea suggests that such a bias is not an inaccurate reflection of local conditions.

35   Chelsea Land Records: Ballou: vol. 17, 495; Slack: vol. 16, 442; Woodruff: vol. 18, 315, and vol. 19, 17.

36   The incidence of family migration was determined from the U.S. Census schedules. Ballou: Child, *Child's Orange County Gazette*.

37   Haywood: Congregational Church Records and Chelsea Land Records: vol. 18, 180. Scales: U.S. Census schedules, 1880; Chelsea Land Records: Stearns: vol. 17, 281; George: vol. 18, 330.

38   L. D. Mason, "Comments on Western Emigration," New Hampshire Board of Agriculture, *Report* (Concord, N.H., 1873), 185–99.

39   "The Wisconsin Emigrant's Song," in Helen Hartness Flanders et al., *The New Green Mountain Songster: Traditional Folk Songs of Vermont* (Hatboro, Pa., 1966), 106–8.

40   Emily F. Hoag, "The National Influence of a Single Farm Community: A Story of the Flow into National Life of Migration from the Farms," U.S. Department of Agriculture, *Bulletin* 984 (1921): 1–55, esp. 35, 51.

41   E. C. Young, "The Movement of Farm Population," Cornell University Agricultural Experiment Station, *Bulletin* 426 (1924); W. A. Anderson, "Mobility of Rural Families I: Changes in Residence and Occupation of Rural Husbands and Wives in Genesee County, New York," Cornell University Agricultural Experiment Station, *Bulletin* 607 (1934): 18; W. A. Anderson, "Mobility of Rural Families II," Cornell University Agricultural Experiment Station, *Bulletin* 623 (1935); C. E. Lively and P. G. Beck, "Movement of Open Country Population in Ohio I: The Family Aspect," Ohio Agricultural Experiment Station, *Bulletin* 467 (1930); and, Lively and Beck, "Movement of Open Country Population in Ohio II: The Individual Aspect," Ohio Agricultural Experiment Station, *Bulletin* 489 (1931); Paul S. Peirce, "Social Surveys of Three Rural Townships in Iowa," *University of Iowa Monographs, Studies in the Social Sciences* 5 (1917); Carl W. Thompson and G. P. Warber, "Social and Economic Survey of a Rural Township in Southern Minnesota," *University of Minnesota Studies in Economics* 1 (1913).

42   Young, "Movement of Farm Population," 75–7; Lively and Beck, "Movement II," 16.

43   Henretta, "Families and Farms"; Clark, "Household Economy."

44   Peter R. Knights, "The Contours of Nineteenth-Century Lives: Lessons from a Study of Internal Migration Based on Boston," paper presented

at the Social Science History Association Annual Meeting, Nashville, Tenn., October 1981; Thomas Dublin, *Women at Work: The Transformation of Work and Community in Lowell, Massachusetts, 1826–1860* (New York, 1979).

45 Records, R. G. Dun & Co.; *Story Norman Goss, Doctor of Medicine of Chelsea, Vermont, 1831–1905* (Boston, 1905); "Bench and Bar," in Child, *Child's Orange County Gazette.*

46 Horace Samuel Merrill, *William Freeman Vilas, Doctrinaire Democrat* (Madison, Wis., 1954), 6–7. Also "Bench and Bar," in Child, *Child's Orange County Gazette.*

47 George H. Steele to William B. Hale, January 9, 1846, George H. Steele Papers, Vermont Historical Society.

48 Manuscript credit ledgers, R. G. Dun & Co.

49 Corwin: *Herald and News* (Randolph, Vt.), April 26, 1883.

50 D. Tarbell, *Incidents of Real Life* (Montpelier, Vt., 1883), 41; also Records, R. G. Dun & Co.

51 C. I. Hood, "Address," in *Old Home Week Celebration, Chelsea, Vermont: 1902* (Lowell, Mass., 1902), 18–25; also Records, R. G. Dun & Co.

52 Carpenter: *Rural Vermonter* (Montpelier, Vt.), November 11, 1887; Corwin: *Rural Vermonter*, December 3, 1886; Hood: "Address."

53 Child, *Child's Orange County Gazette*; and Records, R. G. Dun & Co.

54 Information on the more transient members of the 1880 cohort is from the Manuscript Schedules, U.S. Census, 1880.

6. Their town

1 *Herald and News* (Randolph, Vt.), June 9, 1892.

2 *Manual of the Chelsea, Vermont, Congregational Church* (1888), 32–63, Vermont Historical Society; hereafter cited as *Manual*; Randolph A. Roth, "Whence This Strange Fire? Religious and Reform Movements in the Connecticut River Valley of Vermont, 1791–1843" (Ph.D. diss., Yale University, 1981), 392–415.

3 John Moore Comstock, *Chelsea, Vermont* (n.p., 1944), 33.

4 Hamilton Child, *Child's Orange County Gazette, 1762–1888* (Syracuse, N.Y., 1888), 243; *Manual*, 32–63.

5 *Manual*, 32–63.

6 Ibid.; manuscript records, Chelsea, Vermont, Congregational Church, 1789–1857, Vermont Historical Society, hereafter cited as Congregational Church records.

7 Congregational Church records.

8 Manuscript Town Records, 1788–1919, Office of the Town Clerk, Chelsea, Vt., vol. 2, Town Meeting, April 9, 1838, hereafter cited as Chelsea Town Records.

9 Manuscript records, Chelsea Washington Total Abstinence Society, 1844, Chelsea Historical Society, hereafter cited as Abstinence Society records.

10 Ibid.; *Manual*, 32–63; Chelsea Town Records, vol. 1; manuscript records,

Ladies' Benevolent Society of the Chelsea Methodist Episcopal Church, 1879–1882, Chelsea Historical Society; E. Ralph Walker, *Historical Sketch of the Chelsea West Hill Union Meeting House* (n.p., 1933).

11 Abstinence Society records; Manuscript Schedules, U.S. Census of Population, 1840 and 1850.

12 Jill Siegel Dodd, "The Working Classes and the Temperance Movement in Ante-Bellum Boston," *Labor History* 19 (1978): 510–31; W. J. Rorabaugh, *The Alcoholic Republic: An American Tradition* (New York, 1979), 79–84; Paul Johnson, *Shopkeeper's Millennium: Society and Revivals in Rochester, New York, 1815–1837* (New York, 1978).

13 Joseph R. Gusfield, *Symbolic Crusade, Status Politics and the American Temperance Movement* (Urbana, Ill., 1963), 61–86; Ian R. Tyrrell, *Sobering Up: From Temperance to Prohibitionism in Antebellum America, 1800–1860* (Westport, Conn., 1979), 159–90.

14 Chelsea Town Records, vol. 2, Town Meeting, March 19, 1844.

15 Chelsea Town Records, vol. 2; George H. Steele to William B. Hale, January 9, 1846, George H. Steele Papers, Vermont Historical Society.

16 Manuscript records, Orange County Temperance Society, 1855–1884, Chelsea Historical Society, hereafter cited as Temperance Society records.

17 Ibid.

18 Chelsea Town Records, vol. 2, Town Meeting, March 4, 1862; *Argus and Patriot* (Montpelier, Vt.), March 14, 1876.

19 Chelsea Town Records, vol. 2; Temperance Society records; *Argus and Patriot*, March 23, 1876.

20 *Argus and Patriot*, December 8, 1870; Manuscript Court Records, vol. 21, 106, Orange County Court, hereafter cited as Orange County Court records; manuscript credit ledgers, R. G. Dun & Co., Orange County, Vermont, vol. 16, Baker Library, Harvard University School of Business Administration; manuscript register, Orange County Jail, Orange County Court, hereafter cited as Orange County Jail register.

21 Orange County Jail register; *Argus and Patriot*, June 9, 1870; Orange County Court records, vol. 22, 4–5, 105, 601–2, 605–6.

22 Chelsea Town Records, vol. 3.

23 Ibid., vol. 2 and vol. 3; Edward P. Brynn, "Vermont's Political Vacuum of 1845–1856 and the Emergence of the Republican Party," *Vermont History* 38 (1970): 113–23. Walter Hill Crockett, *A History of Vermont*, 4 vols. (Burlington, Vt., 1938), vol. 3, 419–92.

24 Crockett, *History of Vermont*, 419–92; Brynn, "Vermont's Political Vacuum." Eric Foner also points out the importance of former Democrats in the new Republican party; see his *Free Soil, Free Labor, Free Men: The Ideology of the Republican Party Before the Civil War* (New York, 1970), 149–85.

25 Foner, *Free Soil*, 316.

26 James H. Moorhead, *American Apocalypse: Yankee Protestants and the Civil War, 1860–1869* (New Haven, Conn., 1978), 164.

27   Manuscript records, Orange County Agricultural Society, 1846–61, Chelsea Historical Society.

28   Ibid.

29   Manuscript records, Vulture Engine Company, 1884–1896, Orange County Court, hereafter cited as Vulture Engine Company records; manuscript records, Chelsea Baseball Club, 1876–1877, Orange County Court; *Roster of the H.E.K. Hall Camp No. 28, Vermont Division, Sons of Veterans* (n.p., 1888), Chelsea Historical Society; *Herald and News*, May 4, 1893. On the role of voluntary associations in reducing local conflicts and divisions in nineteenth-century America, see Don H. Doyle, "The Social Functions of Voluntary Associations in a Nineteenth-Century Town," *Social Science History* 1 (1977): 333–56.

30   The newspapers are filled with such notices, especially the *Argus and Patriot* (Montpelier, Vt.), the *Herald and News* (Randolph, Vt.), and the *Rural Vermonter* (Montpelier, Vt.).

31   *Argus and Patriot*, March 5, 1874; *Herald and News*, December 24, 1891, and February 11, 1892.

32   Vulture Engine Company records.

33   *Rural Vermonter*, October 1, 1886; manuscript records, Chelsea Debating Club, 1897–1898, Chelsea Historical Society, hereafter cited as Chelsea Debating Club records.

34   Congregational Church records.

35   Diary of Alvah Carpenter, 1880, in the possession of Carroll Carpenter, Chelsea, Vermont; Diary of Eugene Thorne, 1880, in the possession of Sid Gilman, Chelsea, Vermont.

36   Diary of Alvah Carpenter, 1880; Diary of Eugene Thorne, 1880.

37   Collamer M. Abbott, " 'Gramp' Abbott's Life: Farming in Central Vermont, 1865–1913," *Vermont History* 39 (1971): 31–42; Diary of Alvah Carpenter, 1880; Diary of Eugene Thorne, 1880.

38   Chelsea Debating Club records.

39   James M. Williams, *An American Town* (New York, 1906); W. G. Mather, T. H. Townsend, and Dwight Sanderson, "A Study of Rural Community Development in Waterville, New York," Cornell University Agricultural Experiment Station, *Bulletin* 608 (1934).

40   Of the many surveys of rural communities, few examine long-term change over time. Bruce Melvin, "The Sociology of a Village and the Surrounding Territory," Cornell University Agricultural Experiment Station, *Bulletin* 523 (1931), is an exception.

41   W. A. Anderson, "The Membership of Farmers in New York Organizations," Cornell University Agricultural Experiment Station, *Bulletin* 695 (1938); E. D. Tetreau, "Farm Family Participation in Lodges, Grange, Farm Bureau, Four-H Clubs, School and Church," Ohio Agricultural Experiment Station, *Mimeograph Bulletin* 29 (1930); Perry P. Denune, "Some Town–Country Relations in Union County, Ohio," *Ohio State University Studies*, Sociology Series 1 (1924); and Perry P. Denune, "The

Social and Economic Relations of the Farmers with the Towns in Pickaway County, Ohio," *Ohio State University Studies*, Bureau of Business Research (1927), 18.

42   Robert L. Duffus, *Williamstown Branch: Impersonal Memories of a Vermont Boyhood* (New York, 1958), 61.
43   Ibid., 59–76.
44   Newell Sims, *A Hoosier Village* (New York, 1912); Duffus, *Williamstown Branch*, 131–50. See also Page Smith, *As a City Upon a Hill: The Town in American History* (New York, 1966).
45   Lura Beam, *A Maine Hamlet* (New York, 1957); Duffus, *Williamstown Branch*; Russell H. Farnsworth, *Over Cram Hill* (Burlington, Vt., 1967); Wheeler McMillen, *Ohio Farm* (Columbus, Ohio, 1974); Albert Britt, *An America That Was: What Life Was Like on an Illinois Farm Seventy Years Ago* (Barre, Mass., 1964).

Conclusion

1   *Old Home Week Celebration, Chelsea, Vermont: 1902* (Lowell, Mass., 1902).
2   C. I. Hood, "Address," *Old Home Week . . . 1902*, 18–25.
3   W. H. Davis, D.D., "Address," *Old Home Week . . . 1902*, 11–17.
4   Ibid., 17.
5   Stanley Parsons, *The Populist Context: Rural versus Urban Power on a Great Plains Frontier* (Westport, Conn., 1973).
6   Robert H. Wiebe, *The Search for Order, 1877–1920* (New York, 1967).

Bibliography

Primary sources

Unpublished materials

Cambridge, Mass. Baker Library, Harvard University School of Business
  Administration. Credit ledgers of R. G. Dun & Co., Orange County,
  Vermont, vol. 16, 1840–1890.
Chelsea, Vt. Chelsea Historical Society. Records of the Chelsea Washing-
  ton Total Abstinence Society, 1844.
  Records of the Chelsea Debating Club, 1897–1898.
  Records of the Ladies' Benevolent Society of the Chelsea Methodist
  Episcopal Church, 1879–1882.
  Records of the Orange County Temperance Society, 1855–1884.
  Records of the Orange County Agricultural Society, 1846–1861.
  Entry Book of the Orange County Agricultural Society, 1849–1858.
Chelsea, Vt. Orange County Courthouse collection. Records of the Vul-
  ture Engine Company, 1884–1896.
  Records of the Chelsea Baseball Club, 1876–1877.
Chelsea, Vt. Personal collection of Sid Gilman. Diary of Eugene Thorne,
  1880 and 1884.
Chelsea, Vt. Personal collection of Carroll Carpenter. Diary of Alvah Car-
  penter, 1861–1863 and 1880.
Montpelier, Vt. Vermont Historical Society. Records of the Chelsea, Ver-
  mont, Congregational Church, 1789–1857 and 1845–1880.
  George H. Steele Papers.

Published materials

Barry, Samuel F., and Benton, C. *A Statistical View of the Number of Sheep
  in the Several Towns and Counties in Maine, New Hampshire, Vermont,
  etc. . . . in 1836.* Cambridge, Mass.: Folsom, Wells, & Thurston, 1837.
Beers, F. W. *Atlas of Orange County Vermont.* New York: F. W. Beers, 1877.
Chelsea, Vt. Chelsea Historical Society. *Roster of the H. E. K. Hall Camp
  No. 28, Vermont Division, Sons of Veterans.* 1888.
  Story Norman Goss, Doctor of Medicine of Chelsea, Vermont, 1831–1905.
  Boston, 1905.
Child, Hamilton. *Child's Orange County Gazette, 1762–1888.* Syracuse,
  N.Y., 1888.
Comstock, John Moore. *Chelsea, Vermont.* N.p., 1944.

George, Noah J. T. *Gazetteer of the State of Vermont*. Haverhill, N.H., 1823.

Hemenway, Abby M. *The Vermont Historical Gazetteer*. Burlington, Vt., 1871.

Montpelier, Vt. Vermont Historical Society. *Manual of the Chelsea, Vermont Congregational Church*. 1888.

  Old Home Week Celebration, Chelsea, Vermont: 1901. Lowell, Mass.: C. I. Hood, 1901.

  Old Home Week Celebration, Chelsea, Vermont: 1902. Lowell, Mass.: C. I. Hood, 1902.

Tarbell, D. *Incidents of Real Life*. Montpelier, Vt., 1883.

Thompson, Zadock. *A Gazetteer of the State of Vermont*. Montpelier, Vt., 1824.

  Thompson's History of Vermont. Burlington, Vt., 1842.

Walker, E. Ralph. *Historical Sketch of the Chelsea West Hill Union Meeting House*. 1933.

Wallings, H. F. *Map of Orange County Vermont*. New York, 1858.

Government records and publications

Office of the Town Clerk, Chelsea, Vt. Manuscript Vital Records, 1857–1896. Vermont State Division of Public Records, microfilm.

  Manuscript Town Records, 1788–1919. Vermont State Division of Public Records, microfilm.

  Manuscript Grand List of Taxes, 1837, 1855, 1860, 1865, 1870, 1875, 1880, 1885, 1890, 1895, and 1900.

  Manuscript Land Records, 1850–1911. Vermont State Division of Public Records, microfilm.

  Manuscript List of Enrolled Militia, 1864–1867. Vermont State Division of Public Records, microfilm.

Orange County Court, Chelsea, Vt. Manuscript Register, Orange County Jail.

  Manuscript Court Records.

U.S. Census of Agriculture. Manuscript Schedules for Chelsea, Vt., 1850, 1860, 1870, and 1880. Montpelier, Vt.: Vermont Division of Public Records, microfilm.

U.S. Census of Manufactures. Manuscript Schedules for Chelsea, Vt., 1850, 1860, 1870, and 1880. Montpelier, Vt.: Vermont State Library.

U.S. Census of Population. Manuscript Schedules for Chelsea, Vt., 1840, 1850, 1860, 1870, 1880, and 1900. Washington, D.C.: National Archives, microfilm.

U.S. Department of Commerce. Bureau of the Census. *United States Census of Agriculture: 1900*, part I. Washington, D.C.: United States Census Office.

  United States Census of Religious Bodies, 1926, vol. 2. Washington, D.C.: U.S. Government Printing Office.

U.S. Geological Survey. *15' Series Map*, Barre, Vt., East Barre, Vt., Randolph, Vt., and Strafford, Vt. Washington, D.C., 1957.

Vermont State Board of Agriculture. *Reports.* Montpelier, Vt., 1872–1900 (sometimes published in Rutland, Vt.).

The Resources and Attractions of Vermont with a List of Desirable Homes for Sale. Montpelier, Vt., 1891.

A List of Desirable Farms and Summer Homes in Vermont. Montpelier, Vt., 1895.

Newspapers

American Agriculturalist. New York, N.Y.
Argus and Patriot. Montpelier, Vt.
Aurora of the Valley. Newbury, Vt.
The Country Gentleman. Albany, N.Y.
Herald and News. Randolph, Vt.
Maine Farmer. Augusta, Me.
New England Farmer. Boston, Mass.
New Genesee Farmer. Rochester, N.Y.
Rural Vermonter. Montpelier, Vt.

Secondary sources

Abbott, Collamer M. " 'Gramp' Abbott's Life: Farming in Central Vermont, 1865–1913." *Vermont History* 39 (1971): 31–42.

Adams, Thurston M. "Prices Paid by Vermont Farmers for Goods and Services and Received by Them for Farm Products, 1790–1940; Wages of Vermont Farm Labor, 1780–1940." University of Vermont Agicultural Experiment Station, *Bulletin* 507. Burlington, Vt.: University of Vermont Agricultural Experiment Station, 1944.

American Academy of Political and Social Science. "Country Life." *Annals* 40 (1912).

American Sociological Society. "The Sociology of Rural Life." *Publications of the American Sociological Society* 11 (1917).

Anderson, W. A. "Mobility of Rural Families I: Changes in Residence and Occupation of Rural Husbands and Wives in Genesee County, New York." Cornell University Agricultural Experiment Station, *Bulletin* 607. Ithaca, N.Y.: Cornell University Agricultural Experiment Station, 1934.

"Mobility of Rural Families II." Cornell University Agricultural Experiment Station, *Bulletin* 623. Ithaca, N.Y.: Cornell University Agricultural Experiment Station, 1935.

"The Membership of Farmers in New York Organizations." Cornell University Agricultural Experiment Station, *Bulletin* 695. Ithaca, N.Y.: Cornell University Agricultural Experiment Station, 1938.

Anderson, Wilbert L. *The Country Town: A Study of Rural Evolution*. New York: Baker & Taylor, 1906.

Atherton, Lewis. *Main Street on the Middle Border*. Bloomington, Ind.: Indiana University Press, 1954.

Baron, William R., and Bridges, Anne F. "Making Hay in Northern New England: Maine as a Case Study, 1800–1850." *Agricultural History* 57 (1983): 165–80.

Bassett, T. D. Seymour. "500 Miles of Trouble and Excitement: Vermont Railroads, 1848–1861." *Vermont History* 49 (1981): 133–53.

Bateman, Fred. "Improvement in American Dairy Farming, 1850–1910: A Quantitative Analysis." *Journal of Economic History* 28 (1968): 255–73.

"Labor Inputs and Productivity in American Dairy Agriculture, 1850–1910." *Journal of Economic History* 29 (1969): 206–29.

"The Marketable Surplus in Northern Dairy Farming: New Evidence by Size of Farm in 1860." *Agricultural History* 52 (1978): 345–63.

Bauder, Ward W. *The Impact of Population Change on Rural Community Life: The Economic System*. Ames, Iowa: Iowa State University Department of Economics & Sociology, 1963.

Beale, Calvin L. "Rural Depopulation in the United States: Some Demographic Consequences of Agricultural Adjustments." *Demography* 1 (1964): 264–72.

Beale, Calvin L., and Bogue, Donald J. "Recent Population Trends in the United States and Their Causes," in James H. Copp, ed., *Our Changing Rural Society: Perspectives and Trends*, pp. 71–126. Ames, Iowa: Iowa State University Press, 1964.

Beam, Lura. *A Maine Hamlet*. New York: Funk, 1957.

Bell, Robert Malen. "James C. Malin and the Grasslands of North America." *Agricultural History* 46 (1972): 414–24.

Bidwell, Percy W. "Rural Economy in New England at the Beginning of the Nineteenth Century." *Transactions of the Connecticut Academy of Arts and Sciences* 20 (1916): 319–53.

Black, John D. *The Rural Economy of New England*. Cambridge, Mass.: Harvard University Press, 1950.

Blalock, Hubert M. *Social Statistics*. New York: McGraw-Hill, 1972.

Bogue, Allan G. *From Prairie to Corn Belt: Farming on the Illinois and Iowa Prairies in the Nineteenth Century*. Chicago: Quandrangle Books, 1968.

Bogue, Margaret B. *Patterns from the Sod: Land Use and Tenure in the Grand Prairie, 1850–1900*. Springfield, Ill.: Illinois State Historical Library, 1959.

Boisen, Anton T. "Factors Which Have to Do with the Decline of the Country Church." *American Journal of Sociology* 22 (1916): 177–92.

Bowers, William L. "Crawford Township, 1850–1870: A Population Study of a Pioneer Community." *Iowa Journal of History* 58 (1960): 1–30.

The Country Life Movement in America, 1900–1920. Port Washington, N.Y.: Kennikat Press, 1974.

Boyle, James E. "The Passing of the Country Church." *Outlook* 77 (1904): 230–4.

Bremner, Robert H. *From the Depths: The Discovery of Poverty in the United States*. New York: New York University Press, 1956.

Britt, Albert. *An America That Was: What Life Was Like on an Illinois Farm Seventy Years Ago*. Barre, Mass.: Barre Publishers, 1964.

Brunner, Edmund deS. *The Growth of a Science: A Half-Century of Rural Sociological Research in the United States*. New York: Harper, 1957.

Brynn, Edward P. "Vermont's Political Vacuum of 1845–1856 and the Emergence of the Republican Party." *Vermont History* 38 (1970): 113–23.

Burr, Nelson R. *A Critical Bibliography of Religion in America*, vol. 2. Princeton, N.J.: Princeton University Press, 1961.

Clark, Charles E. *The Eastern Frontier: The Settlement of Northern New England, 1610–1763*. New York: Knopf, 1970.

Clark, Christopher. "The Household Mode of Production – A Comment." *Radical History Review* 18 (1978): 166–71.

  "The Household Economy: Market Exchange and the Rise of Capitalism in the Connecticut Valley, 1800–1860." *Journal of Social History* 13 (1979): 169–89.

Coale, Ansley, and Demeny, Paul. *Regional Model Life Tables and Stable Populations*. Princeton, N.J.: Princeton University Press, 1966.

Cole, Donald B. *Jacksonian Democracy in New Hampshire, 1800–1851*. Cambridge, Mass.: Harvard University Press, 1970.

Conzen, Michael. *Frontier Farming in an Urban Shadow*. Madison, Wis.: State Historical Society of Wisconsin, 1971.

Cox, LaWanda C. "Tenancy in the United States, 1865–1900: A Consideration of the Agricultural Ladder Hypothesis." *Agricultural History* 18 (1944): 97–105.

  "The American Agricultural Wage Earner, 1865–1900: The Emergence of a Modern Labor Problem." *Agricultural History* 22 (1948): 95–114.

Crockett, Walter Hill. *A History of Vermont*, 4 vols. Burlington, Vt.: Vermont Farm Bureau, 1938.

Cross, Whitney. *The Burned-Over District: The Social and Intellectual History of Enthusiastic Religion in Western New York, 1800–1850*. New York: Harper & Row, 1965.

Cubberly, Ellwood P. *Rural Life and Education: A Study of the Rural-School Problem as a Phase of the Rural-Life Problem*. Boston: Houghton Mifflin, 1914.

Currier, Amos N. "The Decline of Rural New England." *Popular Science Monthly* 38 (1891): 384–9.

Curti, Merle. *The Making of an American Community*. Stanford, Calif.: 1959.

Danbom, David B. *The Resisted Revolution: Urban America and the Industrialization of Agriculture, 1900–1930*. Ames, Iowa: Iowa State University Press, 1979.

"Rural Education Reform and the Country Life Movement, 1900–1920."
Agricultural History 53 (1979): 462–74.

Danhoff, Clarence. *Change in Agriculture: The Northern States, 1820–1870.*
Cambridge, Mass.: Harvard University Press, 1969.

Davenport, Charles B. "The Nams: The Feeble-minded as Country Dwellers." *Survey* 27 (1912): 1844–5.

Davenport, Charles B., and Danielson, Florence H. "The Hill Folk – Report on a Rural Community of Hereditary Defectives." *Eugenics Record Office Memoir* 1 (1912).

Davis, Lance E. "The Investment Market, 1870–1914: The Evolution of a
National Market." *Journal of Economic History* 25 (1965): 355–99.

Dawley, Alan. *Class and Community: The Industrial Revolution in Lynn.*
Cambridge, Mass.: Harvard University Press, 1976.

DeJong, Gordon. *Appalachian Fertility Decline.* Lexington, Ky.: University
of Kentucky Press, 1968.

Demaree, Albert Lowther. *The American Agricultural Press, 1819–1860.*
New York: Columbia University Press, 1941.

Denune, Perry P. "Some Town–Country Relations in Union County,
Ohio." *Ohio State University Studies*, Sociology Series 1 (1924).

"The Social and Economic Relations of the Farmers with the Towns in
Pickaway County, Ohio." *Ohio State University Studies*, Bureau of
Business Research (1927).

Dodd, Jill Siegel. "The Working Classes and the Temperance Movement
in Ante-Bellum Boston." *Labor History* 19 (1978): 510–31.

Doyle, Don H. "The Social Functions of Voluntary Associations in a
Nineteenth-Century Town." *Social Science History* 1 (1977): 333–56.

Dublin, Thomas. *Women at Work: The Transformation of Work and Community in Lowell, Massachusetts, 1826–1860.* New York: Columbia University Press, 1979.

"Women Workers and the Study of Social Mobility." *Journal of Interdisciplinary History* 9 (1979): 647–65.

Duffus, Robert L. *Williamstown Branch: Impersonal Memories of a Vermont
Boyhood.* New York: Norton, 1958.

Dykstra, Robert R. "Town-Country Conflict: A Hidden Dimension in
American Social History." *Agricultural History* 38 (1964): 195–204.

Earp, Edwin L. *The Rural Church Movement.* New York: Methodist Book
Concern, 1914.

Easterlin, Richard A. "Factors in the Decline of Farm Fertility in the
United States: Some Preliminary Research Results." *Journal of American History* 63 (1976): 600–14.

"Population Change and Farm Settlement in the Northern United
States." *Journal of Economic History* 36 (1976): 45–75.

Alter, George, and Condran, Gretchen. "Farms and Farm Families in
Old and New Areas: The Northern States in 1860," in Tamara K.
Hareven and Maris A. Vinovskis, eds., *Family and Population in Nineteenth-Century America*, pp. 28–84. Princeton, N.J.: Princeton University Press, 1978.

Ellsworth, Clayton S. "The Coming of Rural Consolidated Schools to the Ohio Valley, 1892–1912." *Agricultural History* 30 (1956): 119–28.

Farnsworth, Russell H. *Over Cram Hill*. Burlington, Vt.: Queen City Printers, 1967.

Fiske, G. Walter. *The Challenge of the Country: A Study of Country Life Opportunity*. New York: Association Press, 1913.

"The Development of Rural Leadership," in "The Sociology of Rural Life," *Publications of the American Sociology Society* 11 (1917), 56–7.

Flanders, Helen Hartness, Ballard, Elizabeth Flanders, Brown, George, and Barry, Phillips. *The New Green Mountain Songster: Traditional Folk Songs of Vermont*. Hatboro, Pa.: Folklore Associates, 1966.

Fletcher, Henry U. "The Doom of the Small Town." *Forum* 19 (1895): 214–23.

Foner, Eric. *Free Soil, Free Labor, Free Men: The Ideology of the Republican Party Before the Civil War*. New York: Oxford University Press, 1970.

Fox-Genovese, Elizabeth, and Genovese, Eugene. "The Political Crisis of Social History: A Marxian Perspective." *Journal of Social History* 10 (1976): 205–20.

Friedberger, Mark. "The Farm Family and the Inheritance Process: Evidence from the Corn Belt, 1870–1950." *Agricultural History* 57 (1983): 1–13.

Fry, Charles Luther. *Diagnosing the Rural Church: A Study in Method*. New York: Doran, 1924.

Fuller, Wayne E. *RFD: The Changing Face of Rural America*. Bloomington, Ind.: Indiana University Press, 1964.

The Old Country School: The Story of Rural Education in the Middle West. Chicago: University of Chicago Press, 1982.

Gagan, David P. "The Indivisibility of Land: A Micro-analysis of the System of Inheritance in Nineteenth-Century Ontario." *Journal of Economic History* 36 (1976): 126–41.

Gates, Paul. *Landlords and Tenants on the Prairie Frontier*. Ithaca, N.Y.: Cornell University Press, 1970.

"Two Hundred Years of Farming in Gilsum." *Historical New Hampshire* 33 (1978): 1–24.

Gelfant, Blanche H. *The American City Novel*. Norman, Okla.: University of Oklahoma Press, 1954.

Gill, Charles Otis, and Pinchot, Gifford. *The Country Church: The Decline of Its Influence and the Remedy*. New York: Macmillan, 1913.

Six Thousand Country Churches. New York: Macmillan, 1920.

Goldthwait, James W. "A Town That Has Gone Downhill." *Geographical Review* 17 (1927): 527–52.

Goody, Jack, Thirsk, Joan, and Thompson, E. P., eds. *Family and Inheritance: Rural Society in Western Europe 1200–1800*. Cambridge: Cambridge University Press, 1976.

Greven, Philip J. *Four Generations: Population, Land, and Family in Colonial Andover, Massachusetts*. Ithaca, N.Y.: Cornell University Press, 1970.

Griliches, Zvi. "Hybrid Corn and the Economics of Innovation," in Robert Fogel and Stanley Engerman, eds., *The Reinterpretation of American Economic History*, pp. 207–13. New York: Harper & Row, 1971.

Gross Robert. A. *The Minutemen and Their World*. New York: Hill & Wang, 1976.

"Culture and Cultivation: Agriculture and Society in Thoreau's Concord." *Journal of American History* 69 (1982): 42–61.

Gusfield, Joseph R. *Symbolic Crusade, Status Politics and the American Temperance Movement*. Urbana, Ill.: University of Illinois Press, 1963.

Haines, Michael. "The Use of Model Life Tables to Estimate Mortality for the United States in the Late Nineteenth Century." *Demography* 16 (1979): 289–312.

Hansen, Marcus. *The Immigrant in American History*. Cambridge, Mass.: Harvard University Press, 1940.

Hartt, Rollin Lynde. "A New England Hill Town." *Atlantic Monthly* 83 (1899): 561–74 and 712–20.

Haskell, Thomas L. *The Emergence of Professional Social Science: The American Social Science Association and the Nineteenth-Century Crisis of Authority*. Urbana, Ill.: University of Illinois Press, 1977.

Hays, Samuel P. *The Response to Industrialism, 1885–1914*. Chicago: University of Chicago Press, 1957.

Henretta, James A. "The Study of Social Mobility: Ideological Assumptions and Conceptual Bias." *Labor History* 18 (1977): 166–78.

"Families and Farms: *Mentalité* in Pre-Industrial America." *William and Mary Quarterly*, 3rd ser., 25 (1978): 3–32.

"Social History as Lived and Written." *American Historical Review* 84 (1979): 1293–1322.

Hester, Seth William. "The Life and Works of Warren H. Wilson and Their Significance in the Beginnings of the Rural Church Movement in America." M.A. thesis, Drew Theological Seminary, 1946.

Higgs, Robert. *The Transformation of the American Economy, 1865–1914: An Essay in Interpretation*. New York: Wiley, 1971.

Hilfer, Anthony C. *The Revolt from the Village, 1915–1930*. Chapel Hill, N.C.: University of North Carolina Press, 1969.

Hoag, Emily F. "The National Influence of a Single Farm Community: A Story of the Flow into National Life of Migration from the Farms." U.S. Department of Agriculture, *Bulletin* 984. Washington, D.C.: U.S. Department of Agriculture, 1921.

Hoffer, Charles R. "The Development of Rural Sociology." *Rural Sociology* 26 (1961): 1–14.

Hofstadter, Richard. *The Progressive Historians: Turner, Beard, Parrington*. New York: Knopf, 1968.

Hofstadter, Richard, and Lipset, Seymour Martin, eds. *Turner and the Sociology of the Frontier*. New York: Basic Books, 1968.

Hoskins, T. H. "New England Agriculture." *Popular Science Monthly* 38 (1891): 700.

Hyde, William D. "Impending Paganism in New England." *Forum* 13 (1892): 519–28.

Jacobs, Jane. *The Economy of Cities.* New York: Random House, 1969.

Jacobsen, Paul H. "Cohort Survival for Generations Since 1840." *Millbank Memorial Fund Quarterly* 42 (1964): 36–53.

Johnson, Paul. *A Shopkeeper's Millennium: Society and Revivals in Rochester, New York, 1815–1837.* New York: Hill & Wang, 1978.

Jones, Douglas Lamar. *Village and Seaport: Migration and Society in Eighteenth-Century Massachusetts.* Hanover, N.H.: University Press of New England, 1981.

Jordan, Holman B. "Ten Vermont Towns: Social and Economic Characteristics, 1850–1870." Ph.D. dissertation, University of Alabama, 1966.

Katz, Michael B., Doucet, Michael J., and Stern, Mark J. "Migration and the Social Order in Erie County, New York: 1855." *Journal of Interdisciplinary History* 8 (1978): 669–701.

Kensler, Gladys, and Melvin, Bruce L. "A Partial Sociological Study of Dryden, New York, with Special Emphasis on Its Historical Development." Cornell University Agricultural Experiment Station, *Bulletin* 504. Ithaca, N.Y.: Cornell University Agricultural Experiment Station, 1930.

Kirkland, Edward C. *Men, Cities, and Transportation: A Study of New England History, 1820–1900,* 2 vols. Cambridge, Mass.: Harvard University Press, 1948.

Kirschner, Don S. *City and Country: Rural Responses to Urbanization in the 1920s.* Westport, Conn.: Greenwood Press, 1970.

Kistler, Thelma M. "The Rise of Railroads in the Connecticut River Valley." *Smith College Studies in History* 23 (1937–8).

Klimm, Lester. "The Relation between Certain Population Changes and the Physical Environment in Hampden, Hampshire and Franklin Counties, Massachusetts, 1790–1925." Ph.D. dissertation, University of Pennsylvania, 1933.

Knights, Peter R. "The Contours of Nineteenth-Century Lives: Lessons from a Study of Internal Migration Based on Boston." Paper presented at the Social Science History Association Annual Meeting, Nashville, Tenn., October 1981.

Kutolowski, Kathleen S. "Freemasonry and Community in the Early Republic: The Case for Antimasonic Anxieties." *American Quarterly* 34 (1982): 543–61.

Kuznets, Simon, Thomas, Dorothy S., Lee, Everett S., Miller, Ann R., Brainerd, Carol P., Easterlin, Richard A., and Eldridge, Hope T. *Population Redistribution and Economic Growth, United States 1870–1950,* 3 vols. Philadelphia: American Philosophical Society, 1957–64.

Lampard, Eric E. *The Rise of the Dairy Industry in Wisconsin: A Study in Agricultural Change, 1820–1920.* Madison, Wis.: State Historical Society of Wisconsin, 1963.

LeDuc, Thomas H. "An Ecological Interpretation of Grassland History: The Work of James C. Malin as Historian and as Critic of Historians." *Nebraska History* 31 (1950): 226–33.

Lipson, Dorothy A. *Freemasonry in Federalist Connecticut*. Princeton, N.J.: Princeton University Press, 1977.

Lively, C. E., and Beck, P. G. "Movement of Open Country Population in Ohio I: The Family Aspect." Ohio Agricultural Experiment Station, *Bulletin* 467. Columbus, Ohio: Ohio Agricultural Experiment Station, 1930.

"Movement of Open Country Population in Ohio II: The Individual Aspect." Ohio Agricultural Experiment Station, *Bulletin* 489. Columbus: Ohio Agricultural Experiment Station, 1931.

Lowenthal, David, and Comitas, Lambros. "Emigration and Depopulation: Some Neglected Aspects of Population Geography." *Geographical Review* 52 (1962): 193–210.

Ludlum, David. *Social Ferment in Vermont, 1791–1850*. New York: Columbia University Press, 1939.

McMillen, Wheeler. *Ohio Farm*. Columbus, Ohio: Ohio State University Press, 1974.

Malin, James C. "The Turnover of Farm Population in Kansas." *Kansas Historical Quarterly* 4 (1935): 339–72.

Mann, S. A., and Dickinson, J. M. "Obstacles to the Development of a Capitalist Agriculture." *Journal of Peasant Studies* 5 (1978): 466–81.

Mason, L. D. "Comments on Western Emigration." New Hampshire Board of Agriculture, *Report*. Concord, N.H.: 1873.

Mather, W. G., Townsend, T. H., and Sanderson, Dwight. "A Study of Rural Community Development in Waterville, New York." Cornell University Agricultural Experiment Station, *Bulletin* 608. Ithaca, N.Y: Cornell University Agricultural Experiment Station, 1934.

Mayhew, Anne. "A Reappraisal of the Causes of Farm Protest in the United States, 1870–1900." *Journal of Economic History* 32 (1972): 464–75.

Melvin, Bruce. "The Sociology of a Village and the Surrounding Territory." Cornell University Agricultural Experiment Station, *Bulletin* 523. Ithaca, N.Y.: Cornell University Agricultural Experiment Station, 1931.

Merrill, Horace Samuel. *William Freeman Vilas, Doctrinaire Democrat*. Madison, Wis.: State Historical Society of Wisconsin, 1954.

Merrill, Michael. "Cash Is Good to Eat: Self-Sufficiency and Exchange in the Rural Economy of the United States." *Radical History Review* 3 (1977): 42–71.

Miyakawa, T. Scott. *Protestants and Pioneers: Individualism and Conformity on the American Frontier*. Chicago: University of Chicago Press, 1964.

Moorhead, James H. *American Apocalypse: Yankee Protestants and the Civil War, 1860–1869*. New Haven, Conn.: Yale University Press, 1978.

Morgan, Phillip. "The Problems of Rural New England: A Remote Village." *Atlantic Monthly* 79 (1897): 577–87.

Morse, Hermann Nelson, and Brunner, Edmund deS. *The Town and Country Church in the United States as Illustrated by Data from One*

Hundred and Seventy-Nine Counties and by Intensive Studies of Twenty-five. New York: Doran, 1923.

Munyon, Paul G. *A Reassessment of New England Agriculture in the Last Thirty Years of the Nineteenth Century: New Hampshire, A Case Study.* New York: Arno Press, 1978.

Nardroff, Ellen von. "The American Frontier as Safety Valve – The Life, Death, Reincarnation and Justification of a Theory." *Agricultural History* 36 (1962): 123–42.

Neely, Wayne Caldwell. *The Agricultural Fair.* New York: Columbia University Press, 1935.

Nelson, Lowry. *Rural Sociology: Its Origins and Growth in the United States.* Minneapolis, Minn.: University of Minnesota Press, 1969.

Nesmith, G. T. "The Problem of the Rural Community, with Special Reference to the Rural Church." *American Journal of Sociology* 8 (1903): 812–37.

Newby, Howard, and Buttel, Frederick H., eds. *The Rural Sociology of the Advanced Societies: Critical Perspectives.* Montclair, N.J.: Allanheld, Osmun, 1980.

Nie, Norman H., Hull, C. Hadlai, Jenkins, Jean G., Steinbrenner, Karin, and Bent, Dale H. *SPSS: Statistical Package for the Social Sciences.* New York: McGraw-Hill, 1975.

Nugent, Walter T. K. *The Structures of American Social History.* Bloomington, Ind.: Indiana University Press, 1981.

Pabst, Margaret. "Agricultural Trends in the Connecticut Valley Region of Massachusetts, 1800–1900." *Smith College Studies in History* 26 (1940–1).

Parker, William. "Agriculture," in Lance Davis, Richard A. Easterlin, and William N. Parker, eds., *American Economic Growth: An Economist's History of the United States.* New York: Harper & Row, 1972, pp. 369–417.

Parsons, Stanley. *The Populist Context: Rural versus Urban Power on a Great Plains Frontier.* Westport, Conn.: Greenwood Press, 1973.

Peirce, Paul S. "Social Surveys of Three Rural Townships in Iowa." *University of Iowa Monographs, Studies in the Social Sciences* 5 (1917).

Pred, Allan. *The Spatial Dynamics of U.S. Urban-Industrial Growth, 1800–1914.* Cambridge, Mass.: MIT Press, 1966.

Riley, Robert A. "Kinship Patterns in Londonderry, Vermont, 1772–1900: An Intergenerational Perspective of Changing Family Relationships." Ph.D. dissertation, University of Massachusetts-Amherst, 1980.

Robinson, William A. *Jeffersonian Democracy in New England.* New Haven, Conn.: Yale University Press, 1916.

Rorabaugh, W. J. *The Alcoholic Republic: An American Tradition.* New York: Oxford University Press, 1979.

Rosenberg, Charles E. "The Adams Act: Politics and the Cause of Scientific Research." *Agricultural History* 38 (1964): 3–12.

"Science, Technology, and Economic Growth: The Case of the Agricultural Experiment Station Scientist." *Agricultural History* 45 (1971): 1–20.

Roth, Randolph A. "Whence This Strange Fire? Religious and Reform Movements in the Connecticut River Valley of Vermont, 1791–1843." Ph.D. dissertation, Yale University, 1981.

Rothenberg, Winnifred. "The Market and Massachusetts Farmers, 1750–1855." *Journal of Economic History* 41 (1981): 283–314.

Rozwenc, Edwin C. "Agriculture and Politics in the Vermont Tradition." *Vermont History*, n.s. 17 (1949): 81–96.

"The Evolution of the Vermont State Department of Agriculture." *Vermont Quarterly* 14 (1946): 163–83.

"The Group Basis of Vermont Farm Politics, 1870–1945." *Vermont History* 25 (1957): 268–87.

Russell, Howard S. *A Long, Deep Furrow: Three Centuries of Farming in New England.* Hanover, N.H.: University Press of New England, 1976.

Rutman, Darrett B. "People in Process: The New Hampshire Towns of the Eighteenth Century." *Journal of Urban History* 1 (1975): 268–92.

Ryan, Mary P. *Cradle of the Middle Class: The Family in Oneida County, New York, 1790–1865.* New York: Cambridge University Press, 1981.

Salmon, D. E., ed. *Special Report on the History and Present Condition of the Sheep Industry of the United States.* Washington, D.C.: U.S. Department of Agriculture, 1892.

Sanborn, Alvan F. "The Future of Rural New England." *Atlantic Monthly* 80 (1897): 74–83.

Saville, John. *Rural Depopulation in England and Wales, 1851–1951.* London: Routledge & Kegan Paul, 1957.

Schlebecker, John T. *Whereby We Thrive: A History of American Farming, 1607–1972.* Ames, Iowa: Iowa State University Press, 1975.

Schmitt, Peter J. *Back to Nature: The Arcadian Myth in Urban America.* New York: Oxford University Press, 1969.

Schob, David E. *Hired Hands and Plowboys: Farm Labor in the Midwest, 1815–1860.* Urbana, Ill.: University of Illinois Press, 1975.

Scott, Roy V. *The Reluctant Farmer: The Rise of Agricultural Extension to 1914.* Urbana, Ill.: University of Illinois Press, 1970.

Shapiro, Henry D. *Appalachia on Our Mind: The Southern Mountains and Mountaineers in the American Consciousness, 1870–1920.* Chapel Hill, N.C.: University of North Carolina Press, 1977.

Shryock, Henry S., and Siegel, Jacob S. *The Methods and Materials of Demography,* 2 vols. Washington, D.C.: U.S. Department of Commerce, 1975.

Sims, Newell. *A Hoosier Village.* New York: Columbia University Press, 1912.

Sinclair, Robert O., and Tefft, Frederick. "Off-Farm Migration and Farm Consolidation in Central Vermont, 1953–1963." University of Vermont Agricultural Experiment Station, *Bulletin* 642. Burlington, Vt.: University of Vermont Agricultural Experiment Station.

Smith, Daniel Scott. "Parental Power and Marriage Patterns: An Analysis of Historical Trends in Hingham, Massachusetts." *Journal of Marriage and the Family* 35 (1973): 419–28.

"A Perspective on Demographic Methods and Effects in Social History." *The Newberry Papers in Family and Community History*, No. 77–4K (1977).

"A Malthusian-Frontier Interpretation of United States History Before c. 1815," in Woodrow Borah, Jorge Hardoy, and Gilbert A. Stelter, eds., *Urbanization in the Americas: The Background in Comparative Perspective*, pp. 15–23. Ottawa: National Museum of Man, 1980.

Smith, Page. *As a City Upon a Hill: The Town in American History.* New York: Knopf, 1966.

Stephenson, Charles. "Tracing Those Who Left: Mobility Studies and the Soundex Indexes to the U.S. Census." *Journal of Urban History* 1 (1974): 73–84.

Stilwell, Lewis D. *Migration from Vermont.* Montpelier, Vt.: Vermont Historical Society, 1948.

Strong, Josiah. *The New Era.* New York: Baker & Taylor, 1893.

Swierenga, Robert. "Towards the 'New Rural History': A Review Essay." *Historical Methods Newsletter* 6 (1972): 111–22.

"Theoretical Perspectives on the New Rural History: From Environmentalism to Modernism." *Agricultural History* 56 (1982): 495–502.

Sykes, James M. "Trends in Vermont Agriculture." Vermont Resources Center, *Report* 7 (1964), 14.

Tarver, James D. "Intra-Family Farm Succession Practices." *Rural Sociology* 17 (1952): 266–71.

Tetreau, E. D. "Farm Family Participation in Lodges, Grange, Farm Bureau, Four-H Clubs, School and Church." Ohio Agricultural Experiment Station, *Mimeograph Bulletin* 29. Columbus, Ohio: Ohio Agricultural Experiment Station, 1930.

Thernstrom, Stephan. *Poverty and Progress: Social Mobility in a Nineteenth-Century City.* Cambridge, Mass.: Harvard University Press, 1964.

The Other Bostonians: Poverty and Progress in the American Metropolis, 1880–1970. Cambridge, Mass.: Harvard University Press, 1973.

and Knights, Peter R. "Men in Motion: Some Data and Speculations about Urban Population Mobility in Nineteenth-Century America." *Journal of Interdisciplinary History* 1 (1970): 17–47.

Thompson, Carl W., and Warber, G. P. "Social and Economic Survey of a Rural Township in Southern Minnesota." *University of Minnesota Studies in Economics* 1 (1913).

Thrasher, Max Bennett. "A New England Emigration." *New England Magazine* 16 (1897): 372–6.

Throne, Mildred. "A Population Study of an Iowa County in 1850." *Iowa Journal of History* 57 (1959): 305–30.

Turner, Frederick Jackson. *The Frontier in American History.* New York: Holt, 1920.

Tyack, David B. *The One Best System: A History of American Urban Education.* Cambridge, Mass.: Harvard University Press, 1974.

Tyrrell, Ian R. *Sobering Up: From Temperance to Prohibitionism in Antebellum America, 1800–1860.* Westport, Conn.: Greenwood Press, 1979.

Uhlenberg, Peter. "Non-Economic Determinants of Non-Migration: Sociological Considerations for Migration Theory." *Rural Sociology* 38 (1973): 296–311.

Vinovskis, Maris. "The Jacobsen Life Table of 1850: A Critical Reexamination from a Massachusetts Perspective." *Journal of Interdisciplinary History* 8 (1978): 703–24.

Vogt, Paul L., ed. *The Church and Country Life.* New York: Macmillan, 1916.

Wade, Richard. *The Urban Frontier: The Rise of Western Cities, 1790–1830.* Cambridge, Mass.: Harvard University Press, 1959.

Welch, Rodney. "The Farmer's Changed Condition." *Forum* 10 (1891): 689–700.

Wells, George F. "The Country Church and Its Social Problems." *Outlook* 83 (1906): 893–5.

Wetherell, Charles. "A Note on Hierarchical Clustering." *Historical Methods Newsletter* 10 (1977): 109–16.

Wiebe, Robert H. *The Search for Order, 1877–1920.* New York: Hill & Wang, 1967.

Williams, James M. *An American Town.* New York: Columbia University Press, 1906.

Wilson, Harold Fisher. "The Roads of Windsor." *Geographical Review* 21 (1931): 379–97.

 The Hill Country of Northern New England: Its Social and Economic History, 1790–1930. New York: Columbia University Press, 1936.

Wilson, Warren H. *Quaker Hill: A Sociological Study.* New York: Columbia University Press, 1907.

Winters, Donald L. *Farmers Without Farms: Agricultural Tenancy in Nineteenth Century Iowa.* Westport, Conn.: Greenwood Press, 1978.

Wohl, R. Richard. "The 'Country Boy' Myth and Its Place in American Urban Culture: The Nineteenth-Century Contribution." *Perspectives in American History* 3 (1969): 77–156.

Woodworth, H. C. "Nute Ridge: The Problems of a Typical Backtown Community." University of New Hampshire Extension Service, *Circular* 68. Durham, N.H.: University of New Hampshire Extension Service, 1927.

 "A Century of Adjustments in a New Hampshire Back Area." *Agricultural History* 11 (1937): 223–36.

Young, E. C. "The Movement of Farm Population." Cornell University Agricultural Experiment Station, *Bulletin* 426. Ithaca: Cornell University Agricultural Experiment Station, 1924.

Zelinsky, Wilbur. "Changes in the Geographic Patterns of Rural Population in the United States, 1790–1960." *Geographical Review* 52 (1962): 492–524.

Zinar, Ruth. "Educational Problems in Rural Vermont, 1875–1900: A Not so Distant Mirror." *Vermont History* 51 (1983): 197–220.

Index